D1544469

The Making of Lee Boyd Malvo

The Making of
LEE BOYD MALVO

THE D.C. SNIPER

Carmeta Albarus, MSW, LCSW

with forensic analysis by Jonathan H. Mack, Psy.D.

 Columbia University Press / New York

Columbia University Press
Publishers Since 1893
New York   Chichester, West Sussex
cup.columbia.edu
Copyright © 2012 Columbia University Press

Cover photos: © CNP/Corbis, © Megan Gayle/Shutterstock
Cover design: Marc Cohen

Library of Congress Cataloging-in-Publication Data
Albarus, Carmeta.
The making of Lee Boyd Malvo : the D.C. sniper / Carmeta Albarus ; with forensic analysis by
Jonathan H. Mack.
         p.   cm.
Includes bibliographical references and index.
ISBN 978-0-231-14310-3 (cloth : alk. paper) — ISBN 978-0-231-51268-8 (electronic)
1. Malvo, Lee Boyd, 1985–   2. Serial murderers—United States—Psychology.   3. Criminal
snipers—United States—Psychology.   4. Serial murders—Washington Metropolitan Area—
Case studies.   I. Mack, Jonathan H.   II. Title.
HV6248.M2747A43   2012
364.152'32092—dc23
[B]
2012008511
♾
Columbia University Press books are printed on permanent and durable acid-free paper.
This book was printed on paper with recycled content.
Printed in the United States of America
c 10 9 8 7 6 5 4 3 2 1
References to Internet Web sites (URLs) were accurate at the time of writing. Neither the author
nor Columbia University Press is responsible for URLs that may have expired or changed since the
manuscript was prepared.

I've felt abandoned, saying, "Father, where art thou?"
But he can not be found.

—LEE BOYD MALVO 7/21/06

CONTENTS

ACKNOWLEDGMENTS

The outcome of this case would not have been possible without the effort of the defense team that was put together to represent Lee Boyd Malvo. Special mention must be made of attorney Craig Cooley, who devoted time and energy to showing the world that Malvo was worthy of the best legal representation the Commonwealth of Virginia could offer, and even after the case was over did not cease his interest in seeing to the growth of this young man. Craig's interest extended to his cooperation for this book. Alas! If only Malvo had met a Craig Cooley before he met Muhammad.

My love and thanks go to my family and friends for their support and encouragement. To the two women who raised me, my mother and my grandmother, Joyce Josephs and Ellen Thomas, who taught me the virtue of giving back; to my daughter, Tamika, and my grandsons, Douglas and Nathaniel; to Conrad, without whose wisdom and critical eye this project would not have come to fruition; to the CVA crew, Eutifan, Alene, Simone, Winnifred, and Maxine, who were there with me as I worked through the Malvo case. To Cessie, my mentor and friend, who introduced me to the field of mitigation and believed in my ability do this work; to the editorial staff of Columbia University Press for their guidance; to Jonathan Mack for agreeing to do the forensic analysis, and to Lee Boyd Malvo for trusting me enough to open up about his life, and to publish this work in the hope that others will learn from his experiences.

In all this I remember the victims, especially those who made the ultimate sacrifice with their lives. Thanks to Cheryl Shaw, the daughter of Jerry Taylor, and Sonia Wills, the mother of Conrad Johnson, for allowing me the chance to speak with them and share in their pain. I acknowledge and am humbled by their strength and their willingness to reach out so that others can learn from this tragedy.

The Making of Lee Boyd Malvo

Introduction

A Nation in Fear—the Crime

On October 2, 2002, the local news reported a fatal shooting in the parking lot of a grocery store in Montgomery County, Maryland. Within fifteen hours, a wave of five fatal shootings in Montgomery County brought residents of the Maryland, Washington, D.C., and Virginia corridor face to face with their worst fear—terrorism in their backyards. "Where will the next strike occur?" was the question in people's minds as chaos gripped the area. Restaurants and many stores closed, plummeting business and commerce to low levels. Many gas stations hung shields around their pumps. Frightened residents, fearing a sniper nearby, nervously danced the "gas station jig," crouched low and shuffling back and forth while they pumped gas.

An oftentimes beleaguered chief of police was constantly on television trying to reassure the public, but to no avail. A *Washington Post* poll conducted on October 24, 2002, asked Washington, D.C., residents what they were most personally threatened by; 44 percent named the sniper attacks, 29 percent the 9/11 attacks, and 13 percent the anthrax scare.

Between October 2 and October 24, the Beltway sniper shootings claimed the lives of ten victims and injured four others. It was barely a year after the September 11, 2001, tragedy, and talk of terrorism abounded. The shootings appeared so random and yet so deliberate, crossing racial, gender, age, and class lines. The northeastern corridor of the United States, indeed the entire nation, was gripped in fear.

Sightings of a white van at or around the time of the shootings had law enforcement officers looking for such a vehicle. Profilers suggested that this was the work of a disgruntled, middle-class white male. While experts gave their opinions and everyday folk tried to make sense of what was happening in the nation's capital, John Allen Muhammad was plotting how best to make the nation pay for the injustice that he felt had been dealt him.

It was not a white van occupied by a disgruntled, middle-class white male that officers should have been looking for. It was a blue Chevrolet Caprice, with a black male veteran of the first Gulf War, forty-one-year-old Louisiana-born John Allen Muhammad, accompanied by seventeen-year-old Jamaican-born Lee Boyd Malvo. At his Maryland trial in 2006, Muhammad would tell the court that he had come to the Washington area in search of his children, who had been taken away by the courts in August 2001: "August 31st was my 9/11," he said.

Muhammad had found the perfect disciple to assist him in his deadly plot. Lee Boyd Malvo's identity and fate had become merged with Muhammad's as he searched for a "hero dad," who would rescue him from his earlier years of abuse, abandonment, and neglect. And so it happened that the fate of innocent people became inextricably pulled into the tortured web of a deluded master and his disciple during those horrific days in October.

The sniper shootings began on October 2, 2002, at 5:20 p.m. when a shot was fired through a window of a Michael's Craft Store in Aspen Hill, Maryland. No one was hurt in that incident. But soon the shootings turned deadly. The victims were a random cross-section of society, innocent individuals going about their daily lives. None had any connection to either John Muhammad or Lee Malvo.

1. James Martin, a fifty-five-year-old program analyst at the National Oceanic and Atmospheric Administration (NOAA), was killed in the parking lot at a food warehouse grocery store on October 2 at 6:04 p.m. in Aspen Hill, Maryland.

2. James L. (Sonny) Buchanan Jr., a thirty-nine-year-old landscaper, was shot dead on October 3 at 7:41 a.m. while mowing the grass at an auto mall in White Flint, Maryland.

3. Prem Kumar Walekar, fifty-four, was killed on October 3 at 8:12 a.m. while filling his cab with gas at a Mobil gas station on Aspen Hill Road, Maryland.

4. Sarah Ramos, a thirty-four-year-old babysitter, was killed on October 3 at 8:37 a.m. outside the post office on International Boulevard in Silver Spring, Maryland. She had just gotten off the bus and was seated on a bench reading a book.

5. Lori Ann Lewis-Rivera, twenty-five, was killed while vacuuming her Dodge Caravan at a Shell gas station on October 3 at 9:58 a.m. in Kensington, Maryland.

6. Pascal Charlot, a seventy-two-year-old retired carpenter, was killed on October 3 at approximately 9:20 p.m. while walking along Georgia Avenue in Washington, D.C.

7. Caroline Sewell, a forty-three-year-old woman, was shot in the parking lot of a Michael's craft store in Spotsylvania County, Virginia, on October 4 at 2:30 p.m. She survived the shooting.

8. Iran Brown, thirteen, was shot and critically wounded as his aunt dropped him off at his middle school in Bowie, Maryland on October 7 at 8:09 a.m.

9. Dean Myers, fifty-three, was fatally shot on October 9, at 8:10 p.m. while pumping gas at a Sunoco gas station in Manassas, Virginia.

10. Kenneth Bridges, fifty-three, was killed on October 11, at 9:30 a.m. at an Exxon gas station off Interstate 95 in Spotsylvania County, Virginia.

11. Linda Franklin, a forty-seven-year-old FBI intelligence analyst, was killed on October 14 at 9:15 p.m. on the lower level of a parking garage of the Home Depot in Falls Church, Virginia.

12. Jeffery Hopper, thirty-seven, was shot on October 19 at 8:00 p.m. in a parking lot near the Ponderosa Steakhouse in Ashland, Virginia. He survived.

13. Conrad Johnson, thirty-five, was shot dead on October 23 at 5:56 a.m. as he stood on the steps of his bus in Aspen Hill, less than a mile from where the sniper shootings had begun twenty-one days earlier. Like Lee Boyd Malvo, Conrad Johnson was born and spent his early formative years in Jamaica.

The sniper shootings in October are not the only incidents that have been attributed to the Beltway snipers. Several other shootings across the country have also been connected to Lee Boyd Malvo and John Allen Muhammad. These include but are not limited to:

1. Kenya Cook, a twenty-one-year-old, was shot on February 16, 2002, in Seattle. The intended victim was her aunt, Isa Nichols, who had testified on behalf of Mildred Muhammad (the ex-wife of John Muhammad) in their child custody case.

2. Jerry Taylor was killed by a shot to the upper body on March 13, 2002, in Arizona.

3. Paul LaRuffa was shot five times at close range on September 5, 2002, while locking up his pizzeria in Clinton, Maryland. Mr. LaRuffa survived the attack. His computer was found in Muhammad's car at the time of their arrest.

4. Rupinder (Benny) Oberio was shot on September 14, 2002, in Silver Spring, Maryland.

5. Muhammad Rasid was shot on September 15, 2002, in Clinton, Maryland.

6. Million Waldemarian was killed on September 21, 2002, in Atlanta, Georgia.

7. Claudine Parker was killed as she was locking up an ABC liquor store on September 21, 2005, in Montgomery, Alabama.

8. Kellie Adams was shot in the same incident as Claudine Parker. She survived.

9. Hong Im Bellenger was killed on September 23, 2002, in Baton Rouge, Louisiana.

THE ARREST

The nation exhaled a collective sigh of relief after John Allen Muhammad and Lee Boyd Malvo were taken into police custody at a highway rest area off Interstate 70 in Myersville, Maryland, on October 24, 2002. The arrest was made when a trucker and another motorist called the police after spotting Muhammad and Malvo sleeping inside their vehicle. African Americans, and particularly Jamaicans, expressed shock and disbelief when the racial identities of the snipers were disclosed. They did not match the supposed profiles.

A dazed Muhammad and Malvo were taken to the Youth Division for separate questioning, as it was clear that their identities were fused as father and son. A memorandum dated October 24, 2002, prepared by Detective Terry Ryan of the Major Crimes Division of the Montgomery County Police, gave details of an interview conducted with Lee Malvo shortly after his arrest and provides a window into Malvo's state of mind at the time. The interview was conducted at a Montgomery County off-site family services facility located in Rockville, Maryland. According to the memorandum, shortly after Malvo was placed in a secured designated interview room, he tried to escape. He had to be forcibly removed and restrained by task force officers. Throughout the interview, he communicated through gestures and by tracing words on the table surface and the wall.

When asked by the interviewing officer if he knew why he'd been arrested, Malvo nodded, but when advised that it was necessary to communicate with the interviewers, he gestured "with fingers to lips, a zipper motion repeatedly." When it was explained to Malvo that there were certain forms that had to be completed and that would require his signature, he responded by making a crumpling-up gesture and throwing motion. He refused to sign anything. He further communicated the following: "I understand my rights. . . . The police want to know about my thoughts. . . . The police are trying to get what I am thinking." As he communicated this, he repeatedly made a noose and hanging gesture. But when asked if he wanted to hurt himself, he shrugged his shoulders and appeared noncommittal.

Malvo was asked during the interview about the $10 million that he and Muhammad had demanded to end the shootings. (This was in reference to a written request they made during their killing spree.) He shook his head. The memorandum states: "The subject then placed his hand, midline from the chest, then placed the hand at a higher level. The subject struck his chest several times while nodding in the affirmative." When it was suggested that the shootings had little to do with the money, Malvo nodded, then gestured that the [police] writer was getting into his head. He later tapped his head and then made a gesture of turning a key on his forehead as if the information he had was locked away.

When asked if he would like something to eat, Malvo responded by tracing the words "Eat one time." He indicated that he consumed one meal per day, in the evening. Throughout this initial interview, the only time Malvo showed any appropriate response was when it was noted that a great amount of evidence had been recovered near the scene of the shooting of the bus driver, Conrad Johnson, and the suggestion made that something must have happened to make Malvo leave the things behind. According to the report, "The subject [Malvo] nodded in the affirmative and his eyes welled with tears."

When Malvo was handed over to authorities in Fairfax County, Virginia, he did communicate verbally while under interrogation at the Fairfax County police station. He said that he took responsibility for all the shootings. He further said that, if he had the chance, he would do the shootings again. Excerpts from the interrogation transcript clearly show that Malvo's words seemed to reflect a distorted sense of reality and altered state of mind. Very often it did not seem he was responding to the interrogators, but rather to Muhammad's commands that had been impressed upon him. The following selected excerpts demonstrate his state of mind at the time, and also hint at some aspects of his training from Muhammad.

QUESTION: How long did you hang around the Home Depot afterwards?

MALVO: Let's see, it's like being, being deep inside a gorge, you can attack people, you don't want to be in there after you hit. Because you've cornered yourself up in something to fight to the death, it's like a wounded animal, don't fight to your enemy wounded you don't hit it crack, once you do that, the crack soldiers are gonna come out, you don't hit top of the line, no, not unless you have to, you stay as far away from them as possible. Because they know what to do there. They're better thinkers and they're faster thinkers; in this world you gotta roll or else you die and you're rolling out dead.

QUESTION: And then what, you guys just drive?

MALVO: Drive away or walk away or run away, and you just do it calm, you've done nothing, just be calm about it, uh, see, that's the whole suspicion, people that do things are frightened, running, screaming, when certain actions, cops can smell it for a mile. Yeah he's suspicious, that's what they do, they're good at it, they will sniff it out, and I'll look them in their face right there, look them in their face and move out of the way.

Regarding the $10 Million Payoff That Malvo and Muhammad Demanded:

QUESTION: If we hadn't have caught you, you'd still be doing it?

MALVO: Right now?

QUESTION: Uh-huh.

MALVO: You would have, you would have given in by now.

QUESTION: But . . .

MALVO: I think you would have given in by now because you didn't know what was coming next.

QUESTION: You mean giving in means we would have paid you off? But if you hadn't been paid off, would you have still continue to shoot and request money?

MALVO: Yeah, we had the resources to keep going.

QUESTION: You did?

MALVO: Yeah, everyone donated.

[Donations are what Muhammad called proceeds from the robberies.]

QUESTION: Where were you getting cash money?

MALVO: You plan for, you plan for war, before war, so you have all your resources before. You, you don't have no money on you, but you have your money.

On His Diet:

QUESTION: Would you ever eat before you shot or do you wait till after you shoot to go eat? Does it matter?

MALVO: I fast.

QUESTION: You always fast when you're gonna shoot?

MALVO: Uh-huh. Fast the whole time, all I had was raisins and maybe crackers and that was it and water.

QUESTION: And you felt fine?

MALVO: Oh yeah, it's a state of mind. I can do as many push-ups as I did when I was eating food, it, it's just a state of mind, that's all it is.

On His Relationship with Muhammad:

MALVO: Since you're asking so many questions, can I ask one question now?

INTERVIEWER: You can ask anything that you want.

MALVO: Where's my father?

INTERVIEWER: Where is he, that's a good question, uh, I know that, and I am basing this on television because he's being interviewed by . . . [Interviewer was referring to biological father, Leslie Malvo]

MALVO: No, no, no, not him—JOHN!

On Why They Were Captured:

QUESTION: Did you want us to catch you?

MALVO: I would prefer to be elusive, unknown, and free.

QUESTION: So why do you think we caught you?

MALVO: My laziness, my lack of discipline.

QUESTION: Your lack of discipline. What does that mean?

MALVO: I departed from something.

QUESTION: You departed from something?
MALVO: Yeah, that I know works for five minutes of pleasure.

(The five minutes of pleasure that Malvo engaged in was sleep. He fell asleep and thus was caught. He blamed himself for deviating from the code of discipline Muhammad used to train him.)

Reflecting on his state of mind at the time of his arrest and during those police interviews, Malvo would state years later: "I was different then. I was way out there. I never allowed myself to feel. I did not care—I wanted to die. Death was my way out. So I did anything and everything to get myself killed. I could not do it, so I wanted the courts to do it for me."

THE TRIAL

In November 2003, in Chesapeake, Virginia, Lee Malvo went on trial for the murder of FBI analyst Linda Franklin, one of the ten people killed in the sniper shootings. Malvo's defense team, headed by Craig Cooley and Michael Arif and including Tom Walsh, Mark Petrovich, and John Strayer, presented an insanity defense. Testimony from mental health experts Dewey Cornell, Ph.D., and Neil Blumberg, M.D., as well as testimony from experts in the areas of indoctrination and cultic processes was presented. Expert testimony was buttressed by lay testimony from a host of individuals, including Malvo's biological father, Leslie Malvo; other relatives; former schoolmates; teachers; and people who had observed the interactions between Lee Malvo and Muhammad at various stages in their relationship. I also testified at both the guilt/innocence and penalty phases of the trial. For much of the trial, Malvo sketched on a legal pad and ignored the proceedings. Una James, his mother, did not testify. Though she was granted a parole visa, like several other witnesses, she expressed distrust of the process and maintained that unless she was granted a regular visa that would allow her free access to travel in and around the United States, she would not attend.

The key evidence in the case was the taped confession that Malvo made at the time of his arrest, when he claimed responsibility for all the shootings. His attorneys argued that Malvo had been coached to "self-destruct" if captured and that the confession was in parts inconsistent with the facts. The defense's position was that the shooting was orchestrated by Muhammad as part of a scheme to kill his wife and retrieve his children, who had been taken from him by the courts, and Malvo was only a pawn molded like a piece of clay by John Muhammad.

The position of lead prosecutor Robert Horan was that Malvo was a willing and equal participant. The prosecution's mental health witnesses were headed by psychologists Dr. Stanton Samenow and Dr. Evan Nelson. Dr. Samenow, who had interviewed Malvo on eight occasions, testified that he saw no evidence of mental illness. Dr. Nelson testified that Malvo had the capacity to tell the difference between right and wrong.

On December 18, 2003, after nearly fourteen hours of deliberation, the jury convicted Lee Malvo of capital murder. A sentence of life without parole, rather than the death sentence that was sought, was later recommended by the jury.

In a courtroom in Virginia Beach, not far from where Malvo was being tried, John Muhammad also was on trial. In that case, the prosecution argued that John Muhammad was the actual mastermind and that although Malvo had claimed responsibility for the shootings, Muhammad was the more culpable. While Malvo claimed that he was to blame for all the shootings, Muhammad proclaimed that he and Malvo were innocent. According to an FBI report dated October 24, 2002, Muhammad claimed that the gun and ammunition recovered from his Chevrolet Caprice were found by Malvo at a rest stop twelve hours prior to their capture.

When the agents tried to play on Muhammad's feelings for Malvo, hoping that he would take some responsibility for the shootings, Muhammad responded that he did not know what they were talking about. He asked to see his "son," and when this request was denied, he stated that he wanted a lawyer. When he was informed that people saw him and Malvo as "monsters, terrorists, and scum for killing innocent women and children," he just stared. Muhammad denied any involvement in the sniper shootings, but admitted that he had traveled to Maryland to find his wife and children. Muhammad had learned through Devoted Dads, a nonprofit fathers' rights group, that his wife, Mildred, was in the area.

Their crimes captured the attention of not only the nation but also the world. Even years after the shootings, interest in Malvo's story has not waned. Media outlets worldwide expressed an interest in interviewing him. In one instance, Malvo's telephone conversations with a producer from ABC were aired on ABC TV's morning program on the fifth anniversary of the sniper shootings. The producer had facilitated a telephone conversation between Malvo and Cheryll Witz, the daughter of Jerry Taylor (one of the victims). In Malvo's conversation with Ms. Witz, he offered apologies for taking the life of her father. Much controversy erupted over the call, given concerns about possible resurgence of trauma suffered by the victim's family.

However, in a telephone conversation with me later, Ms. Witz indicated that her conversation with Malvo provided some level of comfort for her and she believed that Malvo was sincere in his expression of remorse. She expressed the hope that she would be able to have further correspondence with him.

In October 2007, the fifth anniversary of the sniper shootings, two specials aired on cable television: CNN's *The Minds of the D.C. Snipers* and BET's *Muhammad and Malvo*. E! TV's *Too Young to Kill* featured the story of Lee Boyd Malvo. MSNBC and the History Channel also aired specials on the sniper shootings.

Malvo remains incarcerated at Red Onion State Prison in Virginia, where he is in isolation, having no human contact. During a visit with Malvo in November 2009, days before the scheduled execution of John Muhammad, I asked how he was coping with the impending execution. "Fate is taking its course," he responded, adding that he felt pity for the man who took him on his murderous trail. He hoped that Muhammad would come to acknowledge his guilt and beg forgiveness. He was happy to see Muhammad's children on a CNN program about the execution. "I feel so proud of them. Their mother is doing a good job," he commented. John Allen Muhammad was executed by the state of Virginia on November 10, 2009.

MY INVOLVEMENT IN THE CASE

In late February 2003, I received a call from John Strayer, one of the five attorneys representing Malvo. He wanted to know if I would be interested in assisting on the case. My name had been suggested by a well-known death penalty attorney from Virginia. The rationale was that because I am Jamaican born, as is Malvo, it would be beneficial to have someone with the cultural sensitivity that I could bring to the defense team. However, I could only be appointed as an investigator because Virginia, at the time, did not recognize the function of a mitigation specialist, my particular area. That would limit my involvement, since I would be unable to use my clinical expertise, and furthermore I was not licensed as an investigator.

This was the first conflict for me, because a significant part of my professional function is working directly with defendants. Trained as a social worker, I chose a practice in forensic social work, an area where social work and law intersect. As a mitigation specialist, I assist defense attorneys in conducting social history investigations and assessments of criminal defendants. For defendants facing capital punishment, such as Lee Boyd Malvo, this entails a thorough investigation into the person's life so as to gain an understanding of the factors that shaped the individual and contributed to his or her criminal actions. This requires the practitioner to be empathetic and to employ a trained ability to engage the client and his or her family system.

The role of the mitigation specialist has been recognized and endorsed by the American Bar Association as essential to the defense of those on trial for capital crimes. Mitigation evidence is usually presented at the penalty phase of the trial, after there has been a conviction for capital murder. Russell Stetler, the National Mitigation Coordinator for the Federal Death Penalty Resource Counsel and Habeas Assistance Training Counsel Projects, notes that mitigation specialists can come from a wide range of disciplines; however, social work has come to be viewed as the profession most likely to foster the techniques and skills required. Stetler (2007) points out that a mitigation specialist has to have competency in the areas of identifying collateral evidence of mental disorders and deficits, exposure to trauma, brain damage, and substance abuse. He states further that this kind of investigation must be multigenerational so as to identify genetic predispositions, in utero exposures, and intergenerational patterns of behavior, including the historic influences of culture and subculture.

Because the state of Virginia did not recognize mitigation specialists at the time I was asked to assist on the Malvo case, I was asked to emphasize my investigative credentials rather than my clinical expertise. A total of five investigators were requested of Judge Jane Roush, the trial judge for the Malvo case who had appointed Craig Cooley as one of the lead attorneys. Of the five requested, only three were appointed, including me. Upon being advised of my appointment, I was warned of the formidable task that lay ahead, because Malvo's personality was so merged with Muhammad's that he saw himself as one with Muhammad.

A PERSONAL JOURNEY

The knowledge that this case would garner national and international attention was not lost on me. Yet being involved also seemed like a natural progression, given the road that I had traveled to get to that point in my career and my life. I was born in Jamaica, where I was trained and worked as a teacher. My decision to come to the United States was influenced by the desire to provide a better life for myself and my daughter, Tamika Douglas. My journey as an immigrant has been marked by a determination to seize opportunities when they present themselves. Such an opportunity appeared in 1989. For a number of years I had worked as a babysitter, like many other immigrants who get their start by working in the home as a housekeeper or a child care provider. But I also was going to school at night, furthering my education in another area. Even though teaching was my first love, the educational system in the United States was so different from that in Jamaica that I did not want a teaching career in America. I set my sights on law and completed paralegal studies at a local college.

While I was on a play date with the child I was entrusted to care for, I heard of a job opening with a social worker, Cessie Alfonso, who was seeking an assistant with good communication skills. I was informed that her area of social work was very specialized and entailed working with attorneys. I felt it might be a good fit with my own career aspirations. My meeting with Ms. Alfonso was a hit. I found her to be down to earth, engaging, with a keen understanding of cultural issues. Most importantly, she loved people.

One of the early cases I was involved with was that of an African American male whom I felt was innocent. The evidence against him was dubious at best, and I felt that it was an injustice that he was convicted. The jury was out for about nine days and rendered a guilty verdict on the eve of Thanksgiving. He was not given the death penalty, but the unanimous verdict for life imprisonment came back in less than an hour. His name was Robert Douglas and he died trying to clear his name, but he never stopped being a loving and attentive father to his son.

That case had a profound impact on me. "I want to be a lawyer," I recall telling my friends and associates. I felt that I could do a lot more as an attorney than as a social worker, but I was discouraged by an attorney with whom I had worked and who respected and valued the role of the mitigation specialist. He argued that there was need for mitigation specialists and I would serve my career goals better if I obtained a degree in social work. I heeded his advice and earned a master's degree in social work from Yeshiva University, Wurzweiler School of Social Work in New York City.

In 1995 I started my own agency, CVA Consulting Services in Harlem. My experience with Cessie Alfonso and Alfonso Associates paved the way for my transition, and the support I had from Ms. Alfonso made it seem right. Since then I have been involved in hundreds of cases, most of which were death penalty cases. However, the majority were resolved with a plea for a sentence less than death. There have been cases where I have had doubts about the guilt of my client, but for the most part my clients have been guilty as charged and my challenge was not to suggest that they did not commit the crime, but rather to explain the circumstances and mitigating factors that should be considered along with the murder.

MY RELATIONSHIP WITH LEE BOYD MALVO

There was no doubt as to whether or not Lee Boyd Malvo committed the crimes for which he had been charged. There was no doubt as to whether or not he pulled the trigger in many of the shootings. The question that loomed for his defense, and for those around the world who had followed the horrible case, was why. Finding the answer was further complicated by the fact that without Malvo's cooperation, it would be difficult to mount any meaningful defense. Malvo had provided the authorities with a full confession, taking responsibility for all the murders, and he had continued to maintain his guilt. Experts who had met with Malvo and assessed the situation suggested that it would take years for him to come to any true understanding of himself, separate from John Muhammad.

At the time of my appointment I was informed that my focus in the case would be limited to investigating and tracking Malvo's life in the islands of Jamaica, where he was born, and Antigua, where he met John Muhammad. I was told that there would be little value in my meeting with Malvo, given his lack of cooperation. I challenged that position, for even as I recognized the frustration his attorneys might have been feeling, I knew from many years of professional experience that commonality of culture and ethnicity goes a long way in establishing trust, and trust is the hallmark of any successful client–attorney relationship. "I believe that you and your client will be better served if I played a more central role in meeting and working with him," I remember telling Craig Cooley.

I worked hundreds of grueling hours and finally established a relationship of trust with Lee Boyd Malvo. Once that trust was there, Malvo was more inclined to cooperate with his defense team. Ultimately, as previously stated, he was found guilty of capital murder in the death of Linda Franklin, but he was spared the death penalty and instead received a sentence of life without the possibility of parole.

The end of the trial did not signal an end to my interaction with Malvo, however; our communication has extended to the present time. The work that I have done with offenders over the years has fostered my belief that even in the worst of us there is the possibility of redemption. My continued contacts and interactions with Malvo contribute to an even better understanding of this.

In March 2005, the Supreme Court held (in *Roper v. Simmons*) that it was unconstitutional to impose capital punishment for crimes committed while under the age of eighteen. This ruling meant that Malvo would no longer face capital punishment in any of the other murder cases he had pending. At the time, he had already served two years of his life sentence. He had begun to write a journal of his life, tracing his steps from Kingston, Jamaica, into the hands of Muhammad. He knew that it was the desire to have a father that encouraged him to blindly follow Muhammad, and that he would never again be a part of the outside world. But he hoped that his story would be a lesson to fathers and sons, to mothers who have to be both mother and father, and to youth who sometimes are blinded by what they want to see rather than what they should be seeing. He thought it could warn others who might be at risk of going down a destructive path. The account that follows is partly informed by Malvo's own journal, along with my own investigations into his early life; the opinions of his friends, teachers, and family members; and my own impressions as I came to understand him.

My reasons for taking on this project include the fact that the journey that led Malvo to this place is one that begs for understanding. From all accounts, until he met John Muhammad, Malvo was a youth with tremendous potential. His academic pursuits since incarceration confirm the possibility of scholarly accomplishments. Like many who have worked with Malvo over the years, I am faced with the question of what made him capable of murder—and further, what it was about Malvo's relationship with John Muhammad that led him to commit that crime.

Malvo himself has been confronted with these haunting questions. He has tried to retrace the steps that led to his destruction of so many lives. In his journal, he wrote:

> I have been confronted by the shadows on my walls, making faces, as I retraced my steps along the road that led me here. The answer for a very long time has been a cloak of guilt and self-loathing wherein there have been nights when I have asked myself, "Will I choose to wake up tomorrow?" I see now by looking at these walls that they speak to me. No hope,

prayer, wish or fear, or any desire will ever remove them. Like my past they are concrete. I find within myself and many of my fellow prisoners that it is not that we feel unloved but something much worse—we feel unlovable. If a man has never experienced love, then I ask how can we expect him to express it. I surrendered my life to John Muhammad who showed me what I thought was love.

(The reader will see, from the journal passage above and many reprinted throughout this book, that Malvo's writings are very "adult" in their style and word choice. They are presented exactly as he wrote them, with minor edits to correct spelling errors only. His style reflects one method of Muhammad's indoctrination, in which Malvo was forced to memorize various speeches and books, as will be discussed in section 2. In section 4, Jonathan Mack will present a psychological explanation of Malvo's writing style.)

This book goes beyond the point of how Malvo became the sniper to discover the processes of his evolution. As we look into these factors it is important to be mindful of how his actions affected us individually, and collectively as a society. We are also concerned with the question of whether there are other Lee Boyd Malvos out there, and how can we minimize the risk of similar acts of violence.

In writing this work, certain considerations came to mind. Would a book like this affect Malvo's legal status, given the magnitude of his crimes and the numerous jurisdictions involved? (As of this writing, there are no further cases pending against him.) Then there was Malvo's age: he was seventeen years old at the time of the sniper shootings, and even at twenty-seven (when I completed this manuscript), he was still ascending into adulthood. It might seem a bit premature to tell the story of his life, given that he is still developing his own thoughts and identity, and his perspectives might easily change. The decision to write this book at this time is a recognition that Malvo's circumstances have been anything but normal, and that his story might be best told while it is still recent enough to be useful.

Although Malvo is the main focus, this project was also influenced by the interactions that I have had with hundreds of clients. Many of them had no fathers to guide and protect them. Many turned to criminality after going through misguided and violent juvenile stages. Many of them, while incarcerated, have had time to reflect on their lives, and have come to seek redemption and hope for a better future. The lack of a father figure is by no means the only reason behind Malvo's descent into crime, but it is certainly a key theme. I hope that a detailed examination of Malvo's tragic trajectory may provide society with an understanding of some of the factors that can result in criminal consequences.

HOW THIS BOOK IS ORGANIZED

Section 1, "A Father Lost: The Genesis of Reactive Attachment Disorder in Lee Boyd Malvo," chronicles Lee Malvo's travels from Jamaica, the island of his birth, through St. Maarten, Antigua, and then finally to the United States. The narrative of his life is based on writings from his journal and heavily augmented by numerous interviews that I conducted on Malvo's behalf with his friends, family members, and teachers from Jamaica and Antigua, as well as my review of the testimony provided at his trial. In limited instances, it was not possible to interview specific individuals named by Malvo or to confirm his account with third parties. In some instances, where the naming of particular individuals might result in undue scrutiny, their names have been changed (as indicated in the text) or not mentioned. At certain points insights are offered into aspects of Malvo's life that were influenced by a wider social context. Malvo's own writings (including letters and poems), as well as his art, illustrate his emotional development.

Section 2, "A False Father Found: Malvo Meets John Muhammad" describes the first meeting between Malvo and John Muhammad, his perceived "hero" father figure, and examines how his attachment grew and what it entailed. This includes his brainwashing by Muhammad and his engagement in Muhammad's "war against the system."

Section 3, "A False Father Rejected: Separating Malvo from Muhammad" tells of the extrication of Malvo from the psychological control of John Allen Muhammad, including Malvo's plummet into emotional despair as he grappled with the enormity of his actions and his current hope for healing and restitution, as evidenced by his decision to testify against Muhammad in May 2006. This section also addresses Malvo's transformation from the sniper to the person he is now. At fifteen, Lee Boyd Malvo's life was taken over by John Muhammad. Now, in his twenties, Malvo has taken strides to reclaim his identity emotionally and psychologically.

Section 4, "A Forensic Mental Health Analysis of Lee Boyd Malvo," by Dr. Jonathan H. Mack, a licensed clinical psychologist with specialized training and experience in clinical neuropsychology and forensic psychology, provides a more technical, academic explanation of forensic mental health evaluations. It analyzes Malvo based on a review of numerous documents and expert reports and of relevant diagnostic factors that predisposed him to be vulnerable to the destructive influence of Muhammad and involvement in the sniper shootings.

Dr. Mack reviews the roles of the different mental health experts in criminal cases and defines the types of evaluations performed by forensic mental health experts. He also reviews the psychiatric findings and opinions of several psychiatrists, psychologists, and neuropsychologists involved in this case.

Dr. Mack also examines general issues to be considered in forensic mental health examinations, including psychological histories involving various forms of neglect (e.g., abandonment, inconsistent or multiple caretakers) and abuse (emotional, physical or sexual), the developmental age of the brain of the defendant, and the concept of youth as a mitigating factor in capital homicide defense.

Finally, in the epilogue, I examine where Lee Boyd Malvo is today— and how his story, while thankfully unique in its level of tragedy, can illuminate all-too-common family dynamics that often influence the lives of youth.

One such theme in Malvo's story is the lack of a father. Malvo did not attach to Muhammad in order to become a sniper. He attached because he was searching for a father figure and thought that he had found it in Muhammad. Interestingly, Malvo's intellectual attributes did not protect him from attaching to Muhammad, succumbing to his vigorous indoctrination (or brainwashing, as Dr. Mack explains in section 4) and subsequently being taken on Muhammad's murderous trail. Similarly, intelligence does not necessarily offer protection to many of society's youths who are drawn into attachments to gangs, drug dealers, and other negative influences. Parental nurture and attachments is vital to development.

In this book, some of Malvo's voice is retained in quotations from his writings and statements. The quotes that are attributed to John Allen Muhammad are derived from Malvo's own recollection of what Muhammad told him. Some are very long speeches and may not be verbatim. Muhammad maintained that he and his "son" (Malvo) were innocent of the sniper shootings. In his trial at Montgomery County Court in 2006, Muhammad represented himself and thus conducted the cross-examination of Malvo, who was the prosecution's star witness. I was present at that trial and on several occasions heard Muhammad call Malvo "son," which prompted Judge James Ryan to instruct Muhammad to refrain from referring to him as such.

I made a request to meet with Mr. Muhammad, but he declined. There is no confirmation of any of Malvo's statements regarding Muhammad from Muhammad himself. However, over many hours of meetings and interviews I have conducted with Malvo, he has remained consistent in his recollections of what Muhammad told him and of the nature and details of their relationship. Therefore, the words he has attributed to Muhammad may be considered relevant in helping to measure this man's influence upon Malvo.

Other individuals I have interviewed corroborated Malvo's account of his history and, according to the specific knowledge of each individual, portions of his relationship with Muhammad. Based on the work I have done, I take the position that Malvo was deeply influenced by Muhammad. Information from various sources within this book supports that belief. However, others may have a different interpretation. It should be noted as well that much of what Malvo shared in his personal history were his recollections of events; others may recall certain events differently.

This book does not seek to retry Malvo's case. Malvo has admitted his guilt, was convicted, and is serving a life sentence for his many crimes. The book looks at the life of Lee Boyd Malvo, how he became the D.C. sniper, and how the associated tragic chain of events can be used as a teachable opportunity. There are other young black men facing a myriad of issues, including the significant question of the absent father, one factor that made Malvo so susceptible to Muhammad's corrupting influence. For many of these youths, as with Malvo, a sense of purpose has been eroded in the search for identity,. Thankfully, most children are resilient and can and do overcome tragedies. But some are scarred for life. Malvo's story is an extraordinary one, but also one that emerges from occurrences that happen in so many families.

Malvo indicated that his consent to have his story told and his words and art used comes out of the acknowledgment of how his actions affected the lives of the victims and their families. Related to this is his hope that others can be spared a similar fate. Malvo will derive no financial benefit from this book.

MY FIRST ENCOUNTER WITH MALVO

My first meeting with Malvo took place on March 23, 2003. I was accompanied by two of his attorneys, Craig Cooley and Tom Walsh. Malvo was in chains, shackled at his feet and handcuffed. He was extremely polite as he entered the small room in which the interview would take place. I was immediately struck by how young and disarming he looked. Though he had just turned eighteen, I could easily have mistaken him for fourteen. He was also small in stature. I tried to imagine him spouting the venom that was attributed to him in the media regarding his confession, but it was difficult to do so.

I have dealt with many youthful offenders over the years, and there usually is a hardness in them that can easily be discerned. But this was not evident in Malvo. My question as I saw this young man was: Who is Lee Boyd Malvo? As a mitigation specialist, I have to cast aside judgment and view the individual not as the monster portrayed by the media, but as a human being, deserving of empathy. This demands the proverbial effort to walk in the other person's shoes in order to understand his or her experiences and perspective.

The introduction was made by Mr. Cooley. "Lee, this is the lady I told you would be helping us on the case." Malvo looked in my direction and nodded. "And guess what? She is Jamaican," Cooley continued. A slight smile crossed Malvo's face as he sat down.

As Malvo addressed his attorney, I took note of the way he spoke. Strangely, he did not have a Jamaican accent. That in itself was amazing, as it takes a while to so completely lose one's accent. I had been told that he'd been in the United States for less than two years. I made a decision then and there that I would communicate with him in Jamaican patois (a Jamaican dialect), to establish a basis for connecting with him.

As I began speaking in Jamaican patois, the two attorneys were at a loss. It seemed impolite on my part to be speaking in a dialect that neither attorney could understand, but I decided that an explanation could come later. Right then I was faced with the challenge of determining how much of this young man's identity had been submerged. Were there any vestiges of his Jamaican identity left? Could he understand me? Though he maintained an American accent when he responded, it was clear that he knew exactly what I was asking. It was also clear, however, that he had an agenda, and it was not sharing with me his life in Jamaica, which was what I wanted to hear about. It was instead to "educate" me on the injustices that he saw as endemic to American society.

His youthful face was transformed and his eyes became like slits as he launched into a monologue about Jim Crow laws and the oppression of black people worldwide, including the laborers of "Botswene," Ghana, which he claimed to have personally seen in his global travels. I briefly asked him what he thought about Accra (Ghana's capital) and the El-Mina slave castles. He ignored the question and continued talking about the global discrimination against blacks that he had seen. I knew better than to openly challenge him, even as I suspected that he was talking about things he had not actually witnessed or experienced.

Seizing the opportunity to attempt to bond with him through the language he grew up with and through the commonality of our Jamaican experience, I conceded that there was injustice and agreed that the playing field was not fair, but I also suggested that it was not all bad, at least from my perspective. I knew that to establish a relationship based on trust I had to be honest with him, and engage him in some dialogue. That entailed pointing out where we might have some differences in opinion. However, it was clear that he was not hearing what I was saying, as he continued, at times almost in a monologue, to state his position on the oppression of the black man. On several occasions he diverted and railed against the "white man, wearing a black robe," who had the audacity to take the children away from their dad.

Another thing was quite evident: his loyalty to the man he called "Dad." He talked incessantly about John Allen Muhammad and how great a father he was. Malvo's loyalty to and admiration for Muhammad reminded me of his attorneys' warning that his personality was so merged with Muhammad's that it would be impossible bring him to the point where he could be of any use to his own defense. I knew that we did not have the luxury of years of therapy to get him sufficiently detached. Furthermore, it was not my role to be his therapist. My function was to provide assistance in mounting a defense.

That first meeting with Malvo lasted about two hours, and, at its conclusion, I asked him by what name he preferred to be called. "John Lee Muhammad," he said. I presented him with an authorization for release (of records) form that required his signature. He signed it "John Lee Muhammad."

As we emerged from the meeting, the attorneys asked my impression. "That was not a Jamaican kid that I met in there," I told them. Having been a teacher in the public school system, dealing with hundreds of Jamaican adolescents, I felt confident in asserting that Lee Malvo had undergone a "washing away" of his identity. He had spoken so passionately of his experience as a "black man" in this racist society that it was clear he was parroting what had been imparted to him by his "dad."

Neither attorney had been exposed to the Jamaican culture in any real sense. I informed them that Jamaicans, particularly those of Malvo's generation, did not come from a society where they faced victimization because of race. Jamaica's population is over 90 percent black. I asked, "Did you hear how he talked as though he had personally been to Ghana and seen those laborers?" They had heard about his visit to Ghana, and wondered if he had in fact been there. "I bet that he has never set foot in Ghana, or anywhere in Africa, for that matter," I said. I concluded that it was more probabley that Muhammad had visited Ghana and shared with his protégé only the parts that would imbue in Malvo a hatred for the system, which was dominated by white men, or "devils," as he trained Malvo to see them.

As I began my journey back to New York, a 250-mile drive, I made a stop at my mother-in-law's house. I looked exhausted and burned out. She gave me a CD that she said gave her inspiration: *Believe* by Yolanda Adams. "Take this baby and play it." For the months leading up to the trial, I sang along with Yolanda's songs on that CD. It gave me inspiration and hope that the task ahead was doable, for this was a daunting assignment. Trial was set for November 2003; this meant I had only eight months to establish a relationship with Malvo that would result in his giving the cooperation his attorneys needed to mount an effective defense. I struggled with the narrow scope of my role, as defined by the court; to do a social history investigation of his life. Having met with Malvo, I knew I could not simply be an investigator. In order to get at the story of Malvo's life, I had to help him separate from the John Muhammad identification and reconnect to his identity as Lee Boyd Malvo.

Although my formal role did not include that of therapist, it was apparent there would be therapeutic challenges, despite the fact that Malvo's responses to the defense team's main psychiatrist and psychologist suggested a refusal to cooperate with any mental health assessment. My professional experience and my observation of Malvo told me that he was a very disturbed individual, and although he was being treated by the legal system as an adult, he was still a minor and under the influence of an adult father figure at the time of his arrest.

It seemed I was being relied on to penetrate whatever barriers stood between not only Malvo and his attorneys but also Malvo and the psychiatrist and psychologist on the defense team. I had to take an approach that would give the attorneys what they needed primarily—Malvo's timely cooperation for the sake of his legal defense—while also being sensitive to whatever therapeutic needs he might exhibit.

Preparation for trial, I thought, meant not just getting the legal arguments ready but also helping Malvo to be ready for the trial process. Reconciling those two concerns was not beyond my scope as a clinical social worker or my experience as a mitigation specialist. However, Malvo presented a very unique set of circumstances that I knew would test the capacity of my training and practice.

As I reflected on the meeting with Malvo, I was reminded of the characterization made by Dr. Simone Gordon, DSW, the Clinical Director of CVA Consulting, at the time we were asked to assist on this case:

> For those of us who work in the field of forensic social work, particularly in the field of capital mitigation, the task is daunting. Unlike the traditional social work experience, our work is done inside the jails, in high-security facilities with no privacy in circumstances that parallel the incarcerated conditions of our clients, both physically and psychologically. We know firsthand what it is like to enter the world of the chained; of the prisoner without and the prisoner within. Despite our visceral responses to the confined space, which is not usually viewed as a place of safety, creativity, and healing, we are required to do the work. We have to find a way to connect with the person who sits before us. We have to connect with the "disconnected," with a life history of disrupted attachment relationships, not only from the world but from the self.

I had to connect to Malvo under those circumstances.

SUBSEQUENT MEETINGS WITH MALVO

Six days after that first visit, I returned to meet with Lee Malvo (or John Lee Muhammad, as he then preferred to be called). This time we met without his attorneys present. He lectured about the injustices and indignities that the black man faces on a daily basis. "Look at the schools. They are geared to develop sports but not academics. There are more black men in prisons than in college." He talked of veterans he had seen in his travels through the United States. Hundreds, he said, were homeless and living either on the streets or in shelters. "They fought in wars for this country and came back to nothing." It became increasingly clear that I was dealing not just with Lee Malvo but also with another persona, John Allen Muhammad, which seemed more dominant.

After listening to about two hours of the hate-filled rhetoric, I challenged him. "I could understand if I was speaking with an older American black male who had lived with racial discrimination and oppression in the United States, but I am having a hard time relating this to a Jamaican kid who went to one of the best schools on the island." He looked at me with piercing eyes and said emphatically, "We are one," referring to himself and John Muhammad. The way he said this and the emphasis he gave it seemed almost messianic. I acknowledged the father-and-son relationship because he obviously would not tolerate anything else, and I wanted him to feel as trusting of me as possible.

He continued, "The white man gives you guns so you can turn it against yourself." As much as I was trying not to challenge him so early in the process, I felt compelled to point out that he and Muhammad were playing right into what he claimed the white man was doing. "I have sat here and listened to you talk about the white man killing black men, so tell me, how can you justify killing a man who has done so much to uplift the black youth in his community?" (I was referring to Kenneth Bridges, one of the shooting victims, and what I had learned about his community-building efforts.)

There was a trace of anger in my voice. Malvo seemed taken aback by that comment. He wasn't expecting to be challenged. For a couple minutes he was actually silent. His expression softened. However, as though he needed to defend against something that was being aroused in him, he said, "You have to change the system without the system knowing. We don't build because we have no land. We can't start within the system, you have to build a whole new generation and start with the kids."

There was such a disconnect between his response and my comments that it was even more obvious to me that he was parroting what he had been told. He seemed to have a rigid view of the world that could not have been shaped by his experience prior to meeting Muhammad. Should I confront him or should I go along with his remarks? I decided that I would apply a client-centered approach. This was made popular by psychologist Carl Rogers and, as the term suggests, leads to a relationship wherein the needs of the client, rather than of the practitioner, are central to facilitating the client's cooperation and personal growth.

Somers-Flanagan and Somers-Flanagan (1999) cite Rogers's core conditions for a client-centered approach: congruence (or consistency and authenticity in one's feelings toward the client), unconditional positive regard (acceptance or respect for the client as a person of value), and accurate empathy (demonstrating the ability to reflect and respond accurately to the client's feelings or issues).

At the time, I felt that Malvo would be responsive to this method. For one thing, it would contrast with the adversarial dynamic that seemed to characterize his interactions with other members of the defense team. I surmised that it would be counterproductive to allow that dynamic to dominate my interactions with Malvo. I saw in him someone whose personhood and perception of the world, no matter his demeanor or deeds, needed to be acknowledged and affirmed if we were to make any progress.

Sometime later, I recognized that my approach, based on Rogers's principles of congruence, unconditional positive regard, and accurate empathy, could have struck an intuitive chord with Malvo, given his relationship with Muhammad. His unwavering reference to Muhammad as "Dad" begged for an explanation why he had such devotion to a man who had been in his life for only a little over two years. "Tell me. What is it about your dad that you did not get from your other parents?" He responded decisively, "My dad gave me consistency, 100 percent unconditional acceptance, and he led by example."

Another technique I drew upon was what cognitive-behavioral therapists call cognitive reframing. The aim was not to have cognitive therapy sessions per se, but rather to recognize that Malvo's apparent need for thought stimulation or critical thinking might also be a way to establish a relationship that would lead to his legal and personal progress. Cognitive reframing would be complementary to the client-centered approach, particularly as it affirmed for Malvo that I took him and his perceptions seriously.

Through cognitive reframing, I was able to question Malvo's assumptions and emotional biases in a way that helped him realize that there were ways of seeing the world other than that which Muhammad had taught him. It helped that Malvo loved to read and to express his thoughts through art and writing. Accordingly, I could engage him through oral communication and by facilitating his need for ongoing discussions as well as revisions of his art and written communication.

I realized that my questioning of his ideas would be a sensitive issue for him, because his belief system seemed to have become quite rigid and identified with his "dad," Muhammad. I had to question his ideas without giving him the impression that I was arguing with him or rejecting him and Muhammad. Within the client-centered relationship, I could at least engage him in a process of self-monitoring and self-awareness in relation to his thoughts and beliefs, and whether they accurately reflected reality.

From such a process, he would begin to recognize that some of his thoughts and beliefs contradicted his own rational individual personhood as Lee Boyd Malvo, not John Lee Muhammad, and thus also see the necessity and desirability of correcting those thoughts and beliefs.

It was important, for instance, that I recognize key words or ideas in Malvo's speech that held great significance for him. One such idea was the need to save the children and in turn save the world. "So how will you change the system with the kids?" I asked. He gave me a look that suggested he was about to share with me a big secret that only he and Muhammad knew. "Dad was going to start a community of seventy boys and seventy girls, and once they knew themselves and their potentials, they were going to be sent out into different parts of the world to change the system and bring about a just society." The $10 million they demanded from the police, he stated, was to be used to fund that project, which would be in either Ghana or Canada.

He asked me if I had seen *Roots*. I told him that I had. He then asked if I remembered what Tizzy said. At that time I could not even remember who Tizzy was. I countered, "I watched *Roots* before you were even born, and I don't remember what Tizzy said." He again gave me that look suggestive of imparting great truths. "She said this system must change." He then pounded his handcuffed hands on the table and said emphatically, almost in a shout, "This is for Tizzy!!!" He saw the dumbfounded look on my face as I wondered how on earth this kid got caught up in this worldview. Just as suddenly, his features relaxed and he smiled. "If you want to understand me, watch *The Matrix*." He repeated, "Watch *The Matrix*!"

Not wanting to sound uninformed, I asked what watching *The Matrix* had to do with me understanding him. (At the time, I think I may have heard some mention of *The Matrix* relative to the case, but I had not seen the film.) He repeated the directive. "If you want to understand me, watch *The Matrix*." He also had another bit of advice for me. "Read the Willie Lynch speech."

I was not accustomed to receiving such instructions from a client, but I realized that the only way to make any progress with this young man was to understand him from the perspective that he was giving me. As Malvo spoke about Willie Lynch, it was clear that he was repeating not history learned in school, but rather what he had learned from John Muhammad. Yet I would have to begin where this young man was. I had never researched Willie Lynch (a slave owner who supposedly made a speech on slavery in Virginia in 1712) or his purported exhortation to white slave owners as to how to ensure dominance over their slaves. (No historical document supports the existence of a speech by this Willie Lynch, and its authenticity has been challenged by historians.)

Below is a text of the purported Willie Lynch speech:

Gentlemen:

I greet you here on the bank of the James River in the year of Our Lord one thousand seven hundred and twelve. First I shall thank you The Gentlemen of the Colony of Virginia for bringing me here. I am here to help you solve some of your problems with slaves. Your invitation reached me on my modest plantation in the West Indies where I have experimented with some of the newest and still oldest methods of control of slaves. Ancient Rome would envy us if my program is implemented. As our boat sailed south on the James River, named for our illustrious King, whose version of the Bible we cherish, I saw enough to know that your problem is not unique. While Rome used cords of woods as crosses for standing human bodies along its highways in great numbers, you are using the tree and the rope on occasion.

I caught the whiff of a dead slave hanging from a tree a couple miles back. You are not only losing valuable stock by hanging, you are having uprisings, slaves are running away, your crops are sometimes left in the field too long for maximum profit, you suffer occasional fires, your animals are killed. gentlemen, you know what your problems are: I do not need to elaborate. I am not here to enumerate your problems, I am here to introduce you to a method of solving them.

In my bag here, I have a fool proof method for controlling Black Slaves. I guarantee everyone of you that if installed correctly, it will control the slaves for at least 300 years. My method is simple. Any member of your family or your Overseer can use it.

I have outlined a number of difference(s) among the slaves; and I take these differences and make them bigger. I use fear, distrust, and envy for control purposes. These methods have worked on my modest plantation in the West Indies and [they] will work throughout the South. Take this simple little list of differences, think about them. On top of my list is "Age," but it is only there because it begins with an "A." The second is "Color" or "Shade," there is intelligence, size, sex, size of plantation, status of plantation, attitude of owner, whether the slaves live in the valley, on a hill, East, West, North, or South, have a fine or coarse hair, or is tall or short. Now that you have a list of differences, I shall give you an outline of action but before that, I shall assure you that distrust is stronger than trust and envy is stronger than adulation, respect and admiration.

The Black Slave, after receiving this indoctrination, shall carry on and will become self-refueling and self-generation for hundreds of years, maybe thousands.

Don't forget you must pitch the old black versus the young black and the young black male against the old black male. You must use the dark skin slave vs. the light skin slave and the light skin slaves vs. the dark skin slaves. You must also have your white servants and overseers distrust all blacks, but it is necessary that your slaves trust and depend on us. They must love, respect and trust only us.

Gentlemen, these Kits are keys to control, use them. Have your wives and children use them, never miss an opportunity. My plan is guaranteed and the good thing about this plan is that if used intensely for one year the slaves themselves will remain perpetually distrustful.

Thank you gentlemen.

(http://www.duboislc.org/html/WillieLynch.html)

This speech gained some attention, particularly among black men who attended the Million Man March in 1995, where it was referenced by Minister Louis Farrakhan. The "Willie Lynch syndrome" is seen as a pathology that fuels disunity among blacks. Malvo's understanding is that John Muhammad attended the Million Man March. Though Malvo was only ten years old and living in Jamaica at the time, he received a full dose of the Willie Lynch speech after he met Muhammad. Malvo reported that he had read the speech several times and committed it to memory.

After reading about Willie Lynch and reviewing his speech, I surmised that this was one way Muhammad shaped Malvo's views. In addition, I bought a videotape of *The Matrix*. Upon my first viewing, the scene that stood out for me was that of the "superchildren," who seemed to possess extraordinary powers. I wondered if that scene informed the idea, reported by Malvo, of building a compound of select children who would be trained to bring out their own powers. It was unclear, however, how deeply this movie related to the dynamic between Malvo and John Muhammad.

After additional viewings, I arrived at an understanding of the interrelationship with Muhammad and what he had inculcated in Malvo. This process was crucial in unlocking the psychological hold that Muhammad had on Malvo. I began to see how the movie could have made such a strong impression on the young man while he was with Muhammad. There appeared to be a strong father/mentor-and-son motif in the relationship between the two main characters in the movie. From this relationship, idealistic themes such as truth, identity, righteousness and justice, the esteemed place of children, war against oppression and slavery, and bringing a just system into being became important.

In *The Matrix*, the younger character, Neo (which means "new"), seemed to stand in for Malvo. Morpheus, the older character, seemed to stand in for Muhammad. Morpheus is a play on the word "morph" or "morphosis," and the name symbolizes form and change. When he was in the world of the matrix, the Neo character was known as Thomas Anderson. An evil agent constantly refers to him as Mr. Anderson—refusing to call him by his "real" name, Neo. The agent wants to reinforce the idea that Mr. Anderson is a slave to the system. However, in Morpheus's world—the real world—Thomas Anderson has thrown off his slave identity and has become new. He has found his true identity, hence Neo. In Malvo's perspective, this theme in the movie was analogous to the new identity that Muhammad had given him. Malvo insisted that his name was John Lee Muhammad, and even signed his name accordingly. Lee Boyd Malvo was the slave identity that he needed to renounce.

There are two defining moments in the movie that held significance for Malvo. The first is when Morpheus offers Neo the pill of truth, which Neo accepts. Malvo was led to believe that Muhammad was offering him truth. Muhammad used Malvo's curiosity for knowledge and truth to influence him to accept whatever Muhammad said. Malvo saw Muhammad as Neo saw Morpheus—a wise, authoritative father figure who held the key to his future.

The second defining moment in the movie is when Neo meets the Oracle, who informs him that without Morpheus, humanity would be lost. In the film, Neo has to make a choice. He decides that the real world needs Morpheus ("without him we are lost") and so is prepared to sacrifice his own life to save his father/mentor. Malvo believed that he was supposed to sacrifice his own life to save his dad—Muhammad. Malvo blamed himself for Muhammad getting caught, saying he should have been awake and more disciplined. In the interrogation after his arrest, Malvo took the blame for the shootings. He believed that it was better for him to confess and take the blame, as in so doing he would be sparing Muhammad's life.

It is possible that Muhammad used *The Matrix* to facilitate his brainwashing of Malvo. Under the guise that he was imparting truth to an intelligent, but still unlearned prodigy, Muhammad indoctrinated Malvo into believing that the present world system was a matrix designed to keep him in slavery and oppression. Muhammad may have intended to transform or morph Malvo from Lee Boyd Malvo—the slave identity—to John Lee Muhammad. "We are one," Malvo said of their relationship. Muhammad started the process of molding Malvo into his little soldier, ready to fight what he presented as a righteous war. Malvo believed that he had a stake in Muhammad's war, and that it was part of a larger vision to bring about truth and justice that would emancipate the black man. Malvo said Muhammad told him: "You are not supposed to be good . . . this is war."

In painting this larger vision, Muhammad did two things. First, he indoctrinated Malvo into thinking that this new world of truth and justice could only come about through fighting to save the children. Malvo therefore saw himself as drafted into the battle to get Muhammad's children back from his ex-wife after he lost legal custody. "We did everything to get the children back" and "What right does a white judge have to tell a black man how to raise his children" he repeated frequently.

Although Muhammad's apparent focus was his own children, it is possible that one way to influence Malvo was to make it seem that he was part of a bigger vision: to get seventy boys and seventy girls, whom Muhammad would groom to change the system. These kids were to be the best and brightest, Muhammad told Malvo. Malvo was convinced that he was the first of the chosen.

Malvo saw in *The Matrix* the idealistic notion of the primacy of children being truly established. The idea of saving children (from the system) so that they in turn could save the world was impressed upon him. He was convinced that Muhammad already had or would in future put everything in place to fulfill this perfect vision, including the land upon which to build a compound.

Second, it seems that Muhammad used *The Matrix* as a tool of desensitization. In the film, the system is not real. Malvo's early writings and art after his arrest repeated this idea. The system is not real, Muhammad taught him, but an imposition or means of control. Furthermore, if the system is not real, therefore it is not the truth; and if the system is the enemy, then killing becomes necessary to bring into being the greater good. Muhammad apparently wanted Malvo to be so desensitized that he would see even the shooting victims as unreal or inconsequential. As in *The Matrix*, these victims (casualties) were to be seen as merely neural simulations projected as real. Malvo recalled that he watched *The Matrix* over a hundred times and prior to almost every shooting.

Malvo recalled Muhammad constantly reminding him that someone had to make a change in the world, and Malvo was that person. Like the Neo character, Malvo took the concept of sacrifice and validation very seriously. He believed that it was up to him to save Muhammad, even to the point of giving his own life. Accordingly, he at first refused to cooperate with his lawyers because, as he said, he would never let them use him against his dad. He saw his lawyers as part of the system that Muhammad had told him was the enemy. Conversely, even though Malvo also saw the detectives and police as part of the system, and hence the enemy, he was willing to "cooperate" with them by taking total blame because they were presumably there to facilitate his need to sacrifice himself.

It is significant that during the interrogations after his arrest, Malvo tried to avoid answering questions when he believed the interrogators were trying to trap him into incriminating Muhammad. He was not so hesitant, however, in providing answers that incriminated himself, and that he believed could be used to seek his execution.

As I discussed *The Matrix* with Malvo, I asked him whether my understanding of the movie comported with what he had learned from it. As I spoke, a pleased look came over his face, as if I had arrived at some knowledge others had failed to grasp. He indicated that he was impressed with how well I understood what *The Matrix* was about.

Having an understanding of the significance of the film to Malvo's relationship with Muhammad, I was able to realize the depth of loyalty Malvo felt toward this man he called "Dad." I could also see why Malvo felt that he was the one to be sacrificed. As though putting me on notice, Malvo intoned that he would not succumb to any persuasion to go against his father. "They want to use me to kill my dad." "Who wants to use you to kill your dad?" I asked him. "These crackers," he responded. "But it's not going to happen." As he repeated this, he pounded his cuffed hands on the table. "I love my dad to death," he declared.

At this point I recognized that it was useless to challenge this devotion. Instead, I joined him in defense of a father (Muhammad) who had given him what he saw as true affirmation. I concurred with him, stating that "they" had to be crazy to think that he could be used to kill his dad. Malvo smiled, clearly satisfied with my response and feeling that I understood and appreciated his love for Muhammad.

For the first five sessions with Malvo, the overriding themes were oppression of blacks, not only in the United States but globally, and the loss of Muhammad's children. His rambling rhetoric was oftentimes interrupted with "Sorry, Dad." When I asked what he was sorry for, his face fell, and with eyes downcast, he responded that he fell asleep. He was the sentry and should have stood guard while Muhammad slept, but he was tired and he fell asleep. He blamed himself for the arrest.

Then he would go back into more rhetoric: "There is no difference between Jamaicans, Africans, black Americans, Guyanese, we are all black people. But America is the only place where blacks have the resources to make changes for black people all over the world. When I walk down the street, they don't see a Jamaican. They see a black man."

As I looked at Malvo sitting across from me, looking more like a fourteen-year-old than an eighteen-year-old, I could not help but say, "They don't see a man, they see a kid who really should be in school. So tell me, why I am sitting here and you sitting there across from me charged with first degree murder?" He didn't directly respond, but his eyes became teary. "Everybody is talking about the kid who got shot, but I am a kid too," he said woefully. Without going into any details, he said, "My dad wanted me to take a head shot, but I couldn't. Something inside me would not make me do it. I'm glad he survived."

I challenged him. "Can you understand why the kid who was shot generated so much attention and outrage?" He looked up at me again, with eyes that were far removed from the horrific acts he had committed, and said, "Yes, children are special. But as for me, nobody really cared. The only person who mattered to me was my dad. He's the only one who loves me." He recounted an occasion when he was shoved by a patron in a coffee shop, and Muhammad sprang to his defense. Muhammad grabbed the man's arm and almost broke it, then gave the man an ominous warning: "Never lay your hands again on my son." Malvo smiled as he recounted that incident. He was convinced that Muhammad had his interests at heart.

The meek persona that spoke with the voice of a hurt child was quickly replaced with an angry intonation. "We did everything to get the children back. Everything! Yet they took them away. How can a judge tell a man how and where to raise his kids?" he asked me. I responded that when the matter of custody arises, the court has to decide what is in the best interest of the child and, in the case of Muhammad's children, the judge might have felt it was better for the mother to have custody. "But he was the best father a kid could have. I never saw him hit his children. Not once. He was good to them. He was good to all children."

As I tentatively brought up the subject of Malvo's life in Jamaica, he spoke passionately about his biological father, Leslie Malvo. "He gave me balance. My dad was the nurturer." That balance was upset when the bond with his biological father was broken. He spoke of a deep longing to regain that nurturance and love, and this was what he found in John Allen Muhammad. I recognized that he was reliving his own pain at being taken away from his biological father and joining Muhammad in his grief for his children. In many ways Muhammad was the longed-for hero dad, the type of father who fights for his children, and that Malvo wished he'd had in his biological father.

The bonding with Muhammad took place on the island of Antigua, after Malvo's mother, Una James, left him to travel to the United States. Una reportedly traveled with illegal documents bought from Muhammad, who was residing on the island with his children at the time. Shortly after Una left, Malvo suffered an attack of rheumatic fever, a condition that plagued him as a child. He was near death when Muhammad went in search of him. Muhammad found Malvo and nursed him back to health. Finally, it seemed to Malvo, he had the father he'd been looking for. I realized I had to travel to the islands of Jamaica and Antigua to get a full understanding of the foundation of Malvo's attachment to Muhammad. I had to understand the lives of the parents who had him and then abandoned him. For though his attachment to Muhammad began in Antigua, Malvo's vulnerability to this kind of attachment started in Jamaica.

1 A Father Lost

The Genesis of Reactive Attachment Disorder
in Lee Boyd Malvo

MALVO'S EARLY LIFE IN JAMAICA

On February 18, 1985, in Kingston, Jamaica, Lee Boyd Malvo, the son of Una James and Leslie Malvo, was born. However, his story does not begin there. To understand Lee Malvo and the forces that shaped him and facilitated the persona of John Lee Muhammad, we have to understand the legacy his parents handed to him.

Leslie Malvo, born in St. Andrew, Jamaica, on December 26, 1947, traces his paternal lineage to Spain. According to Leslie, his father, Burby Malvo, was a World War I veteran who relocated to Jamaica after the war. Leslie stated that the correct spelling of the family name is actually Malveaux. "Is when him come to Jamaica dat dem spell it Malvo," he said.

Leslie Malvo sounded proud of his mixed heritage, citing his complexion and "good hair," which he inherited from his father, who he said was almost white. Burby and his Jamaican wife, Agatha, had seven children; Leslie was the last. (Both are deceased.) Leslie Malvo spoke of a loving home. "My father never beat me yet," he said with a satisfied smile on his face. He recalled as well that his mother, though the disciplinarian in the home, punished with a loving hand.

Leslie did not have the benefit of a high school education. He went as far as the sixth grade. He admits that academic learning was never one of his strong points. He was good with his hands, and after leaving school he learned masonry. To this day he earns his livelihood as a mason. While proud of his lineage, he seems a man of humble bearing, not given to airs, and with very simple needs. One such need was to have children who would bear his name and validate his sense of paternal pride.

Lee Malvo was Leslie's third child; he had fathered two other children by two different women. A fourth child was born to yet another woman after Una had Lee. Leslie's behavior is not unusual in the Jamaican culture, where many men have children by different sexual partners and often play a minimal role in the lives of their offspring. In Jamaica, it is not uncommon for children to be raised by single mothers with little or no support from fathers. The father's absence does not stop him from taking pride in the number of children he has.

Chevannes (2006), former dean of the Faculty of Social Sciences at the University of the West Indies, notes that within the African-Caribbean context, fatherhood is not only a matter of functional role but also a question of identity—that having children is a part of the construction of manhood. Fatherhood is a status and also a role that men are expected to play—providing for their children and being the guardian of their moral development, particularly for the boys.

Unfortunately, as Chevannes (2006) also points out, the tenuous role of fathers within the construct of the family has led to a crisis of masculinity and fatherhood. He attributes much of the dysfunction to the cumulative effects of Jamaica's troubled colonial past, the ill effects of migration, urbanization, and neoliberal economics—all of which have led to the loosening of family bonds and responsibility.

To Leslie Malvo's credit, despite the historical and sociocultural context, he did try to be a good and loving father. Rohan Malvo, Leslie's first son, said he had a close relationship with his father and that he could depend on him for support. Leslie's pride in being a father was especially evident after Lee Malvo's birth. "Of all my children, Lee look like me the most," he remarked. He expressed delight in Lee being light-complexioned and very intelligent. Leslie believed too that he had found the "love of his life" in Lee's mother, Una James.

Una's lot in life was quite different from Leslie's. She was born on September 8, 1964, in the rural district of Niagra, St. James. Her parents, Adolphus and Epsie James, had a tumultuous relationship marked by violence, which spilled over to affect the children. According to Marie Lawrence (née James), Malvo's maternal aunt and older sister to Una, both of her parents showed signs of psychological dysfunction. Epsie James has a history of mental illness and was a patient at the Bellevue (Mental) Hospital in Kingston prior to her involvement with Adolphus. Adolphus James was an alcoholic who was brutal to his family, especially when he came home drunk.

According to Marie, after suffering years of abuse, Epsie James decided that she was tired of it. One morning shortly after her husband left for work, she packed her bags, took her two daughters, and left the home. They traveled to another parish, St. Elizabeth, where they settled in a small district called Nain. She farmed the land for ground provisions such as yams, pumpkins, and bananas; cleaned houses; and washed clothes in order to support herself and the girls. Life was hard. It felt even harder for Una, who felt her potential was being wasted.

Marie stated that Una was the more academically inclined of the two sisters and yearned for an education. Una recalled that she would walk miles to find her father and ask him to pay for her schooling. He refused. Marie said she also made a similar request of her father, but no money was forthcoming.

At age sixteen, after completing the ninth grade, Una opted to escape the doldrums of her life in St. Elizabeth by moving to the capital city of Kingston. There she found work as a live-in maid, but wages were low and life remained hard. She recalled that she had to wash, clean, cook, and do everything else to keep the household running. Her job was akin to that of an unpaid maid. She was able eventually to obtain accommodations with an older relative, but the living conditions were crowded and conflicts developed.

Despite the indignities Una suffered, she still aspired to improve her life. She worked during the day and attended classes at night, in English, mathematics, accounting, and shorthand. She said that despite her efforts, she did not get affirmation and support from her family. Rather, she was abused. It was in the midst of her despair that she met Leslie Malvo.

When Una became pregnant by Leslie, he saw this as a turning point in his life. He felt positive about settling down and providing for Una and his unborn child. Whether or not Una's pregnancy was planned is debatable; she has made assertions on both sides of the issue. According to both parents, Malvo was a good-looking baby, happy and content, and according to his mother, cried very little. He was also a healthy baby who reached his developmental milestones at a much earlier age than the average child. According to Una, when she looked at her young son she recalled that education was what she had wanted most as a child, so she could grow up to be whatever she wanted. She was determined to do everything she could to ensure that her son would have a good education.

DAD THE NURTURER

Malvo's earliest memories are of interactions with his father, Leslie. Malvo recalled that he and his father developed a quick bond. His father was the nurturing parent. According to Malvo, he did not make much of a fuss at home, thus allowing Malvo to be a child, to play and break things. Malvo said that when he was two years old Leslie bought him a tricycle, and they spent a lot of time with that tricycle. Though he was quite young, Malvo carried fond memories of that period of his life. He remembered that he always wanted to be a pilot, and his father encouraged him. He recalled that even when he tried to draw, his father made something out of his scribbles. When he did well at a task, his father was there to encourage him, and when all was not right, his father reassured him with a smile.

An incident that stood out for Malvo illustrates how important it was to have the balance his father provided. In pretending to be a pilot, young Malvo was playing with his miniature plane and moving around obstacles that he imagined were skyscrapers. During his play, he broke a cherished porcelain vase that belonged to his mother. He recalled sobbing as he looked at what he had done and worried about his mother's reaction. Even though Leslie tried to reassure Malvo that Una would not be allowed to chastise him, Malvo was not convinced. His fears were confirmed when he heard his mother shriek, "Lee!!!" after she saw the broken vase that Leslie had carefully placed in a box. However, as she reached for Malvo, Leslie stepped forward. "Leave the boy alone. I broke it. You'll buy another one next week!" For Malvo, his father was his hero.

Leslie's devotion to Malvo and Una did not go unnoticed. Some young men who knew the family went as far as to suggest that Leslie was the "perfect father." In the impoverished community of Waltham Gardens in Kingston, it was unusual to see a father being so attentive to his son. In a society where absent fathers are not only tolerated but also excused, it was refreshing to onlookers to see the bond they had. Lloyd Barrett, a neighbor and friend of Leslie's, said that Leslie's relationship with Malvo was an inspiration, and that he learned how to be a good father by watching Leslie. Lloyd and other men from the community remembered that Malvo was with his father so often that he was affectionately called "Pardie," meaning that he was seen as his father's little partner. Malvo's father also called him "Little Man."

While Leslie was the nurturer, Una was a hard taskmaster. She exercised the fire-and-brimstone kind of discipline with which she'd been raised.

Unlike the relationship Malvo had with his father, the relationship with his mother was, to use Malvo's term, an "inconsistent one." He learned very early that she had certain expectations for him that seemed to extend beyond the normal expectations that a mother has for her child. She ruled him with an iron fist, and playing was seen as an intrusion on her efforts to make her son studious. So there was to be no playing; at least when Leslie was not around.

Leslie recalled that Una inflicted excessive punishment on Malvo when he was not there. He remembered that Una would beat him for any insignificant thing, with her fist or anything that was close at hand; she also pinched him often. Leslie recalled that she would beat Malvo as though she were beating a grown child. He would see the evidence of the beatings when he came home from work; although Malvo would have completed his homework, he would be sitting in a corner. "He could not move from that corner," Leslie recalled. According to Leslie, to get his son away from that punitive environment, he would take him to the corner shop on his bicycle and buy him ice cream.

Malvo had early recollections of his mother imposing demands on him. He could not have been more than three or four years old when she started demanding that he learn to read, and he was expected to study his words until the lights went out. According to him, his mother tried to instill in him that his father had little or no ambition, and she was determined that he would not follow his father's path. He wrote: "Even when my father and she were on good terms, she would scold me, 'Don't do this like your father.' She was also fanatical about education, and overzealous about religion."

Una James indicated that it was her aspiration to make something of her life even while she lived with Leslie. The impression conveyed was that Leslie, who was almost twice her age, did try to do for her what her father had failed to do. For instance, when she informed Leslie of her desire to do sewing and fashion designing, he bought her two Singer sewing machines and sent her to trade school.

To ensure that Malvo received academically what she had been denied as a child, Una placed him in preschool at age two. This school was called Nanny School, named for a Jamaican national hero, Nanny of the Maroons, and located in the community where they lived.

In contrast to Una's all-business approach, Leslie liked to be jovial and laid back. He was a regular domino player on Oakland and Waltham Park Road. This domino spot was like many others found in poor communities of the island, where men gather to play and drink. One can hear the tap-tapping of the dominoes on tables or makeshift stands. Shouts of "six-love" boom over the chatter of men (and occasionally, brave women) as they wager on the games. In close proximity there is a bartender raking up sales of Red Stripe beer and Dragon or Guinness stout, and of course the popular Over Proof Jamaican White Rum.

According to Leslie, he was quite content with his simple life. He wanted to own his own home and provide for the family, ensuring that Una got to start her business and "Little Man" went to the best school that he could afford.

Although Leslie was content, his gambling habit was a sore point because Una felt it affected the family finances. Leslie disagreed, saying that although he gambled, he was able to provide adequately for his family. Reportedly, a dispute over his gambling practices erupted into a violent confrontation. Leslie hit Una in her face and she retaliated by striking him with a machete. Malvo saw this and cites it as one of his early memories.

The bickering about finances illustrated that the income Leslie earned was not sufficient to realize his dream of owning a home, especially when some of his earnings went toward gambling debts. So in 1988, when he was offered employment as a mason in Grand Cayman, he seized the opportunity. This meant that he had to leave his family and travel to Grand Cayman, where he was contracted to work and reside for up to six months at a time.

Leslie loved the Waltham Gardens community, but it was not the best place to raise a son who held so much promise. So prior to taking up his assignment in Grand Cayman, Leslie decided to move his family to a better neighborhood. Malvo was three years old when they moved to a house in the Washington Gardens area, a safer residential neighborhood. This home was much larger and comprised living and dining areas, with separate bedrooms for the parents and for Malvo. Unlike the residence on Oakland Road, it had indoor plumbing. There was also a lawn in front.

For Malvo, the nicer, safer surroundings were inviting, but his mother's temperament did not change. He could not enjoy the lawn because of her prohibitive rule about going outside. He was sent to one of the best private schools in the area, which provided him with a solid educational foundation, but according to him, it was all study and no play. When his father was at home, he felt happy. He continued to rely on his father to offset his mother's rigid approach to parenting. However, with Leslie's long spells away in Grand Cayman, those precious times were fewer and far between. He recalled that his mother frequently reminded him that his father was not there to "spoil him."

When Leslie left for the contract work in Grand Cayman, he assured Una and Malvo that his decision was for the benefit of all of them. According to him, he worked and sent money by Western Union at least twice per month. He stated that after everyday expenses were taken out, he sent the balance to be saved for the purchase of a home.

Leslie returned to Jamaica on major holidays: at Christmas, at Easter, and in August for the Jamaican independence holiday. He usually brought goods for the home, including TVs, radios, appliances, and toys and clothes for Malvo and Una. Leslie said that he had J$18,000 (Jamaican currency) in an account at Victoria Mutual Building Society in Kingston at one point. This was the equivalent of US$3,600. He decided that he was ready to start saving toward buying a house. From the J$18,000, he took J$10,000 and opened a certificate of deposit account. He said that it was a joint account with Una. The bank, he recalled, had advised him that if he allowed the money to remain for a year, he could get a mortgage of up to J$100,000. He recalled ruefully that he could have bought a house for J$80,000 to J$100,000 at the time. Life was good, and he felt that he, Una, and Malvo would remain together as a family.

MALVO IS TAKEN AWAY FROM HIS FATHER

According to Una, she became frustrated with Leslie's reluctance to have her join him in the Cayman Islands. She felt that this signaled he was having an affair—an accusation that Leslie denies. According to him, he could not have his family join him until he had his own place. He insisted that he had every intention of "doing the right thing" by Una. He recalled that he had even purchased an engagement ring for her, and wanted to surprise her upon his return to Jamaica. Malvo remembered that his primary focus while his father was away was the anticipation of his father's return home.

Leslie had a visit scheduled for August 1990, to celebrate independence day. However, by then Una was ready to move on with her life, without Leslie. She decided that finding her sister, Marie Lawrence, from whom she had been estranged, would be the first step to ending the relationship. She knew that Marie lived somewhere in the parish of St. Ann, close to Brown's Town, but did not know the exact location. Eventually, she learned the details and set about finding her. Though years of separation and bitterness had kept the sisters apart, they reportedly hugged when they saw each other and expressed joy at their reunion. Una informed Marie she needed a new start and wanted to leave Kingston. Endeavor, where Marie lived, was located in the hills of St. Ann and seemed a perfect hideaway for Una. It seemed unlikely that Leslie would be able to find her and Malvo there.

According to Leslie, he was scheduled to arrive in Jamaica on Monday, August 6, 1990. On Friday the 3rd, he sent Una US$200 via Western Union. She collected the money and then, according to him, emptied the joint account prior to his arrival. She packed up everything in the house and moved to Endeavor. Malvo was aware of what was happening and was crushed, but he felt confident his father would find him and take him away from his mother. Una disputes that the money was all Leslie's and stated that she had contributed a significant portion of it as well. She insists that she did not "steal" Leslie's money.

Upon his return home, Leslie was shocked when he did not see the woman he expected to marry and his beloved son. The landlady was surprised to see him. "Brown Man," he recalled her saying, "What you doing here? Una move and gone with everything." Leslie was devastated. He gave his landlady a portion of the rent and went to the bank to see whether the money in the joint account was gone as well. To his dismay, the account was empty. His dreams of a life with Una and Malvo were dashed.

Leslie returned to the old neighborhood at Oakland Road, where he informed his buddies that Una had left and taken Malvo and everything else with her. "We could not believe it. He was too good to that woman and little Pardie," his friend Lloyd Barrett recalled. "He was like a lost man. No one on the corner could believe that Una had left him, and the fact that she had taken Malvo was the worst blow of all. That child was his life."

According to Leslie, he began his search for the truck that had moved his family. He walked for miles, asking every truck driver in the surrounding area if they remembered moving a family from Right Hand Crescent in Washington Gardens. He finally found the driver and made his way to Endeavor, but when he arrived Una was not there.

According to Leslie, he caught up with Una the following day and confronted her. He begged her to give the relationship a chance, but she refused. She told him she left him because she heard he was having an affair. He tried explaining that he was not cheating on her, but her mind was made up. He recalled the utter devastation he felt as she rejected his pleas. By then Una had started a small retail shop in Endeavor. Malvo, in the meantime, had to adjust to a new community.

Malvo recalled that his mother began a process of erasing all similarities with Leslie. "You're just like your puppa [father]," he remembered her saying as she tried to remove whatever traits she saw of his father. These included the toy guns and toy soldiers his father had given him.

It should be noted that toy guns and toy soldiers were popular playthings for little boys in Jamaica. Such toys given to Malvo by his father, Leslie, might now seem unfortunate choices, but they were not intended or perceived at the time to be anything other than play objects. Nevertheless, Malvo recalled that his mother burned them. The toys were replaced with nursery rhymes, which, according to him, he had to read to his mother.

Malvo had to adjust to other difficult changes. One day Una and her sister had a disagreement, which resulted in Una moving to a neighboring district. Una also had another boyfriend, Norman (not his real name). Malvo felt protective of his father's interest, so he resented his mother's relationship with Norman. Malvo showed his dislike in ways that resulted in beatings.

Home became an unhappy place for Malvo. Gone were the days when he could look forward to going home to Dad, and be treated to ice cream and a ride on his bicycle. He dreamed of those days when he sat on Leslie's knee as his father toppled the dominoes on the table. "Six love!!" Though only months had passed, it seemed like an eternity. He dreaded returning home to his mother and Norman after school. So he learned to hang out after school in order to postpone it as much as possible. When he did get home, he would be severely punished.

Malvo said that the beatings and comparisons to his father did not have the desired effect. As he walked around Brown's Town aimlessly, he thought only of his father and hoped that he would rescue him. Though Una asked Malvo what was wrong, she would not listen to his explanation. He recalled that whenever he explained that he just wanted to have his father around, his mother would slap him across his face angrily for even mentioning it. He felt despair. He was unable to understand why his father had not yet returned to save him from what he saw as the tyranny of his mother and her new lover. Early depression had begun to set in.

LAST ATTEMPT AT REUNION

Leslie said that he made about three trips to Endeavor, but to no avail. The last visit occurred after he returned to Jamaica from another one of his work stints in Grand Cayman. He was laden with gifts for Malvo and Una. Malvo has memories of this:

In his last attempt to create some amicable reunion, my dad returned in the summer of 1991. He came well dressed in two cars, one carrying him, the other carrying boxes of toys, books, clothing, and other gifts he bought Mom and myself. He made a huge impression in the little town square from which the shop was only a stone's throw. While they spoke I was stuck on my father like a bee on pollen. We talked, and being myself I filled him in about [Norman] and how Mom beat me for him. He confronted her and asked her while searching my scalp for wounds. "Why did she bust the boy's head?" he asked. "Una, how much time me afi tell you that you can't beat him like sey him a no animal!" [Una, how often do I have to tell you that you can't beat him like he is an animal.]

Malvo cherished the hope that Una would give his father a second chance. He tried in his own way to foster an atmosphere of congeniality between his parents. He even got a water coconut and two straws meant for them to share. Una would have none of this. Leslie begged her to return to him, but she refused. Leslie saw how disappointed Malvo was, so he took him for a walk. During the walk Leslie opened a package he had brought for his son. In it were two flight jackets. One was black leather and the other was silver, with what seemed to Malvo like a million military tags all over it. Malvo recalled the good feeling he had because his father remembered that he wanted to be a pilot.

A reunion was what Leslie had hoped for, but all he left with that evening was a promise that Malvo would be allowed to see him on the holidays. Malvo was filled with despair. Leslie was not able to stand up to Una as he had hoped, and thus failed to take Malvo with him as the boy wished. He was disappointed. He reflected on the times when his father had stood up to his mother. Where was the hero he had once cherished?

To make matters worse, the beatings increased after Leslie's last visit. Malvo noted that his mother was angry that he had told his father about the abuse. It seemed to him that after his father left, the beatings from his mother became laced with vengeance. He felt no love at home, and there was no reprieve from the abuse he suffered. Furthermore, the rift between Una and her sister, Marie Lawrence, meant that Malvo could no longer visit with Marie's children.

This was very upsetting to Marie and her girls, as they were aware of the frequent beatings. One of Marie's daughters, Stacy Ann, recalled that she had visited the shop that Una was operating and observed Una beating Malvo. He could not have been more than six years old at the time. Una was hitting him all over his body with a belt, and despite the fact that Malvo's nose was bleeding, Una did not stop. Marie recalled her daughter running to her to tell her that Una was "murdering Lee," but when she went to the shop to try to stop the beating, Una turned on her and she had to leave. On another occasion, Una was beating Malvo with such fury that Marie intervened to try to stop it. Una grabbed a pair of scissors and threatened to stab her with it. Had it not been for Marie's husband, who was present, she feels that Una would have caused her serious harm. Malvo felt isolated because there was really no one who could come between him and his mother's abusive attitude. His only escape was when he went to school.

Malvo was transferred to Brown's Town Basic School, which provided a better academic curriculum than the basic school he was attending. He did well. Brown's Town was the nearest commercial center to Endeavor. Lula Bradshaw, the principal of the school, has fond memories of Malvo. She described him as an intelligent and giving child. He was the head boy during his last year at the school, which meant that he was the best overall in academic and social attributes. Ms. Bradshaw said Malvo showed a propensity for sharing that was outstanding. He was exceptionally intelligent but also not selfish with his knowledge, sharing what he learned with the other children. Though Malvo was only six years old, Ms. Bradshaw saw in him the potential for greatness. Upon graduation from the basic school, he was adorned with many awards and certificates, but a picture of his graduation shows a sad little boy. "There was no dad to share the joy with me," he wrote.

Malvo said that his mother was prone to severe mood swings. He remembered that she would be happy one moment and twenty minutes later would glare at him and curse under her breath. He remembered that her mood swings were especially evident when he and his mother were alone and, curious child that he was, he would ask her questions. Sometimes she answered him patiently, even tenderly. Other times she glared and sent him to bed.

In many of my interactions with Una James, I have experienced her moods myself; we could be having a reasonable discussion, and then without warning she would spring to her feet and begin railing against everything and everyone around her, including me. She would lash out at the government for not stepping in to get Malvo away from Muhammad; then in the same sentence, she would lash out at Malvo, blaming him for the problems she faced and stating that she wished she had aborted him.

There were also inconsistencies in what she wanted for him. Malvo gave his mother credit for teaching him how to draw. However, as he developed that skill, he remembered her insisting that she wanted him to be a doctor, not an artist. She would replace his crayons and pencils with medical toys, such as stethoscopes.

Malvo said he felt like a "puss kitten," a term referring to the way cats and their kittens are generally treated in Jamaica. They are not prized as pets as in many other countries. In Jamaica, cats are ignored or worse, stoned. He felt abandoned. Like a "puss kitten," his life seemed to be worth nothing. He longed for attachment and began to identify with a stray cat he saw, which he imagined shared a similar need for connection. He begged and cajoled his mother to allow him to take the cat in. He promised that he would house train it.

Malvo found comfort in his pet cat, Charlie. When put in context, this is startling, as generally children in Jamaica grow up seeing cats as wild and suspicious creatures that are not allowed indoors. In that context, a cat's only purpose is to hunt mice. It is culturally normative for Jamaican children to grow up stoning and hitting cats; it is not acceptable to take cats inside and sleep with them.

A beating that made an indelible impression on Malvo came about because of his cat. Malvo recalled that Charlie urinated on the bed. Una screamed like Malvo had never heard her scream before. Then, he recalled, she hit him in the head until he bled. The screaming, he said, hurt more than the physical blows. She insisted that he get rid of the cat and threatened that she would not stop beating him until Charlie was gone. He recalled feeling tremendous anger toward his mother, but he was not able to lash out at her. Malvo recalled that he got Charlie, placed him on the steps, and hit him with a broom as hard as he could. Malvo said that whenever Charlie returned to the house, he had to hit him until he went away. It could be argued here that much of the anger that Malvo felt toward his mother was being displaced onto the cat. After the cat stopped coming to the house, Malvo, who had been potty trained from when he was one year old, began to wet the bed regularly.

He recalled the emptiness that he felt when he could no longer have Charlie as a source of comfort. While to an American audience, this stoning or hitting of the cat may be seen as indicative of future sociopathic behavior, this would not be the case in Jamaica where, at that time, cats were common victims of animal cruelty.

Significant as well is that Malvo was unaware of the memories his cat stirred for his mother. Marie Lawrence, Una's sister, remembered that she and Una had shared a cat as children. According to Marie, it was the only "toy" they had. They were very poor and could not afford regular toys, so, despite their father's objection, they got a stray cat. Their father's reason for not wanting a cat in the house stemmed from folklore that cats are like vampires and suck the blood of children. Thus, they had to hide the animal from their father. When their father found it in the home, he killed it. "We cried so hard, because we really loved that cat," Marie recalled.

No dogs, no cats, no pets, and no interaction with his cousins left Malvo even more isolated. His loneliness was more palpable when his mother left him to go into Kingston to buy goods for her shop. She bought food items and dry goods, which she then sold to tourists in the neighboring town of Ocho Rios. Sometimes she would be gone for days at a time. On such occasions she left Malvo with babysitters. Years later, Malvo remembered an incident of molestation perpetuated by a babysitter. This was a memory that he had repressed, and it did not resurface until much later; it will be discussed later in the book.

Occasionally, Una took Malvo with her to Kingston. On one such occasion they returned only to find boxes of perishable goods, including chicken, chicken backs, turkey necks, beef, and mutton, all spoiled. They saw about two dozen vultures circling the shop. Upon opening the door, they were greeted by a foul stench, because the meat had sat for five days in a completely enclosed space. Una was informed that the landlord had turned off the electricity because of an unpaid bill. Una blamed her sister, Marie, for the landlord's action. Marie, in turn, blamed Una for failing to pay the electricity bill. Malvo was mortified and scared. He feared a showdown between the sisters.

> Mom was not the crying type, so she got a machete and walked down the street, [Norman] accompanying her. Well, Aunt Marie also wanted to fight. [Norman] and John, Marie's husband, separated the sisters. The festering wounds between sisters made Endeavor seem gloomy in all future prospects. So we packed up and returned to Kingston.

LIFE IN A WAR ZONE

When he was seven years old, two years after he was taken to the hills of Endeavor, Malvo returned to Kingston, but not under hopeful circumstances. Waterhouse, a volatile community in Kingston, was one of the few areas with rental housing that Una could afford. Malvo and Una lived in a tenement yard shared by several residents who each had their own living space.

Malvo was anxious about the relationship between his mother and Norman. Norman accompanied them to Kingston and seemed intent on remaining with the family, even though he had to sleep elsewhere because there was not enough room for him. In those cramped conditions, Malvo longed for the days with his father in that nice home in Washington Gardens. However, he had to cope not only with Norman but also with life in Waterhouse, one of the dangerous garrison communities in Kingston.

Garrison communities are known for their strong allegiance to either of the two major political parties, the Jamaica Labour Party (JLP) or the People's National Party (PNP). In exchange for living in certain areas, residents are expected to demonstrate loyalty to whichever party controls that area. This allegiance is defended against outside influence and enforced within by area leaders, often called Dons, and their subordinates. The power assumed by or invested in these leaders includes administering or executing systems of "justice," rewards and punishment, and economic and social benefits upon residents.

After the move to Waterhouse, Malvo was enrolled at the Rousseau Primary School, where he started second grade. This school is adjacent to some of the roughest areas in Kingston. Nevertheless, it reportedly had an excellent record and was seen as a haven in a community fraught with violence.

Malvo was a student there for two years. Teachers described him as "enthusiastic," "optimally rounded," "excellent in all areas," and having "good rapport with students and teachers." The teachers who knew and taught him saw great promise in his future. They stressed that Malvo not only was smart academically but also showed interest in other school activities. Because of his demeanor, Malvo impressed his teachers as a child from a middle-class home where all his material and emotional needs were being met. However, nothing could be further from the truth.

In fact, Malvo felt transplanted to a war zone where he had to be on constant alert. In Waterhouse he did not have the luxury of staying out late in order to delay facing the unpleasant conditions at home. He had to return immediately after school due to the risk of getting shot in the streets, by either gunmen or the police.

Malvo's first exposure to gun violence occurred when he was about seven years old and on his way to school. A police raid had occurred earlier, and the incident sparked a violent exchange between the police and gunmen.

Malvo heard that as the gunmen ran through a tenement yard, a stray bullet killed a pregnant woman. The police raid and the tragic result did not sit well with the area Don, who instructed his supporters to take action. They took their reprisal on a few police officers at a roadblock.

Malvo remarked that out of necessity he had learned what to do whenever there was gunfire, so he fell on the ground when he heard the shooting. However, fearing that he was still in harm's way, he decided to run. He began running in the direction of the gunmen, who surprisingly were not running away from the police. And the police, Malvo noted, did not seem to be running toward their target. He saw further that this was because a trap had been set for them. (In many of the garrison communities, entry and exit are denied outsiders when the metal grates covering large, wide trenches beneath the road surface are removed.) On this occasion, as soon as the police drove into the community the metal grates were removed, preventing them from leaving.

In his flight, Malvo saw a youth of about fourteen years old behind a wall. The police were behind Malvo, shouting at him to take cover, and were oblivious to the youth behind the wall. Malvo recalled the youth communicating with his compatriots with sounds similar to the chirping of birds. One policeman was so focused on stopping Malvo from running to his death that he did not see his own death coming. Malvo recalled what he witnessed:

The young man pointed with his right hand holding the gun between the space in the wall and with his left motioned to me to hit the ground, I dropped and started hollering, "Don't kill me, don't kill me, I won't say anything." I heard a bang. I thought I was shot but when I looked behind me, the head of the policeman was basically gone. I got up and the young man who had shot "Babylon" (as policemen are called in these communities) called out to me to stay put. When the coast was clear, he grabbed me, gently placed me behind the wall, and told me that he would return and tell me when to come out.

I don't know how long he was gone. I was not checking the time. I was too busy looking at the dead policeman. The young man returned, and I will never forget that face. He flashed me a smile, then lifted me from my hiding place and told me to go home. But in an instant the smile evaporated: he shook the revolver and patted it on his leg. He looked at the policeman, then looked at me, and his message was clear. Hear no evil, see no evil, speak no evil! In the garrison there is an unspoken rule that if you snitch they kill not only you but your immediate family, extended family, cat, dogs, babies—everything related to you. The policeman's was the first in a trail of bodies that I would see over the next few years. Most would be strangers like the policeman on the ground in front of me, while others would be family.

There was no school for Malvo that day. The community was so tense after the shooting of the police officer that it took a couple of days for the streets to calm down. Malvo told his mother what he had seen and she comforted him, happy that he was not killed. Living in a war zone, however, meant that he had to learn ways to survive the violence. Malvo recalled being saved by that youth, who spared his life even though he had witnessed the murder. That was unusual, as witnesses are usually eliminated as well, particularly if they are not well known as part of the community.

According to Malvo, though he was a newcomer, he wanted to be known and liked by the local men. This was his way of ensuring protection. So he began to chat with the men on the corner. In talking with them, he felt sure that they would keep him out of harm's way and alert him to danger whenever it was imminent. One day, as he talked to one of them, the man placed his hand over Malvo's mouth to make him shut up. Then he heard the whistles and the shout of "Babylon!" That meant the police or the army was close at hand. He was told to go home, and everyone scattered.

Malvo went home and told his mother what he had heard, that there was going to be a raid, and this meant all precautions should be taken to avoid being caught in the crossfire. He told her that the men on the corner sent him home. Back on the street, conditions were still violent. Malvo's focus was avoiding becoming a victim. He saw another body not long after the first incident he described. This time he was returning from school and witnessed another battle between a gunman and the police. This time, the police shot the gunman. In these areas, the police often engaged their targets in the midst of law-abiding citizens, which did not make the police popular among the residents. Furthermore, the police raids and curfews stopped people from earning a living, and every so often, an innocent bystander could be shot.

Despite the violence in his community, Malvo also had some fond memories. Christmas was a happy occasion, especially when children were given treats. Malvo recalled a popular reggae artist, Shabba Ranks, bringing a "trailer load of toys" for the area kids. Shabba Ranks's generosity to the children of the community was not lost on Malvo, who dreamed of a time when he too could bring joy to depressed children. He imagined flying all over the world and bringing back gifts at Christmas. Such dreams again brought back memories of his father returning from Grand Cayman laden with gifts for him.

That particular Christmas was also special for Malvo because he was allowed to spend part of the holidays with his father. Leslie was living in the more peaceful residential area of Duhaney Park, where residents did not have to dodge bullets when coming home from work or school. Malvo wished that he could stay with his father permanently. He told his father of the times he'd narrowly missed getting shot, and he told him about Una's boyfriend, Norman, and the abuse Norman and Una meted out to him. Leslie decided to accompany Malvo to Waterhouse to see exactly where his son lived. Norman was not interviewed and so could not confirm or deny any role in beating Malvo, but Leslie confirms that his son told him about Norman beating him and his mother allowing it. Leslie recalled that he confronted Una about it; he was outraged and castigated her for bringing his child into such a dangerous living situation. He remembered that Una would have none of this and told Leslie to leave, which he did, but not before a final plea for her to return to him; however, this was ignored. That holiday was the second to last visit Malvo had with his father.

Despite the setbacks Una encountered, she continued to strive for financial independence, which she hoped would enable her to provide for herself and her son, whether or not she received support from Leslie. She enrolled in a vocational school where she took more courses in fashion design and sewing. She worked hard as a self-employed seamstress. She bought fabric and made shirts, pants, and uniforms for hotel workers. She traveled to the tourist resort towns of Ocho Rios and Montego Bay to sell her merchandise.

As a result of her industriousness, Una was able to make a down payment on a home in a housing development named Greater Portmore. This enabled Norman to move in with her and Malvo. Shortly after the move, Una's relationship with Norman deteriorated. Malvo recalled the conflict that characterized the relationship. He felt caught in the middle, especially when these conflicts led to physical altercations. As young as he was, Malvo felt he had to stand up on his mother's side in such fights.

Eventually Una ran out of money and had to give up the house in Greater Portmore and move back to the violent Waterhouse community. Malvo recalled that they moved in with a cousin named Precious, and her husband and four children. This was an unsafe and unstable arrangement for Malvo. Precious reportedly was in conflict with the area Don, mainly because he was uncertain about her political allegiance.

Malvo recalled that Precious was given an ultimatum to move out of the area in a week or face the consequences. On the last day, as she loaded her things into the truck, gunmen came to make sure that she was leaving. Malvo was posted at the gate to sound the warning if he saw the gunmen approaching. "Them coming!" he shouted. But rather than hurrying to leave, Precious grabbed a knife and stormed the gate. Una grabbed Malvo and jumped behind the fence. Within minutes, the confrontation ended with a bang. Through a hole in the fence, Malvo saw Precious's head blown away by a bullet. Malvo was about eight years old, and in less than a year he had witnessed three murders.

Forced to find alternative accommodations, Una and Malvo moved in with a neighbor, Mrs. Gray (not her real name). Their presence on the premises provoked an altercation between Mrs. Gray and her landlord, who demanded more money because of the additional occupants. Una joined in, siding with Mrs. Gray. The landlord was forced to run away, but not before he made an ominous threat: "Next time I'm gonna kill somebody." Such a warning, coming on the heels of Precious's death, had to be taken seriously. Una decided that it was time to move on, but Malvo was once again caught in the middle of conflict. He recalled:

> Mrs. Gray fled to friends, Mom and I with her. Well, we forgot to take some clothes so Mom decided we had to sneak into the house to get some clothes and the money in her handbag. The landlord was posted there, and as soon as we entered the yard—not through the front gate but over the backyard fence—and walked around the corner of the house, our eyes locked with a man with a bandage on his arm and something black and metallic in his hand. He pointed and shouted and we took off. In the process Mom and I got separated. Lost, I wandered aimlessly looking for my mother, as the police were about to start a raid. I ran in the midst of them, grabbed an officer, and told him that my mom and I were separated as we were running from the landlord, who was trying to shoot my mother. Then I explained the entire exodus since Greater Portmore. The officers returned to Mrs. Gray's apartment (if you can call it that) and, after asking a few questions of the neighbors, soon reunited me with my mom, giving her some words of advice. "You need to get this child out of this area."

Una asserts that the advice of the police officers is what prompted her to think seriously about migrating. She recalled that the officer was impressed with Malvo's intelligence and saw in him the potential for success, but recognized that his life was at risk in such a bad environment. Una said that she knew the only way she could give Malvo the opportunity to succeed was to travel abroad.

Despite their tenuous relationship and the harsh discipline that Una inflicted on Malvo, she strove to improve the economic prospects for both of them. Furthermore, Malvo and Una had grown closer after Norman was out of their lives. Malvo even formed a few cherished memories of doing fun things with his mom. Knowing how much it meant to her for him to do well, Malvo excelled in school. He aspired to be the perfect child and the perfect student.

Though he still longed for his dad, Malvo realized that he and his father might not live in the same home like before. Even though he had siblings by his father, he was his mother's only child, so there were no siblings with whom he could bond. It seemed that she was all he had. Una remembered that because Malvo was such an insightful child, she could sit him down and have intelligent conversations with him. She told him about her plans to travel abroad, and he supported those plans. According to her, Malvo was not like other children his age. "He knew that I wanted a better life for him," she said.

MIGRATION AND ITS IMPACT ON FAMILIES

Una's desire to migrate was not unlike that of many Jamaican mothers who choose to leave their children behind in search of a better life overseas. Once she decided to do it, Una made arrangements for her things to be stored and safeguarded. Her other concern was what to do with Malvo. She could not take him with her, so she had to leave him with someone. In Jamaica it is common for parents who decide to migrate to leave their children with a relative. Ensuring that the child is in a nurturing environment helps to alleviate the trauma of the separation and reduces the risk of the child going astray.

In "Understanding the Impact of Parental Migration on Children: Implications for Counseling Families from the Caribbean," Pottinger & Brown (2006) point to an estimated one in five Caribbean children being a child of an immigrant. They cite four forms of migration that allow for immigrants to remain involved in the development of their country of origin. The first is seasonal migration, in which the parent travels for six months at a time to work in the host/receiving country. In many cases, a person can remain legally in the host country for up to six months and will engage in unauthorized employment. This allows for travel back and forth to the host country as long as a valid visa is in place. The second type is serial migration, in which parents migrate singly or together with the intention of sending for the family at a later date. The third type is parental migration, in which the parents migrate for a defined time or indefinitely, but have no intention of having their children live in the overseas country. The fourth type is family migration, where parents migrate with their family.

The effects of separation between the parent and the child at migration can be somewhat tempered by the environment in which the child is left. In a familiar environment, with strong family connection, there is less harm for the child. Ironically, the last of the D.C. sniper victims, Conrad Johnson, a Jamaican, was also left behind as a child when his mother, Sonia Wills, migrated to the United States. She recalled that when she left her son, he was two years old. However, she was able to leave Conrad with her sister, who provided him with love, nurturing, and constancy.

For Una, finding someone with whom she could leave her son was not an easy task. She was isolated from her own family and, given her estrangement from Leslie, there was no one in Malvo's paternal family to whom she could turn. She had to look outside of the family. She turned to a woman she had met when they were training as seamstresses, who lived on the outskirts of Barbican, a community in the suburbs of Kingston. The first time Malvo met this woman was the day before his mother left for St. Maarten.

THE ROLLING STONE YEARS

Malvo was nine years old when his mother first traveled overseas. This was the first of many separations and interestingly, according to Una, it was Malvo who sought to dry her tears as she said good-bye. He reminded her that she was leaving so she could build a better life for them. While reassuring his mother that she was doing the right thing, Malvo also felt the emotional trauma of the separation. Later on, he would write in his journal:

> Mom looked at me and laughed, and then she walked away. It was a good thing she didn't turn around because I was crying. Silent beads of tears

rolled down my cheeks. I would not mouth the sounds. I just let the tears fall, standing like an immovable boulder and watching my mother get smaller and smaller as the distance increased between us. A true statement—the gap between us would only grow greater over the years, the void in me that neither of us could ever fill.

Malvo made an effort to settle into the home of his mother's friend. He was registered at the nearby Barbican Primary School, and did well there. However, according to Malvo, his presence in the home caused tension between this woman and her spouse. Malvo claimed that the woman's spouse beat him, particularly when the woman was not at home to protect him. He said that he wrote to his mother about the abuse, but she never responded. Ultimately the woman informed Una that the arrangement had to end. It was 1995, and Malvo was ten years old.

Realizing that she had to place Malvo somewhere else, Una sent him to his father. Malvo wanted Leslie to keep him permanently; he thought that living with his father could bring stability to his life. He had come to cherish his memories of life up until age five, the last time he and his parents all lived together. But to Malvo's disappointment, Leslie said he could not keep him. Malvo was devastated and felt abandoned.

Leslie has since said that he refused to keep his son because he lived part time in the Cayman Islands and part time in Jamaica, and it would have been difficult to have someone stay with Malvo when he had to travel to Grand Cayman. However, Malvo felt that his father's refusal lay more in the fact that the woman his father was living with saw the boy as an intrusion rather than as part of the family. This was the last time Malvo spent any time with his father.

Following Leslie's refusal, Una made arrangements for Malvo to spend the summer holidays with her in St. Maarten. He felt severely hurt by what he saw as rejection by his father, but he tried to make the best of the visit. Una was cleaning houses seven days a week and also working in a store. She had a new boyfriend who actually took a liking to Malvo, and whom Malvo recalls with fondness. At ten years old, he was beginning to feel hopeful of settling down in a family environment with his mother and a new father.

However, St. Maarten was hit by Hurricane Luis in September 1995, and this made Malvo's staying impossible. The hurricane was devastating; very little of St. Maarten was spared. Hotels, yachts, homes, and businesses were demolished. Looting was rampant. The hurricane destroyed the feeble, hutlike structure in which Una lived. She lost everything and had to seek shelter with friends. She faced difficulties trying to recover economically. Furthermore, she could not enroll Malvo in school because she was not a legal resident. He had to return to Jamaica, but to whom could she send him? Malvo's father had refused to keep him, and the only other person whom she could turn to was her sister, Marie Lawrence. She decided to put away her animosity toward Marie and reach out to her for help. Marie (whom Malvo calls Aunt Marie) responded favorably.

When Malvo was returned to Jamaica, he was ten years old and already had been uprooted ten times. He wondered what life would be like back in the remote hills of Endeavor, where his Aunt Marie lived. He still held out hope that one day he might live with his father, though Leslie's outright refusal had been a crushing blow. When he landed at the airport in Kingston, there was no one to meet him. He followed his mother's instructions to take a taxi from the airport to Endeavor, where his aunt would be waiting. He was relieved when he reached Endeavor and saw his Aunt Marie, her husband, John, and his two cousins, Carlene and Stacy, waiting for him. He had brought suitcases of clothing, gifts for his aunt and her family, and several hundred U.S. dollars.

> Things went smoothly for the first month or so, but I came to learn that Aunt Marie could be as harsh as my mother, and downright mean at times. My aunt was a very irrational and eccentric woman, although she could be gentle when she was in a good mood. Her mood swings were similar to my mother's. After about a month she began to complain that my mother was not sending any money for my upkeep. In the country, we lived on several acres of farmland; we raised goats and pigs and grew yams and potatoes. There were orchards in which tangerine, grapefruit and orange trees grew. The hillsides were filled with blackberry bushes that seemed to bear fruit year round. The farm became my refuge.

Always looking for a surrogate parent who showed him affection, Malvo found such a person in Ms. Diane (not her real name), his aunt's neighbor. He had formed a bond with Ms. Diane on his previous stay in Endeavor. Upon his return, Malvo resumed that connection. He spent as much time as possible at Ms. Diane's home.

Marie, who admits using corporal punishment, said that the discipline she administered was done out of love for Malvo and her desire that he be a well-behaved child. She reported that when she took Malvo to register at the Gibraltar School, she instructed the teachers to "Spare the eye." Such an instruction means that the caregiver can beat any part of the child's body but should stay away from the eyes. Unlike the United States, where corporal punishment is disallowed in schools and hitting a child as a means of discipline is discouraged in the home, in Jamaica, this treatment is accepted. A common expression is "Spare the rod and spoil the child." However, in a caring learning environment, Malvo did not require the beatings that his aunt had instructed the teachers to inflict. Rather, he was an exceptional student who was generous with his classmates. His past teachers even speak of how he offered to carry their bags up the hill to the main road.

Ms. Spence, one of Malvo's teachers, was still using charts made by Malvo as teaching aids in her classroom when I interviewed her in 2003. She and the other teachers at Gibraltar recognized Malvo's potential. Despite missing nearly half a term, he was able to pass the Common Entrance Exam, the test the government used at the time to select students for entry into high school. In order to prepare for the exam, Malvo took extra classes for two months and received tutoring from Ms. Spence and Ms. Diane. His high scores ensured a placement at York Castle High School, a prominent school in neighboring Brown's Town.

Passing his exam brought praise from his mother, and he recalled being awarded with a Super Nintendo that she brought him on a visit from St. Maarten. However, she was very upset with what she saw as his lack of care for the things she had given him. Carlina, one of Marie's daughters, recalled the anger with which Una attacked Malvo for not being more careful with his clothes. Carlina remembered that Una punched Malvo so hard that he fell to the ground. Una also blamed Marie for not caring for Malvo as she expected, and she removed him from the home. According to Marie, however, it was more a case of Una not fulfilling her financial obligations in sending money for her son's upkeep.

Despite the harsh discipline and inconsistent care from Aunt Marie, Malvo felt torn about having to leave Endeavor. He would miss her and his cousins, but mostly he would miss the bond he shared with Ms. Diane. As he went over to her house to say good-bye, Malvo wondered if he would ever see her again.

Una searched for another home for Malvo, because she was going to return to St. Maarten. A friend of hers, Sonya Hodges, lived in Trysee district, close to York Castle High School. Sonya had known Malvo since he was a toddler in Kingston, and so she seemed like a good fit for him. She lived with her two children, Mika and Marvin, both college students. Marvin became like a big brother to Malvo. He treated the boy with affection and tried to shield him from the bullies in the community. Sonya Hodges recalled Malvo residing in her home on two different occasions. The first time was for about a year. The agreement was that Una would send money for Malvo's upkeep; but though the funds were not as forthcoming as was expected, Sonya treated Malvo like he was her youngest child. She recalled that it was a pleasure having him live with her, and the only problem she had was that he would return home from school late. She described him as having a curious mind and envisioned Malvo becoming a doctor or a lawyer.

> I was eleven years old when I entered the gates of York Castle High School, filled with dreams and aspiration long gone. Mom sewed my khaki pants and shirts and took a lot of pictures, then departed as usual. School was a two-mile trot in the mornings; I would awake at 5:00 a.m. and prepare myself for school. I would get there before 7:45 a.m. and school began at 8:15 a.m. Most of my first year was spent frolicking. I did poorly and was placed twenty-fifth out of fifty-three students. The next semester was not much better; I was twentieth in my class, and after that I was stuck between tenth and fifteenth.

Malvo was popular at York Castle. He even had a girlfriend, Kaitlin (not her real name), with whom he shared his hopes and dreams.

> I can freely say she knows me more intimately than anyone else. With her, I discussed my dreams, fears, family problems, and future concerns freely. She was quiet, never yelled, studious, adventurous in her own way; very expressive though she kept that a secret. She was one of the only consistent figures in my life. We agreed that we would abstain from having sex. We were both Christians and I explained that I would not want any child, especially mine, to live the life I was living. Being a teenage father did not fit into my vision of a future—and, lest I forget, my mother would kill me if I became an unmarried father, I told her.

At York Castle, Malvo associated with the sons and daughters of professionals. He recalled that he was a "nerd," as were many of his friends. Though he made some good friends, it was a little hard for him to fit in.

> From the beginning, my best friends and I were bullied. We were small in stature, and talkative, but hung out by ourselves. The older boys, usually

seniors, and sometimes even prefects [class monitors] used to pick on us. We were caught at the restroom or auditorium, our pockets ransacked and lunch money stolen. We complained to our homeroom teacher, Ms. Maxwell, who did her best to resolve our grievances. Unfortunately, that did not help the situation.

An incident that stood out for Malvo was when he was attacked in the boys' bathroom by two of the bullies. They held Malvo's hands behind his back, and although he tried to free himself and get in a few punches, they overwhelmed him. He was pushed into one of the bathroom stalls, where each of his attackers urinated in the toilet. They then took turns holding his head in the toilet and flushing. He did not report the incident to the school because it would be his word against the perpetrators', and he did not want the added burden of being identified as a snitch. This left him with a profound feeling of helplessness and abandonment, as he had no father or mother he could look to for protection.

Malvo recalled that he went to Marvin, who then confronted the bully and warned him not to mess with Malvo again. There was a decline in the attacks, but the bullying did not cease entirely. Malvo said he suffered some hard lessons as he tried to relate to others in the community, even as he tried to feel like just a regular kid. He recalled that on one occasion, although Marvin advised him not to, he went over to the community center to try to get into a cricket or soccer game. He wanted to show that he was not just a nerd, proficient only in school and church.

However, rather than playing any of the games, he was drawn to a discussion about airplanes. He saw an opportunity to indulge his passion for the subject of planes and flight, with knowledge gleaned from talks with his father in earlier days and subsequently from his research at the library. He dominated the discussion, but it ended badly for him. Malvo was beaten up by an older boy who did not take kindly to losing the debate, and also divested of all his clothes and forced to go home naked. When he arrived home, according to Malvo, Sonya and Marvin were not pleased that he'd gone to the community center, and they punished him.

This embarrassing incident haunted Malvo. He was eleven years old at the time and just trying to act like a regular kid, but he was punished for his efforts. His mother visited that summer and he told her about the incident, hoping that this time she would remain in Jamaica and not leave him again. She gave him yet another beating for being disobedient, but she agreed that it was best to find another place for him to live. Sonya remembered Una telling her that she was moving Malvo to a home in St. Elizabeth. Sonya recalled that she advised Una that Malvo needed some stability and she should consider not sending him away again. But Sonya recalled that Una was adamant.

UPROOTED AGAIN

After removing Malvo from Sonya's care, Una decided to reach out to other family members for assistance. She thought of an aunt, Blossom Powell, with whom she had lived during her teen years and for whom she herself had provided child care assistance. She felt that this aunt, a former teacher, would be an ideal guardian for Malvo. Aunt Blossom was seen as a God-fearing woman who had a healthy respect for education. However, as Una found out, her poor health made it impossible for her to care for Malvo.

Rather than turning Malvo away, Blossom asked her daughter, Semone Powell, about taking care of him. Semone's initial answer was no, as she did not feel she could take responsibility for a twelve-year-old boy. She later agreed to keep Malvo after Una impressed upon her that she really needed someone to care for him.

Semone had recently graduated from a teachers' college and was quite young herself—only twenty-one. However, she saw in Malvo a hunger for love and acceptance, and she was impressed with his inquiring mind. Within two weeks Malvo was transported to the Powells' home, where he felt a part of the family. At the time, Semone was still on summer vacation and job hunting, and this gave them an opportunity to become acquainted.

For Malvo, the Powell home was a big difference and a welcome change. The Powells were devoted Seventh-Day Adventist Christians and attended church at least twice weekly. Malvo was introduced to vegetarian dishes, and was happy to be part of a family that had structure and discipline. He was hopeful that finally he had stability and a family he could call his own. At the beginning of the fall semester, Malvo moved with Semone to her new home. He wrote:

> Semone had a parenting style that was the complete opposite of any approach I had ever encountered. We sat down and she asked me what I expected from her. She saw the look of astonishment on my face. My expression said, "What?" Then she explained that she had certain expectations of me and vice versa. She did not believe in corporal punishment

and would not engage in it. She said that we would create a contract. I would keep my end of the bargain and she would keep hers.

She explained that she would not lie to me. She will spend lots of time doing activities with me, listening to me, and so on. She smiled, and then explained my end of the bargain. I would listen to her, and remember that as my guardian she was responsible for me. I might not always agree with her decisions, but she was open-minded and willing to make the necessary changes in her life to accommodate my wishes, or to find a compromise. She said that I should openly and freely discuss my problems with her. She said things to me that I never thought I would ever hear. Her actions were always positive and encouraging. When I was wrong, she explained where I was wrong. When I did well she commended me on how well I had been doing. She pointed out my strong points but she explained and showed me why so-and-so was wrong. She gave me as much time as I needed to question her, and I in turn, actually comprehended what she was saying.

Semone and Malvo bonded very quickly, and he opened up to her. She felt that there were certain decisions that she as a guardian had to make in his best interests, particularly related to his education. She had the benefit of seeing what his grades were like at York Castle, and she recognized that he was not working to his full potential.

Semone felt it was unreasonable to expect Malvo to travel from her home in Mandeville to Brown's Town, where York Castle was located. This required him to take several different buses. She decided to spare him such a long commute and enrolled him at Spalding High School, which was closer to her home. According to Malvo, he agreed that it was better to attend a school that was closer.

In September 1997 Malvo was registered at Spalding High School, where Semone was a teacher. He was twelve years old at the time. Malvo's report card from Spalding shows that he did exceptionally well. He scored As and Bs, and his behavior was excellent. The principal, teachers, and schoolmates have recalled Malvo's time there. One teacher, A. Wilson, the textbook coordinator, recalled Malvo passing by the library and volunteering to help her catalogue and store the books. She said he was an avid reader;s he would read whatever he could and then engage her in discussion about it. He sought explanation and clarification from her. She said Malvo was not only book smart but also a regular kid who interacted well with other students and was a delight to have around.

Semone spent additional time with Malvo on his schoolwork, and he thrived under her care. She said that though Una had left money with her, it was not sufficient for Malvo's upkeep. Nonetheless, she and Malvo were happy. When Malvo was not doing schoolwork, they played board games and studied the Bible together. He noted that Semone even put plans to further her education on hold because she saw her responsibility to him as a priority.

Semone remarked that it was not only her education that she put on hold, but other teaching assignments that she could have taken where she could have gotten a teacher's cottage to live in. But these assignments would not have been suitable for Malvo to get a quality education.

Semone said that after a while Malvo began to share with her some of the traumas of his life. He told her about the separation from his father and how his mother had moved out all their belongings when she left. Semone understood this to have been a significant trauma in Malvo's life, particularly after he shared how disrupted life was afterward. He expressed joy about having her as his guardian and the hope that he could remain with her until he completed high school. He expressed his dreams of becoming a pilot, and she advised him on what he needed to do to realize them. She also recognized the fear that Malvo harbored of his mother. He begged her not to tell Una his secrets. She felt obliged to give him as structured and loving an environment as she could.

According to Semone, Una was socially and mentally challenged and saw Malvo as a burden. She remarked that if Una was angry at anything, she would take it out on her son. She recalled that when he first came to her home he was fearful that she would beat him. She remembered an incident when he had fallen off her father's bike and had scratched his leg. He ran to the bathroom and hid because he feared he would be beaten.

Semone also recalled Malvo's fear of being uprooted. She tried to reassure him that everything would be fine. She remembered his reaction when she started looking for another place to live because her landlord was irascible and they needed more space. When she told Malvo of her decision to move, his reaction gave her some insight about what he had suffered before. She recalled that Malvo threw a tantrum, screaming and jumping up and down like he was crazy, saying that he was tired of moving. "Why can't adults understand that constant moves are hard for kids?" she recalled him asking her. She was astounded by his behavior but tried to explain that they were not going to be constantly moving. She remembered him saying he had never lived in one place for even a year without being uprooted.

As her resources dwindled and the promised funds from Una failed to materialize, Semone's ability to care for Malvo was tested. Semone recalled Malvo saying that if he could contact his father, then his father would send them some money. There was the unspoken fear that like the other care providers before her, Semone would soon tire of having to spend her money on him, and he would once again be uprooted. However, after being assured that Semone would keep him and not send him away again, Malvo settled down in the new place.

The house that Semone rented was within walking distance from the school. This meant it took Malvo less time for travel to and from school, and he also had the opportunity to interact with the neighborhood kids. For the first time in a long time, he was feeling like a normal kid. Semone and Malvo worked together to make the limited funds cover their basic needs. Semone recalled that she spent whatever spare money she had on Malvo.

However, Semone noticed how much he talked about his father. Though his mother had insisted that he list his father as deceased on his school records, Malvo still yearned for those days when they had lived together. Semone recalled being disturbed about this desperate need Malvo had for a father. She was afraid that he was susceptible to bonding to any adult male who showed him any kindness. This made her even more determined to spend quality time with him, and she silently vowed to try to locate Leslie. She enlisted her boyfriend to help locate him. In the meantime, Malvo appeared content with the way Semone related to him.

Semone recalled that Malvo was an obedient child who would do his work without complaint. She remembered that she would give him an allowance from her monthly pay and he would buy ice cream. However, he would always want it in a cone and would bite the end of the cone off and suck the ice cream through. She would have him sit over a towel and use a rag to wipe the cream off his face while admonishing him that he was too old to eat ice cream in that manner. This is noteworthy because the happiest times that Malvo recalls with his father was when they would go to the ice cream shop. From as early as he could remember, he'd eaten just the way Semone described it.

MALVO'S MOTHER RETURNS

Semone and her boyfriend located Leslie and planned to take Malvo to his father. Unfortunately, before they could, Una showed up. Unbeknownst to

Semone and Malvo, she was back on the island. She discovered that Malvo had been transferred from York Castle High School and she was outraged. She had not been consulted about the school transfer and she was not prepared to give authorization. She came to Semone's home to claim what was rightfully hers. Semone and Malvo were playing games when they heard an urgent knock on the door. Malvo wrote:

> I go to the door, see my mom, and took to my heels in the opposite direction, I ran behind Semone, and shouted, "She is going to take me!" Semone told me to calm down and told me that I was being silly. My mom stood at the door and watched me and Semone conversing. She comes home and I'm not even appreciative, was her attitude. She put on her ugliest face and came into the room, talking rapidly to Semone.

Semone remembered how she tried to explain to Malvo that there was no way that his mother would be coming to take him away, given that he was doing so well. "You don't know my mother, that's what she always do," Malvo had told her. Semone recalled Malvo saying, "Come on, Semone, let's put her in a taxi and send her away. Please don't let her take me."

Semone stood astonished and wondered where Una's sudden hostility came from. She tried to explain that she was doing the best she could for Malvo with limited resources. "How dare you take him away from York Castle?" Una demanded. Semone tried to explain that the travel to York Castle would be too great a commute for Malvo and, furthermore, given that she was a teacher at Spalding High School, it seemed like the best alternative. However, Una was not in the mood to be rational. Malvo recalled how enraged Una was as she walked around the house, ripping doors open, making a fuss about the unwashed laundry and the food in the refrigerator, accusing Semone of doing something to Malvo.

Semone recalled that she finally had to raise her voice—the first time Malvo had ever heard her do so. She got Una to be quiet for one minute. "If I knew your address, I would have informed you that I had to transfer him," she recalled telling Una. She went on to say that in the five months she'd had Malvo, they'd been living off her measly teacher's salary. She further pointed out to Una that Malvo was healthy, happy, and doing well in school. Malvo recalled that his mother was not willing to accept any explanations.

Malvo recalled that despite how he felt and how much he wanted to remain with Semone, he knew that he would have to go with his mother eventually. He recalled his mother insisting that she leave with him, but he asked if he could spend the one last night with Semone. He remembered how angry his mother was and that she chastised him for not being happy to see her after she had been gone for so long. He had no choice but to leave with her.

According to Malvo, that night was one of the worst he had experienced to date. His mother was outraged that he dared to choose staying with Semone over going with her. He remembered her saying, "I am the one who brought you here and I can take you back out." She told him that they would return the following morning to Semone's place to pack his things and leave. She told him further that he should repudiate Semone in her presence. Nothing else would satisfy her. Semone, on the other hand, felt certain that Una would calm down and see that it was not in Malvo's best interest to remove him.

Malvo recalled there was a showdown the following morning. Una wanted her son, and nothing or no one would stand in the way of her getting him. Semone showed Una Malvo's report card, pointing out that he had done very well in comparison to how he had been doing at York Castle. But according to Malvo, his mother responded to Semone with grunts and nasty looks. Malvo remembered that Una even took out a camera and began taking pictures of him, the house, the refrigerator, and the unwashed basket of laundry. Semone tried to explain that the clothes were not washed because the water to her home had been turned off due to a broken pipe. The only water that could be used was for cooking and for bathing. But Una did not listen. She told Malvo to pack his belongings and leave with her.

Semone remembered telling Una that there might come a time when her assistance might again be needed, but she remembered Malvo saying that that time would not come. According to Semone, she was traumatized by how Una reacted to her, but she was even more shocked by Malvo's response. According to Semone, Malvo told her that he wanted to be with his mother and that he would never need her again. "It was a like a stab in my heart," she remarked. "I could not believe it was the same child that I had grown to love, saying those hurtful things."

Unknown to Semone, Malvo denounced her because he was forced to do so by his mother. Malvo wrote: "That was one of the hardest things I ever did, but when I told her that I would not need her again I was telling the truth." He packed his clothes, but he left one item, a favorite shirt, among her clothes. "I left that shirt, which was my favorite, hoping that she would understand." Semone recalled finding the shirt among her dirty laundry but thought that it was left by mistake. Not until years later, during the course of my investigation, did she learn why Malvo had left it behind.

Semone recalled that after Una removed Malvo, she sought counseling to deal with what she saw as a rejection of everything she had done for him. She remarked that it was so painful for her that she vowed not to have children of her own. The next time Semone saw Malvo was in court, when she went to testify on his behalf.

Una took Malvo with her to St. Elizabeth, which bordered Manchester, the parish where Malvo had been living with Semone. Malvo wrote that he could not understand his mother. Everything for him was confusing. He recalled his mother demanding that he excel in school, but when he did, she moved him once again. He tried asking her why she had taken him away from Semone. But, as he recalled, she responded with a slap and commented that as his mother, she had the authority to do whatever she wanted with him.

> Every time I opened my mouth I'm rewarded with a slap or some kind of punishment. I got beatings at least twice daily for a few good hours with my mouth closed. I stayed out of her way, while she stayed on my back. The abuse was a twenty-four-hour a day thing, a lecture about my disobedience, worthless traits, my heartlessness, my causing her to be a failure.

Christmas break was over, and Una was successful in getting Malvo re-registered at York Castle. Records show that Malvo was readmitted to York Castle in January 1998. He was placed in the eighth grade, with the classmates whom he had left when he was transferred to Spalding. In addition, Una was able to locate a boardinghouse that was walking distance from the school.

Malvo was also fortunate to be placed with the same homeroom teacher, Ms. Maxwell, who took a keen interest in the welfare of her students. After Una saw to Malvo's readmission and his acceptance at the boardinghouse, she left the island again. Malvo recalled that there were no hugs, no parting words of affection, only threats. "Let me get any bad report and see what I do to you," he remembers her saying.

LIFE AT THE BOARDINGHOUSE

Malvo described the Robertsons' (not their real name) boardinghouse as a huge white house that sits atop a hill overlooking the green pastures of

Brown's Town, St. Ann. Many students from York Castle High School lived there at some point during their high school years. Mr. Robertson was the pastor of a small Pentecostal church, and he also owned a hardware store. His wife owned and operated a bakery. Malvo wrote: "Mr. Robertson was a tall man, with a baritone voice, a quick smile, and good counsel. Mrs. Robertson was a kind lady who was very religious, even-tempered and business-oriented. They had three children. The youngest was Marie Robertson, who was a student at a teachers' college."

Malvo reported that he "chameleoned" himself to try to fit in with the new household. He had been wrenched away from the comfort of Semone and the opportunity to spend the Christmas vacation with her family, but he knew that he had to make the situation work for him. He felt it made no sense crying over lost dreams. With all the students gone home for the holidays, Malvo spent most of his time with Marie, the Robertsons' daughter, or with Mr. Robertson.

> I did the best I could to fit in. I spoke when I was spoken to, kept my head in my journal, and completed the chores to which I was assigned—mainly preparing for school. I cleaned my shorts, sorted the books in my closet, and prepared my uniform. And, of course, my church clothes. We attended church approximately three times weekly—Sundays, Wednesdays, and sometimes Fridays. For much of the Christmas holidays, I was the only boarder in the Robertsons' home. All the boarders had homes to return to. At the end of the holidays I was introduced to my fellow boarders, all eight of them.

From the outside, it seemed Malvo was settling in well. The living conditions were good. The Robertsons fostered a wholesome environment for their boarders. There were rules that had to be followed. Homework had to be completed by a certain time and television watching was restricted. Marie Robertson recalled that Malvo spent a great deal of time by himself, looking out the window. It was at this time too that he started writing a journal. He said that the idea came to him because he had so many thoughts that were bundled up inside him and no one he could share them with, so his journal became his confidant.

Marie recalled that when Malvo was not in a reflective mood, he would join her in the family quarters, where he would assist her with her college projects. She has kept her student project, "Foods of the World," for which she received an A. In the acknowledgments she credited Malvo for the invaluable assistance he provided in drawing the maps and flags of the countries represented, and his drawings of the dishes and fruits. She recalled that he was the only boarder who offered to assist her, and she delighted in his presence. He was a talented artist and curious by nature, she thought.

Malvo's talent was noted, but his teachers and some of his close friends saw that all was not well. Mr. Johnson, Malvo's geography teacher, said that Malvo was one of his better students, with great academic potential, but he felt that potential was not being fully realized. Mr. Johnson also noted that Malvo seemed in need of a mentor or a father figure to whom he could become attached. He tried to hide the turmoil in his life, but his attitude began to change for the worse. Malvo indicated that he went through periods of feeling depressed.

> When I was left alone, as I was on most weekends, I sneaked out, went downtown and played a few video games, or I went to the library, where I stuck my nose in a journal I was keeping and did my homework or at least half of it. Then I'd arrive home just in time before the Robertsons arrived. My instructions were to complete my assignments, study, do laundry, and prepare for church. Come Sunday mornings, I would be ironing a wet church shirt, can't find the tie, found two socks of similar color. I usually got a speech from Mrs. Robertson. "You know I'm going to complain to your mother, and you know she doesn't play." When my behavior got worse she'd give me a few threats of a beating that she never got around to delivering.

Though his mother called the school every Friday to inquire about him, Malvo saw that as a bothersome routine he was forced to go through. According to Malvo, the calls were full of complaints about his schoolwork or his loyalty to her. He recalled that Una would badger him on the phone about his missing her birthday or not writing her, or about him being worthless. She would also warn him that she could come back to straighten him out.

In the meantime, Malvo was retreating more into himself. In the middle of the semester the payments for the boarding stopped coming. Malvo recalled that this went on for a while before Mrs. Robertson said something about it. He recalled that she sat him down and told him what the situation was. Nevertheless, she continued to provide his meals and give him lunch money. To the other boarders, nothing had changed. But Malvo knew that he was an inconvenience. He was feeling more and more depressed. He recalled that the same thing had happened when he was with Semone, but she was family.

Memories of the role his father had played in the early years would come to Malvo. Though his father had once rejected the idea of keeping him, he wondered if Leslie's attitude might have changed. Maybe he could gain his father's acceptance by telling him how well he had been doing, and that he had passed his Common Entrance Exam and was attending York Castle High School.

One Friday, after the other boarders left, Malvo decided to go in search of his father. It was always painful for him to sit alone in a corner and watch the other boarders go home with their parents on weekends. He knew the Robertsons' routine; they were usually out of the house by 6:00 a.m. on a Saturday, so they would not notice him leaving. On a Saturday morning in mid-April 1998, he sneaked out and made the trip into Kingston.

His father was playing dominoes in the same Waltham Park/Oakland Road neighborhood Malvo remembered so fondly. Malvo felt encouraged because his father was happy to see him. He was moved as his father came to greet him and then brought him back to the domino table where, like old times, he was acknowledged by his father's buddies. Leslie and Lloyd Barrett remember that last visit. However, the visit did not have the happy ending that Malvo hoped, because his father again did not agree to keep him. Malvo wrote:

> I told him that I was in high school now, in my second year, that I was boarded out and that Mom was in St. Maarten. I couldn't find the courage to tell him my real reason for coming to see him; that I needed somewhere to live and I had no one else to turn to. I was hoping that he would be able to read my eyes the way he used to when we lived together. Then he could always know when I was hurt or when I was scared and I could depend on him to make it right. Well, to my disappointment, he gave me a few hundred dollars [Jamaican; US$5–10] and sent me packing. He didn't say what I had expected. Obviously he had no intention of "keeping any Pinckney" [child] as he had shouted into the phone two years earlier when my mother asked him to keep me.

After that rejection, Malvo concluded that his mother was justified in listing his father as deceased in his school records. What was the use of having a father if he was not there for you when you needed him most?

He made his way back to the Robertson home in Brown's Town, tearful and heavyhearted. That weekend Mrs. Robertson told him that she would not be keeping him for the next semester because his mother had not been sending any money for his upkeep.

Malvo recalled that shortly after the disappointing visit to his father, his mother returned from St. Maarten. However, this time she had been deported and had lost quite a bit of money. He remembered that she was in a foul mood, and the fact that she was very displeased with his report card made matters worse. Malvo recalled that all the teachers, except the science teacher, had a complaint. His conduct was good and he had academic potential, but he was not performing to the best of his ability. The report card was in contrast to the preceding one from Spalding High, when he was living with Semone. Then he had been placed first in his class, his best performance since he entered high school. This time, at York Castle, he was placed 22 out of 54, with an average of 63.5 percent, far below expectations. On top of this, Mrs. Robertson gave Una a report on his behavior at the boardinghouse.

He wrote:

I knew I had it coming when Mrs. Robertson invited my mom to "stroll downstairs and see my handiwork." Mom returned with a few torn textbooks that she found along with a pair of underwear from my neighbor's doorstep, a bucket of mildewed uniforms that I never got around to washing, a pile of dishes I had accumulated over the last week but would not wash, among other things. She actually made a list of all the things she found, a list for which I would be severely punished. Mrs. Robertson made it very clear. "Ms. James, you will have to find someplace else to house this young man." Dragging me by the ear, Mom went downstairs and packed my stuff while slapping, punching, and cursing me. Mrs. Robertson gave me all three bags of my belongings (my mildewed clothes, dog-eared books, and my sketch pads). We took the stuff and headed for St. Elizabeth, where my mom had an apartment.

According to Malvo, his dismal performance in school was not the only bad news that awaited his mother. Upon arriving home in St. Elizabeth, she was greeted by her landlord, who told her she had to move. His source of discontent was Epsie James, Malvo's grandmother, whom Una had left in her house.

SUICIDE ATTEMPT

Malvo recalled that he could sense his mother's frustrations. It appeared to him that nothing was going right for her. He felt that he was the one upon whom she vented her frustrations; she recounted all his misdeeds and punished him severely for them. He wrote:

> I'm sitting in a chair in a corner, the belt or broomstick is close at hand and she begins listing my wrongs on her fingers. The more she goes on, the more aggravated she gets, and then whap! Just like that, the blows come running in mid-sentence; it was like she had ten hands. It really didn't matter where the blows connected, just that they connected. I had welts from head to toe, a swollen left ear, and black-and-blue spots on my ribs.
>
> As the days went along, she would leave in search of a new apartment. Finding none, she would return and beat me more frequently and extensively, as she became more incensed with my grandmother's antics. My grandmother would begin preaching that it was Una's sin that brought her all this. "God is telling you something!" Then Mom would turn her rage on me. She was enraged about losing her money and getting deported; she talked about it all day, and when I slipped, I got punched, shoved, and yelled at, as she reviewed the list, which went further and further back. "You are completely worthless and have no ambition like your father. Not only are you a disgrace, sometimes me wonder if you are my child." I just listened, wishing that I could disappear. That it would all go away. I did not want to be there any longer.

Given her problems renting a house, Una decided to build one on a half-acre of land she had purchased two years before. She found a nearby contractor and bought the lumber, cement, and building blocks needed for the job. Malvo recalled that he accompanied his mother to the work site, where he assisted as a laborer and where according to him, his mother worked as hard as or even harder than the workmen. However, he received little encouragement for his efforts, and when things did not go right, he was the one punished. He recalled being told so often by his mother that she wished she did not have him that he began to feel it would have been better had he not been born. During one of the daily beatings, he finally decided that he'd had enough. He wrote:

I finally escape the blows by running out of the house. I return from Dudley's mango orchard and go to the back of the yard. It's dark now and the carpenter shop beside the house is closing. Blacka, a fellow who works there, was closing up. He saw me plotting something and said, "What are you doing, Lee? You all right?" "Yeah, I'm fine."

I find a tree and make a knot in a rope made out of sheets. I test its strength, place it around my neck, and tighten the sling and sit on a limb. I'm shaking, crying, and I yell my mother's name. She finds me. I tell her to stop, stay where she is, I'll save her the trouble. "You don't have to batter me anymore."

She and Blacka, spend a good hour or two talking me down. She keeps talking, and Blacka disappears. In a few minutes, I see him under the tree. I get mad, jumped when a hand grabs my waist, pulls me up, takes the rope off my neck, brings me down. My fighting ceased! Mom runs to my side, takes me into the house, and her face was pale, drained of blood. She begins crying as she gives me a lecture about fear.

This was the first time that Malvo attempted to end his life. For that night at least, the beatings stopped. However, according to Malvo, his mother's tears were short-lived. She soon returned her attention to the construction of the new house. The builders were behind schedule, and some of the workmen were incompetent. He recalled that one wall collapsed because the beams were improperly fitted, forcing her to buy additional blocks. She again turned her attention on him and what he had and had not done. He recalled getting an "ass-whopping," after which his mother opened the door and told him to go and kill himself. He remembered her saying that it would be cheaper burying him than living with him. He wrote:

She urges me to go and kill myself. I walk away, find a corner, and meditate on her words. I spent all night going over my life stage after stage, year after year. I tied a couple of pieces of rope together and really thought about making another attempt at taking my life. I had just had enough. But for some reason I lost the courage and the will to do it.

From that point on Malvo kept to himself. He said that he fell into a kind of melancholy mood and went with the flow. If his mother was in a good mood and detected a change in his attitude, she would hug him and ask him what was wrong, why was he not talking? However, a couple of hours later she would tell him that he was the worst thing that had ever happened to her. He remembered that simple conversations ended up with his being struck because he did not answer in time. The beatings were relentless, and after a while, he did not even feel the blows. He just removed himself.

RETURN TO TRYSEE

The summer of 1998 passed, and thirteen-year-old Malvo was scheduled to return to school. It was not possible for him to travel from St. Elizabeth to his school in St. Ann, and furthermore, Una's house was unfinished because she had run out of funds. She turned to her friend Sonya, who had cared for Malvo during his first year at York Castle High School. Sonya consented to take him again.

By then, Una had obtained a replacement passport and was setting her sights on traveling to a different island. Despite the daily dose of abuse he received, Malvo did not want her to leave him again. He was so tired of shifting from place to place that he just wanted her to stay home. He thought that if he did really well that semester, maybe she would stay. He decided to engage the vice principal and the guidance counselor at York Castle to intervene on his behalf.

Malvo went to the vice principal's office to explain why he thought it was important that his mother stay home. The guidance counselor sided with his mother, who said she had to travel because she was the sole provider. The vice principal, Esme McLeod, was more understanding of Malvo's concerns. She recalled the discussion that took place in her office as she pled the case that he needed a stable home.

Ms. McCloud told Una that Malvo needed a stable home, somewhere to settle down. He should not be moving from place to place, as it did him no good. She recalled trying to impress upon Una that Malvo was an intelligent child who could do well if he had a steady support system. She said that Malvo was in need of a parent in his life.

Ms. McCloud is also the mother of Malvo's good friend, Andrew McLeod, who also attended York Castle at that the time. She recalled Andrew telling her that Malvo suffered from the lack of a steady home. "He would tell me, 'Mommy, I feel so badly for Lee. He has no one.'" At the end of the meeting, Una informed Malvo and the school officials that she would be traveling to another island, Antigua. Malvo recalled that as he and his mother walked out of the office, he stopped, shook his head, looked at her right in her eyes, and said, "Don't you feel it, Mom, that you are losing me. Can't you see it?"

However, Una had made her mind up that only migration could give her what she wanted in life. She was struggling to provide books, uniforms, and all the things that a child needs for school, and she was not getting any assistance from Leslie. Although Malvo told her she was losing him, she felt it would be worse if she did not earn enough to pay for his upkeep. Two weeks after leaving him with Sonya, and before she left for Antigua, she paid Malvo a visit. She wanted to know how much he would need for schoolbooks. She gave him J$1,300 to buy the books he would need, some of which could be bought used. He assured her that the money she gave him would be used to buy all the books, with the exception of two that he could borrow from the library for the year. He bade her farewell and headed off to school.

I go to school thinking everything is fine. I return home that evening and am surprised she is still there. For the first time in ages she gives me a hug, waltzes me into the house, shuts the door, and closes the window. I'm wondering what have I done now. With an air of indignation, she holds in her hand my correspondence to my girlfriend. There were several cards and other gifts. I looked at the box where I'd hidden this stuff, thinking that surely no one will ever find it or even think to look here. It had been working for three years, but as the saying goes, all good things must come to an end. And what an end this would be.

She started going through them [his cards to Kaitlin] one by one . . . "You never sent me one card, not one Valentine's or birthday card in three years. How many cards you buy her?" I looked at her with disgust. She took up the belt and started hitting me. I looked at her in defiance and decided I would not cry or holler. She said, "Oh! So now you think that you are a man now, grown up and tough, so you want to fight?" I stood there and stared her down. She looked at the belt, smiled, tossed it on the bed and started punching me instead. My efforts to block the blows only made her erupt again. The woman really lost it, going into a crazy frenzy. Sonya came up from the shop and started banging on the door. "Una, Una, Jesus Christ you a go kill him! Unaaaa!" She opened the door and pulled my mother off me. I was on the ground; my mother had forced me down and was sitting on my back, using the same belt.

I don't remember getting up, because in fact I was knocked out. I do remember waking up in the morning and hearing Sonya telling my mother, "Una! Una! You can't beat him no more. I heard the boy hollering all the way down the shop yesterday. Una, you are mad, you could have killed him!"

Malvo was left bruised and battered after this beating. He recalled that for two days he could not move; he had to rest in bed to heal his wounds. He recalled that he had to lie on his stomach because his back felt broken and his butt was swollen. He could not sit down. His hands were black and blue, and his rib cage hurt. The only place untouched was his head. Una was outraged that he dared to have a female in his life. Even an innocent relationship was a threat to her and her ambitions for him. "Who was this girl?" She wanted to know the girl's name and threatened to kill him if he did not tell her. With Sonya's prodding, he admitted that the girl was a classmate, but he dreaded what this knowledge would mean for him and Kaitlin. He was not so much worried about himself as he was concerned for her.

Sonya recalled that beating and the fury that was unleashed. Her memory was that Una had also found a picture of the girlfriend Malvo was supposed to have had. "I still have that picture with me to this day," she remarked.

A week after the confrontation, Una went to the school. She asked Ms. Maxwell about Malvo's relationship with Kaitlin and was assured that Malvo and Kaitlin were good friends and that the relationship was not harmful. Two weeks later Una left for Antigua, but made arrangements to send Ms. Maxwell money for Malvo's school lunches. She wanted to ensure that none of the money she sent could be spent on this girlfriend of his.

Things went well for about a month or two, and then Una stopped sending money. There was no lunch money sent to Ms. Maxwell and there was no money for Sonya either. After a while, Malvo began to show signs of neglect. He recalled that Sonya tried to keep him on track even though she was not receiving any payment from his mother. Malvo began to stay out late and was not doing well at school. Sonya and Marvin, who tried to enforce discipline, did not see any signs of improvement. Malvo was basically ignored, and things kept going downhill. If he did not get J$50 from Sonya out of her own pocket, he did not have lunch.

I was attending school looking like a bag of rags, and the teachers for once had not complained about my mouth for months. I didn't appear at the volleyball or basketball court. I just sat in class and chilled out by myself. A few friends tried to cheer me up, but it didn't work.

A TEACHER'S RESCUE

His teacher, Ms. Maxwell, recalled that it seemed as though Malvo had re-treated into a world of his own. He was unkempt and listless. It was apparent to her that he was being neglected at home. It pained her to know that a boy with his intellect and charm might be written off if corrective measures were not taken. There was a limit to what steps could be taken to improve his situation in a rural part of the island. Even in the main cities, Kingston and Montego Bay, few government resources existed to help children in trouble—to intercede and have the child placed elsewhere.

Ms. Maxwell knew that money was not forthcoming from Una. Many days she provided lunch for Malvo. She decided that she would ask her father to allow Malvo to live with her family. Once her father agreed, she reached out to Una and offered to take Malvo at no charge until he completed high school.

The Maxwells have fond memories of the time Malvo lived with them. Their home is a modest-looking five-bedroom house, which Mr. Maxwell built with his own hands. The house was more than adequate to accommodate another member of the household. They indicated that they were a Christian, God-fearing family. Mr. Maxwell was a farmer and his wife a homemaker. They only had daughters, so were delighted to have a "son" in Malvo. The environment was wholesome and for the first time in a long time, Malvo felt that he belonged to a family.

At the Maxwells' I was given my own room. I became a part of a family; they treated me as if I had always been there. I talked a lot less and did my work, attended school, and put some effort in the last few months of the school term. I'd been maturing a little bit, but the thought was hitting home that I better start acting right. I would be on my own in three years, tops, if I were lucky. My position on the ratings board jumped from sixteenth to ninth. Mr. Maxwell and I hit it off from the start; we talked a lot about pretty much everything. On weekends we spent our days on the farm. I had my own little plot. I planted cabbage, carrots, and bell peppers. It was great. Watching plants grow is a good feeling.

When I was not checking out my seedlings, I was down by the river investigating bugs and plants. Or down the street having fun with some classmates. I helped as much as I could. Ms. Maxwell's sister had a little shop. I helped out on weekends, sitting behind the counter doing my homework, and serving up a few bottles of Red Stripe beer and tonic drinks. At the end of the term I looked out at the commendations, an A, a B, and two Cs; "Not bad," I tell myself. "I'll get straight As next semester." I remember standing in the auditorium watching the stage. I was thinking that when I walked off, I would have my diploma and ten CXCs [credits from the Caribbean Examinations Council, the body that administers final-year exams for high school seniors] to my name.

Teachers and students alike saw the potential in Malvo. His best friend at the time, Onykeya Nevins, recalled that Malvo was an excellent student whose attitude to his studies was far ahead of the other students'. He recalled that only about 40 percent of the students usually did their homework, but Malvo always did his, and went above and beyond what was required in the assignments. Nevins recalled that Malvo would do extra research so that whatever he did was well presented. Malvo was not a selfish student, as he would share information with the other students, providing help and explanations when asked. This observation is similar to that made by one of his teachers and quality that was seen in Malvo by others. Much later, when I was assigned to his case, he would do research for a member of my staff to whom he had become attached and would offer suggestions as she embarked on her studies. This speaks to his need to be liked and accepted.

Nevins and Malvo did a number of assignments together, and Malvo was an avid contributor to class discussions. He might raise his hands ten times during a session, and would not relent until he could make his contribution. Much of the information that he brought to the class came through extra research. Despite his seriousness toward work, Malvo was able to get everyone to laugh. He had a great sense of humor, Nevins said.

However, it was obvious to Nevins that Malvo had a great need to belong. He felt that the absence of a parent had an even greater impact when Malvo saw other children interacting with their parents. When Malvo visited Nevins at home, Nevins could see how much he yearned for family interaction.

While living at the Maxwells', Malvo felt a need to grow in all facets of his life, including spiritually. Although he was raised nominally as a Seventh-Day Adventist and attended Sabbath services, he had never been baptized. He told Nevins that he wanted to become a Christian. This was not surprising to Nevins, who recalled that Malvo usually espoused Christian values.

Nevins felt that Malvo's commitment to Christianity was sincere and was reflected in his attitude. He recalled that Malvo would walk away from confrontations even when he was in the right.

Malvo also shared his thoughts with his pastor, Lorenzo King. Reverend King remembered when Malvo said that he wanted to be baptized. "I had to meet with him and explore if this was something that he wanted or if he was doing it because someone wanted him to do it. And I was convinced that this young man had reached a stage in his life where he was ready to serve the Lord." Malvo was baptized by Reverend King in 1999. Reverend King said that on the evening of the baptism, Malvo walked two miles to the church, bringing his clothes with him.

> That summer just as things were looking up and I had the promise that I could live with the Maxwells for as long as I wanted, my mother called and informed Ms. Maxwell that I would be migrating to Antigua to live with her. She [Ms. Maxwell] was to take me to the airport on such-and-such a date and put me on the plane. [Mom] had sent the ticket and the necessary funds I would need to travel. I had conflicting feelings because, on one level, I wanted to be with my mother, but I didn't want to leave the Maxwells. At this point, the future wasn't looking all that bad after all. Ms. Maxwell saw that I didn't want to leave. While I was packing I looked across the bed at her and shook my head. She came over and hugged me. "I know, Lee, you don't want to go, but she is your mother (sigh) and I have to send you." The night before I was to leave I found myself staring at the light bulb. I reached up and placed my hand on the light and held it there until it seared into my flesh. Yet I couldn't feel the pain.

Ms. Maxwell said that the journey to the airport was one of the hardest she had ever undertaken. She had seen how well Malvo had done during the months that he lived with her family. Everyone had grown to love him, and it was understood that he would remain a part of the family throughout his high school years and even into college if he so desired. She had hoped that because no payment was expected for his stay, his mother would have let him remain until he graduated. However, Una said that she was now established and had a nice home, so Malvo could join her.

Ms. Maxwell had to infer that all was well for Una, and that finally she would be there for Malvo as a mother should. Nonetheless, there was pain in Ms. Maxwell's heart as she watched Malvo go through the airport. She wondered whether his mother would leave him again or finally give the boy stability.

LIFE IN ANTIGUA

In the summer of 1999, Malvo arrived in Antigua. He was fourteen years old and hopeful that at last he would be with his mother permanently. Though he was sorry to leave the Maxwell family and his friends, he saw his mother's summoning him as a signal that she would not separate from him again. Malvo was essentially still the obedient, dutiful child who associated stability in his life with a parent or authority figure. He still wanted to do the right thing, and the right thing was whatever that parent or authority figure said. He felt sure that his mother was now ready to reassume and reassert her parental responsibility in his life. This was what she was trying to communicate to Malvo and the Maxwells, he hoped, when she said she was now stable and ready to have him join her.

Malvo discovered that his mother lived in a one-room shack with no bathroom facilities. Malvo's bed was two cinder blocks with a piece of plywood laid across them and a foam mattress on top. His mother's "business" was an icebox from which she sold beer and juice. Her "house" was a far cry from the comfort of the Maxwells' home from which he had been uprooted. However, he had learned to adjust over the years each time he was deposited in a new environment, and he decided that he would adjust to this new situation too. He wrote:

At the time that I joined my mom she was a self-employed peddler on Queen Elizabeth highway in St. John's, the capital of Antigua. In my mind, I didn't confront my feelings about my mother or toward my past. I just moved along with the flow. I masked my feelings well. I remained cautiously hopeful that even in this one-room shack where I settled with her, we could be like a family. For the remainder of the summer holidays, I helped my mother peddling during the carnival festivities. I sold soft drinks and jerk chicken. I was more mobile; moving along with the crowds, selling drinks, liquor, and snacks.

Despite the fact that Una's work and living conditions left much to be desired, she was able to enroll Malvo in one of the best private high schools in Antigua. And so, in September 1999, Malvo entered the Seventh-Day Adventist High School in St. John's. He recalled:

> The school, a Christian institution, was small but well staffed. The marked difference was the quality of the teaching staff. The teachers were on the whole much more engaging. They were actually interested in what students said. They were quick to correct but slow to scold. The work was well structured; you knew exactly what the teachers' objectives were and how we would achieve them. Dr. Aaron, the school's principal, could be abrasive in style, mostly serious, not at all wishy-washy. But she could be affable when she decided that the occasion called for it.
>
> I had to give my mother her money's worth, as she swore she would stop wasting her money on me if I didn't. She destroyed my address book and divested me of my phone card, to ensure that I could not maintain contact with my girlfriend, Kaitlin. I decided to focus on no-nonsense subjects: the sciences, information technology, computer, and business subjects.

According to Malvo, they made barely enough to eat and pay rent. Most of his tuition came from Thomas (not his real name), a man with whom his mother was involved romantically. Malvo saw him as an endearing, grandfatherly person, but he was uncomfortable with his mother's relationship with Thomas. Malvo noted that Thomas had a wife who was ill at the time, and furthermore, Malvo felt his mother's relationship with Thomas was not good in the sight of God. Malvo felt helpless and unable to affect the situation one way or the other. He told his mother that he was displeased, but she responded that she was doing what she needed to do to ensure he had the best education possible. That response is in keeping with observations made by one of Una's employers in Antigua. This gentleman (name withheld) remarked that Una could enter a room of men and immediately size them all up and determine which one would suit her needs best. He went on to state that Malvo was like a valuable piece of jewelry that you leave at the pawn shop but then go back to retrieve, or like a prized bull or chattel. He opined that Una wanted to do the best for Malvo, perhaps so he could do his best for her.

Malvo also felt that he was an investment, as his mother had saved the Western Union receipts that showed the money she had sent to Jamaica for his upkeep. She conveyed the impression that she expected optimal returns.

Malvo, on the other hand, only wanted stability and was determined to give Una whatever she wanted as long as she did not leave him again. He was to be disappointed in January 2000, when Una decided that she was going to St. Maarten to try her luck at getting into the United States.

Malvo recalled that his mother paid four hundred dollars for the January-to-March school term and two months' rent, with a promise that she would send more money. Thus, less than six months after Una had removed Malvo from the comfort and stability of the Maxwells' home, she left him again. This time she left him on his own. He was still shy of his fifteenth birthday.

Malvo recalled that Una called him frequently. However, being left alone in Antigua was a harsher blow than the times Una had left him in Jamaica. At least in Jamaica he had relatives and other caregivers who could be asked to take him in. In Antigua, he literally had no one. After she had left him there, he decided that he would never trust his mother again.

Given past occasions when his mother failed to send money as promised, Malvo decided to rely on himself to make up for the shortfalls. He had learned the value of putting money aside. And from the time when he was in Jamaica, he had learned to save most of the money Una gave him. Whatever money he saved in Antigua, however, was not enough to sustain him. Thomas visited him every two weeks and gave him EC$50, but this was not enough to cover his expenses. So he decided that the best way to earn some cash was to make bootleg music CDs. He used his savings to buy a secondhand computer, a Zip drive, and a burner. Then he started stealing the CDs he needed in order to make copies.

At first he stole the latest CDs, made copies, and resold them at a much lower price. The first two months he was able to get enough money for the rent by doing this. Soon he started to steal other things too. His haul ranged from art supplies to a play station. This behavior was a far cry from the Lee Malvo who, less than a year before, had professed his desire to be a baptized Christian. Then he was in the loving and supportive environment of the Maxwells' home, but in Antigua he had no support. He was determined to do whatever he could to remain in school.

Though he lived under precarious conditions, Malvo tried to conceal what his true circumstances were. His best friend at the school he attended in Antigua was John Sewsankar, the son of a pastor. John, who testified for Malvo at his 2003 trial, said that he would have been more than happy to ask his parents to allow Malvo to live with them. But Malvo had built up an image at school that he was doing okay and living in a stable home. He was careful not to let his friends visit him, lest they see that he lived in a shack. Malvo's teachers also did not see anything amiss. He presented himself as a well-groomed scholar who came from a middle-class home.

However, there was one friend, Kenric (not his real name), who discovered that Malvo was living alone in a shack with no running water. After that, the two started going out on jaunts together, stealing for survival in whatever way they could.

The shack in which Malvo lived was adjacent to the house of the landlord, Ernest (not his real name), lived with his family. Ernest said that about three or four months after Malvo arrived, Una left him there alone. Ernest said he asked Malvo for his mother in the second month after her departure, as the rent was not being paid. Malvo told him that his mother was off the island but did not give him her phone number. Ernest noted that Malvo was still a minor, and he could not in good conscience evict him. He disconnected the electricity, however, and told Malvo that he had to get a lantern or some other means of light. He stated that Malvo was a quiet youth who went to school regularly and, to his knowledge, was not given to any kind of misconduct in the community. He added that Malvo could be seen playing basketball with the other boys in the neighborhood.

Ernest saw that Malvo needed mentoring because, even before Una left, it was questionable whether she was giving Malvo the right exposure. In that regard, Malvo recalled that his mother had many suitors whom she brought to the shack. He said he felt uncomfortable, as he had to endure the sounds that came from the makeshift wall that had been erected. He tried to close his mind to what occurred behind the wall and focus on a possible time in his life when that experience would be a distant memory. After his mother departed and left him alone in the shack, he struggled to maintain that focus.

> I had no electricity in the hut, so I hung out after school at the library and did my homework. I would leave the house about 5:20 a.m. or so, no later. My food was down to a few cases of lentils, sugar, and twenty pounds of flour and I had about $100 on hand. Well, I had three shirts and three pairs of pants. . . .
>
> Some days, I slept in an abandoned house that was right beside the main street and next to a streetlight by which I could read. [Kenric], who was aware of my situation, told me about some guys who were smuggling drugs and that I could make some money doing that. But I told him that was not in the cards for me. I just wanted to get through with my exams

and take it from there. I was determined that I shall do well in school despite what I had to endure and one day I would become a pilot and fly far away.

I went back to the shack between June and July to cook some beans and wash my clothes, but that's pretty much the only time I went there. Ernest couldn't catch up with me when I wasn't there. By that time I had destroyed the interior walls of the shack with my fists, so it was really just a one-room plywood hut with an outdoor toilet and sewer water running right along the back of the house—a backyard filled with grass, filth, and garbage. When the rain fell that summer, it flooded, and I donned galoshes and went off to school. I did my final exams in July and got on the Honor Roll.

This was an early sign of the pent-up anger that festered in Malvo: the aggression he states that he felt but suppressed. It was this anger that Muhammad would later tap into.

ST. MAARTEN FOR THE SECOND TIME

After being away for seven months, Una decided to send for Malvo. Her ultimate goal was to reach the United States. She had no intention of returning to Antigua if she could manage that. She made a contact in St. Maarten and paid someone to transport her and Malvo by boat to St. Thomas, U.S. Virgin Islands. At the time she told Malvo to join her, he was desperate, hungry, angry, and tired of hiding from Ernest the landlord.

As the plane took off, however, I began to feel nervous. I had that empty feeling in my stomach. This is what it's like, this is the way it has always been when I contemplate facing my mother. It's a love/hate thing, my mother being the kind of woman one hates to love. Surely she wouldn't find anything to nag about—at least I hoped so.

Una was there to greet Malvo at the airport in St. Maarten, but he noticed that she was fidgety and had a half-smile, which for him signaled trouble. He knew he had to settle in and make the best of the situation. Una was living in another one-room apartment, not much different from what Malvo had left behind in Antigua. He recalled her going through his clothes, his books, and whatever else he had brought with him. Then the complaints began. She was displeased with his writing and the messy condition of his clothes. When his mother inspected his report card, he thought she would have given him credit. Instead she started to berate him, saying that he was just like his father. It sounded like she was accusing him of not trying hard enough, even though he was getting the opportunity that she had wanted as a child. He wanted to tell her about the harsh conditions in which she left him in Antigua, and how he had to do his homework by streetlight, and that he hoped for a hug and some acknowledgment that she loved him. However, he thought better about saying anything to her. Again he just tried to adjust as best he could.

Malvo learned that his mother was having a relationship with a man to whom she had paid money for passage to St. Thomas. (This man shall be called Claude.) Days turned into weeks, and Malvo began to wonder whether they would ever get on the boat. When he mustered up the courage to ask his mother what was happening, she told him what Claude had told her: "Sometime next month." It was becoming clear to Malvo that Claude was stalling.

As time passed, Malvo grew more irritable and resentful. July gave way to August, with no indication he and his mother would ever leave. It would soon be time for him to register for school, any school. But here he was, hoping that he would finally reach America. Malvo recalled the heated arguments between his mother and Claude as she pressed for a date of departure to the United States. Malvo felt caught in the middle, as he was drawn into more than one confrontation between them, where he felt obligated to stand up for his mother. Malvo recalled that after one such heated exchange, which bordered on becoming violent, his mother was able to recover her money from Claude. After that, Una set her sights on a return to Antigua.

THE RETURN TO ANTIGUA

Without Malvo knowing, Una had contacted Thomas, her previous boyfriend, about her intent to return to Antigua. Thomas confirmed that Una called him to say she was returning. Thomas confirmed too that he told Una he was prepared to assist her, if they continued their relationship. He promised that if she settled down with him, he would build her a house and see to her and Malvo's welfare.

Thomas decided that the shack in which Una was living was not good enough for her, so he rented her a bigger place. His wife had died, and he was willing to commit fully to Una. He impressed upon her that he could help support her in business and, if only she did right by him, he was willing to pay Malvo's school fees.

I returned just in time to unpack my bags and get back to the Seventh-Day Adventist School. My greatest worry was avoiding Ernest, an impossible task since the little island had such a small population. At least our living accommodations were much better. Thomas had rented a spacious two-bedroom house with indoor plumbing for a change. He also had paid, in full, my tuition.

My mother had bought quite a lot of clothes for resale and I had to do my part in selling them. My workday began on Friday, and I worked through the weekend. I made very good sales, mainly to young men wanting jeans, T-shirts, dressy clothes, formal wear, perfume, and the like. Soon we had a clientele of about thirty to forty customers who patronized us every weekend. Several more were on the pay-as-you-go plan.

Mom, during the weekdays, dressed and made sales in banks and other small office buildings. At a very quick rate, we were beginning to make progress. Mom would travel twice per month to buy new stock. Finally, things were looking up.

JOHN MUHAMMAD IN ANTIGUA

Someone else had chosen to come to Antigua and put certain plans into effect. His name was John Allen Muhammad. Unlike Una, who was trying to get into the United States, Muhammad was running from the United States with his children. Joan Green (not her real name), the person with whom Muhammad first stayed in Antigua, remembered how she initially became acquainted with him. A cousin of hers had called from Washington State and asked her to give him accommodations. Muhammad arrived on March 28, 2000, with his three children.

Although Joan picked them up at the airport, she figured out later that if she had been allowed to enter the airport terminal and ask for him, she would have realized that something was not right. At the time, she was unaware that he had traveled under the name Thomas Allen Lee, and she would have asked for John Williams, his name before he formally changed it to John Muhammad. His children traveled as Fred Allen Lee, Theresa Lee, and Lisa Lee. According to Joan, they only had carry-on luggage or backpacks. She recalled asking Muhammad how long he intended to stay, and he said six weeks.

Joan said that about a month after his arrival, Muhammad said he wanted to return to Washington for a brief period in order to get some souvenirs. He asked Joan if she could look after his children until he got back. She recalled that she started wondering about Muhammad's intentions and began to question his children. She said that the girls would frequently respond, "Ask my brother." As time went on she began to have suspicions, especially after she heard of the "name game." Muhammad would give one of the little girls a dollar for each time she remembered to say the name he had given her.

Joan also felt that Muhammad was working on the children subconsciously. She said that after they went to sleep, Muhammad would ask her to lend him her CD/tape player, and he would play something on it all night. She could not say what it was, but she thought the practice strange because he waited until they went to sleep to play it. Charmaine, Joan's daughter, corroborated what her mother said. Charmaine was also disturbed by Muhammad's practice of having his children repeat things before they went to bed and then playing the tapes while they slept. "He was subliminally indoctrinating and hypnotizing them," Charmaine remarked. She also had the impression that John was gathering an army because he always had a group of kids following him around.

Joan said that the "name game" suggested to her that the children's true identities were hidden. So in Muhammad's absence she asked the children about their mother. Joan said that John Jr., the oldest of the three, told her that his father had visitation rights but had taken the children away from their mother, and that they had made stops in three different states before finally reaching Antigua. Hearing this, Joan felt that Muhammad had stolen the kids. When he called that night to speak to the children, she told him he should come and get them right away. Muhammad told her he could not get a flight until the end of May. She told him she would take the children to the airport to leave them with the authorities if he did not come immediately.

Muhammad was back in Antigua the next day with a letter purportedly from his wife, Mildred, giving him permission to take the kids on a vacation. Joan recalled that he then gave her an envelope and told her that it should only be opened if something happened to him. After she realized Muhammad's deception, she decided to open the envelope and found the children's correct names and birth certificates inside.

According to Joan, she felt bad about telling Muhammad to take his kids immediately, but she could not trust him. It seemed to her that he loved his kids because he was so protective of them, but she had her doubts about his veracity and intentions. She said Muhammad was big on making an impression and would boast that he had many businesses. "He had ten businesses, but he stole my daughter's health book," she recalled. From what Joan observed, he had a way of attracting respect from the neighborhood children. They looked up to him. She remembered that he had a magnetism that drew them to him. "The kids would gather around him and take in all he had to say to them. They loved him," she said.

Wanda Roper (not her real name), another Antiguan who interacted with Muhammad, recalled that he was very impressed with her son, Albert; he said Albert was very bright, and he tried to entice him and one of her nephews to go to the United States. She said that Muhammad called her son "Albert Einstein." She remarked that Muhammad too was very bright and seemed capable of storing information in his head without writing it down. She recalled that he would ask questions and record the answers in his head. She said this mental capacity was how he got a lot of information from people with whom he associated. She felt that was how Muhammad had gotten the name of his supposedly Antiguan mother.

Joan recalled that Muhammad had asked her how to go about obtaining an Antiguan passport, but she chased him away because she knew he had lied about having an Antiguan mother. He also obtained information about his children's classmates and stored this as well. She eventually told Muhammad that he had to leave her home. He went next door and set up a tent, where he and his children slept for about two nights. He later found accommodations at the home of Charles and Euphernia Douglas, next door to the school where his children were enrolled. The Douglases were Jamaican, and like many Jamaicans residing in Antigua, they were hopeful of getting a visa to enter the United States.

The Douglases were happy to accommodate the well-spoken, imposing American man. Euphernia recalled that Muhammad was a very good father. "He took care of his children. He paid attention to them, checked their schoolwork, and took them to the beach. Muhammad supposedly wanted his children to know the Caribbean and later Africa." She said that Muhammad was wonderful with all kids. He occasionally went to the school and talked with the teachers. If a child fell and got hurt in the schoolyard, he would take the child to the Douglases house and dress the wound.

Keshna, Euphernia's daughter, described Muhammad as the perfect father and counselor. She pointed out that though he was not married to anyone in the house, he was a provider. He volunteered to pay the entire rent, and he provided whatever he thought was needed for the house. He told Euphernia to make a list of necessary food and household items, and then he took her to the store and paid for what she listed. As a father, he seemed attentive, caring, and disciplined. The children had to address adults as "Sir" or "Ma'am." Keshna said that she benefited from Muhammad's advice with regard to the rocky relationship she had with her boyfriend. "He was very perceptive. He saw and sensed the problem before you said anything," Keshna said.

The Douglases saw Muhammad as a "take charge" person. They recalled an occasion when Charles Douglas had an altercation with another man outside the house. Just as the argument was about to get physical, Muhammad stepped outside and took charge. "He spoke to my husband as though he was giving him military orders. 'You listen to me now. Stop this and get inside,'" Euphernia recalled. Her husband did as Muhammad instructed, and the confrontation ended. "He had an air about him that commanded respect," she said.

What the Douglases and others did not know then was that Muhammad had a dark side. They were exposed to the heroic image he portrayed: that of a military man who had served his country and now was willing to serve and protect those around him.

MUHAMMAD, THE MILITARY MAN

FBI reports indicate that Muhammad first served in the National Guard from 1978 to 1985, after which he enlisted in the military. At that time his name was John Williams. He served with the 64th Engineer Company during the first Gulf War. His unit helped to inspect, catalogue, and destroy extensive stockpiles of Iraqi chemical weapons.

Based on a memo from attorney Michael Arif to Malvo's legal defense team, dated July 16, 2003, an entry in John Williams's military records dated August 1982 indicated, "Sgt. Williams demonstrates professional competence in the accomplishment of all missions assigned, especially in the areas of initiative and attainment of results." It further states that he "has exhibited his technical skills both in combat and construction areas during the accomplishments of all tasks and projects assigned to him."

By 1991, however, after he'd been sent to the Gulf, there was a change in Muhammad's attitude. In a military report dated November 14, 1991, one Keith Burpee stated that Williams was placed in his squad after he was involved in an incident with a missing M16, for which no one could prove he was at fault. In February 1992, Muhammad was charged with aggravated arson, but no action was taken. There was also an incident involving a grenade. Allegedly, Muhammad had ignited and discarded an M14 TH3 (an incendiary grenade) on the floor of a sleeping tent. The grenade burned three cots. Significant as well is a military report dated January 25, 1993, citing Muhammad's confrontation with another soldier, coincidentally named Lee. The report read, "Williams allegedly stepped into Lee's face and told him, 'Brother to brother, back off or you will be the first slaughtered. There is no place that your family will be safe and the people that are supporting you will go down also. This I promise you.'"

Muhammad was not trained as a sniper, but an article on time.com dated October 24, 2002, "Sniper-Suspect's Military Record Revealed," stated that there was one area in his military career in which Muhammad was outstanding: his marksmanship. Muhammad's Marksmanship Badge carried an "expert" rating—earned by the ability to hit 36 out of 40 targets at distances ranging from 25 to 300 meters.

In an article in the *Washington Post*, November 8, 2002, written by Marcia Slacum Greene, a *Post* staff writer, Mildred Muhammad recalled that Muhammad wanted to be a career soldier but returned from his tour of duty in the Persian Gulf a changed person. "When he got back he was an angry man. I didn't know this man. The one I knew stayed in Saudi Arabia." Mrs. Muhammad also stated that Muhammad had told her of the discrimination that he suffered in the military and related a particular incident that left him "seething." She remembered him telling her that he was hogtied, arms and legs cuffed behind his back, after he was accused of tossing an incendiary grenade into a tent. She recalled that it was as though he had developed a dual personality, demanding that everything be done with military-style precision.

In the article, Mrs. Muhammad described what she saw as Muhammad's skill at playing mind games. "He knew exactly what words to use to push your buttons. He studied everybody he was around. He knew what words to use in order to get you to do what he wanted. He would study your anger and how fast it would take you to calm down. . . . He is always thinking. His mind is never idle." She recalled as well that he was very controlling and remembered that he once changed their home phone number without telling her. He would taunt her until she yelled at him, then he would lower his voice, give her a penetrating look, and ask why was she upset and what had he said to upset her. The article quotes her as saying, "His [Malvo's] life was over from the time he said 'Hi John.' He just did not know it."

2 A False Father Found

Malvo Meets John Muhammad

I t was during the early days of October 2000 that Malvo first encountered John Muhammad. This was in St. John's, Antigua, at an electronics shop Malvo visited to use the computer and play video games. The shop, operated by Jerome and Leonie Martin, was affectionately called Zaza Yellow's. It was a popular spot on the island, as it provided a variety of computer and electronic equipment for the children of the neighborhood, including Malvo.

> I enjoyed the PC games they played there. The shop was usually crowded with my peers but I usually found a little corner and watched the others play. Occasionally, I had a chance to play a few games myself. On several Fridays, I noticed a father and son laughing and joking as they played Microsoft Flight Simulator. The boy was flying from the outside cockpit view, and his father joked, "Nice scenery, but remind me not to fly with you." The father smirked, and his son looked at him with quizzical but amused eyes. "Well, I thought most pilots should pay close attention to the instrument panel," the father said.

In seeing the camaraderie between father and son, Malvo was transported to the days when he played with his father. There were no computers or flight simulators, just a paper plane made by his father, and they would "pretend fly" while negotiating around the furniture, making sure not to break anything. Malvo noted the similarity between how his father used to play with him and how Muhammad related to his son.

Malvo recalled an occasion when John Jr., Muhammad's son, took a break from the controls to get a drink. Malvo noticed how John Sr. sighed when his son resumed the flight controls, because John Jr. was flying into trouble. Malvo noticed that Muhammad feigned ignorance, challenging John Jr. to pay attention to the fight panel. John Jr. cocked an eyebrow in his father's direction, then took up the challenge. Malvo stood there and watched, enthralled by the interaction. He wrote: "The level of trust, their open camaraderie, and the communication between them was something I'd always dreamed of but until then had never experienced since my mom took me away from my dad."

Malvo saw another quality in John Muhammad that struck him as special. According to Malvo, when Mr. Muhammad addressed a child, he did it no differently than he addressed an adult. Muhammad seemed to give kids his undivided attention. According to Malvo, Muhammad had a way of letting everything "freeze" when he was talking with someone. He noticed that Muhammad actually listened. He would place a small kid on a stool so that communication took place at eye level. He never interrupted until that child finished making his or her point. Then Muhammad rephrased what the child said to make sure of the point, and then he'd give his response.

Malvo was impressed also with the level of respect that Muhammad generated among adults and children. When Muhammad was not at the shop, it was boisterous, but as soon as he stepped in, everyone straightened up. Malvo remembered seeing a toddler, about two or three years old, who was "hell on wheels." The child's mother could not get her to settle down. Muhammad caught the toddler, lifted her from the floor, and asked her name. Suddenly the child became shy. After four or five questions, amid smiles and encouragement, Muhammad got this little girl to sit beside him quietly all evening. Muhammad was a like a Pied Piper. He just had that power with young people, from babies to children in their late teens. Malvo gawked in awe of the effect Muhammad had.

At this time, Una was doing reasonably well with her informal trading. Thomas provided her with the money to travel to different islands to buy clothes and household articles, which she, with Malvo's help, would sell. She ensured that Malvo settled back into school. He was scoring average to above average in all subjects and his conduct was good. Though his teachers felt that he had the ability to perform even better, he was still on the honor roll.

However, Malvo could not feel comfortable, as he knew his mother could leave him at any time. She still had her sights set on traveling to the United States, and she continued to ask about anyone who could provide her with a visa. She was told of an American man, John Muhammad, who could sell her one.

Una went to his residence on Rose Street, where he lived with the Douglases. To Malvo's surprise and delight, Muhammad was the same man he had observed in the electronics shop with his son. He was very businesslike as he struck a bargain with Una. Malvo recalled that as his mother and Muhammad engaged in conversation, he got acquainted with Muhammad's son, John Jr. Malvo noted that John Jr. was called "Little Man," the same nickname Malvo's father used to call him.

> Little Man and I hit it off when we learned we both wanted to be pilots. I made the girls laugh and immediately was made to feel welcome. Every day, after this meeting, I visited Mr. Muhammad. When he was absent, I spent time with the children. Mostly, I would go on an errand to give him information or money. I'd make whatever excuse I could just to be back in his presence. Plus I loved the vitality of his children. They took me in their hearts as if they had known me for a lifetime.

According to Malvo, his mother promised that as soon as she put the funds together she would pay Muhammad to bring Malvo to the United States to join her. She also told Malvo that he should go to Thomas for anything he needed. Malvo had grown to like Thomas and was uncomfortable with the deception. He remembered his mother telling him that what she was doing was best for both of them and that Thomas would be okay financially.

Malvo remained troubled by how his mother manipulated this man. Thomas thought the money he gave Una, which she used to buy the visa, was actually for one of her business trips. He was building a house for Una and Malvo and making plans for them to settle down in Antigua. His was going to acquire a store for Una in the capital, where she could sell her merchandise and also open a small restaurant.

Before departing, Una received all the necessary paperwork, an address in the United States, and a life story. Malvo recalled that his mother had to memorize the information to ensure a smooth entry. Thomas recalled being told by Una that she was leaving for one of her routine trips to St. Maarten. She called some days later to inform him that she had not gone to St. Maarten but instead was in the United States. "She really tricked me," he said. According to Thomas, Una did promise that as soon as she had matters taken care of, she would return to Antigua.

MUHAMMAD THE SAVIOR

As she had done previously, Una left Malvo by himself in Antigua. He was fifteen years old and still attending school. This time he felt a little better because he was in a house and not a shack. Additionally, he was feeling more and more like he had found a family in Muhammad and his children. He continued to attend school regularly and completed his exams. Then he fell gravely ill with rheumatic fever. The illness was a significant event in his life, as it served to cement his relationship with Muhammad, whom Malvo saw as coming to his rescue.

> I had a terrible fever and my joints ached. It was a recurrence of Rheumatic Fever I had contracted as a child. I was not able to get out of bed to call for help or to get food. My tonsils were swollen and I was unable to eat. Two days went by while I was in that condition but I could not get out of bed. Then Mr. Muhammad came by one day and found the back door slightly ajar. Upon entering he saw me in bed, sweating and almost delirious with fever. He called his personal taxi driver, and he lifted me out of bed and carried me out in his arms because I was too weak to walk. He took me to the doctor and then to his place of residence and introduced me to Mrs. Douglas, or Auntie as everyone calls her. I was fed with fluids and soup. He was able to get medication, and within a few days I was up and about. What was truly amazing was that he spent a lot of time ensuring that I was okay and he never asked for payment.

After this rescue, Malvo and Muhammad went everywhere together. They were like disciple and guru: Muhammad spoke and Malvo listened. Finally Malvo had found someone in whom he could confide. He shared his life story, how his mother had taken him away from his father when he was young and how that left a void in his life. He recalled how Muhammad listened intently. Malvo told of his father's refusal to take him when he wanted a place to stay. He shared with Muhammad the brutal beatings that he'd suffered and that he felt unloved and abandoned.

Muhammad also shared his life story with Malvo. Malvo recalled Muhammad pointing out similarities in their experiences. At the time there was no apparent reason for Malvo to doubt Muhammad; his words had the ring of paternal sincerity and sympathy. Furthermore, he said just enough to impress Malvo that they were brought together by shared history and experiences. Malvo heard of Muhammad's abandonment by his father and loss of his mother. Muhammad related that he too had been raised in an abusive environment, by his grandfather. He suffered a similar fate as Leslie: his wife cheated on him and took all his money, destroying businesses they had built together. According to Malvo, Muhammad assured him that they had met not by coincidence but by destiny. Muhammad then began to introduce Malvo as his son.

In order to increase Muhammad's acceptance of him, Malvo practiced speaking like an American. He helped customers to obtain illegal entry into the United States. Soon Malvo knew the ins and outs of getting Antiguan passports, U.S. visas, birth certificates, Social Security numbers, and IDs through Muhammad's contacts. Malvo had to memorize phone numbers and addresses. He recalled that he was able to grasp the operation of the business within two weeks. Muhammad introduced him to customers and acquaintances as his son or his nephew, depending on the circumstances.

Wanda Roper, who had met Muhammad earlier, said that he introduced Malvo to her as his son. At the time, Muhammad had been living in Antigua for months. One day he told her he was going to get his son at the airport. He later came with Malvo and told her this was his son by a Jamaican woman. Malvo then told her he had resided in Antigua before and had attended the Seventh-Day Adventist School.

Leonie and Jerome Martin, owners of Zaza Yellow's electronics shop, also recalled Malvo being introduced to them as Muhammad's son. Leonie remarked that she challenged the claim that Malvo was an American because, although he spoke with an American accent, there were certain inflections that sounded Jamaican. "You're not an American," she recalled telling him. But Malvo insisted that Muhammad was his father and that his mother was a Jamaican.

Despite their doubts, it seemed to Leonie and Jerome that Muhammad had a positive effect on children. For instance, Leonie's grandson came down with a head fungus and Muhammad was able to get medication, which he said was used in the military for similar fungi. Leonie and Jerome were impressed because the medication worked. They reiterated that

Muhammad was greatly admired by both children and adults. Leonie remembered that he was intrigued by her young son's computer skills and intellect. Muhammad offered to take her son to the United States, but she refused.

Though Malvo was spending a great deal of time with Muhammad, he continued to reside at the house where his mother had left him. At one point he stayed with Thomas, who had suffered a broken leg and needed assistance. Malvo respected Thomas*, who had lways been very kind to him. For the entire time that Thomas was recuperating from his injury, Malvo stayed at his residence and worked as much as he could for him. Thomas confirmed that Malvo assisted with the laundry and all the domestic chores, including feeding the pigs, chickens, and rabbits. "I actually enjoyed the work," Malvo recalled.

Thomas remembered Malvo coming to his residence accompanied by a man who claimed to be his uncle. Thomas said that he tried to look out for Malvo, and that Malvo was welcome to stay in his house. Nonetheless, when Malvo decided to live with Muhammad, Thomas felt he did not have the authority to stop him because Una had not specifically asked him to be the boy's guardian.

Malvo confirmed that he was planning to leave Thomas's house and live with Muhammad when Thomas's leg was healed. He was troubled by the way his mother deceived Thomas, so, when he stayed with him, the memories associated with that relationship might have been overwhelming. Malvo said that he discussed with Muhammad the possibility of living with him. Muhammad agreed, saying it would be good for his children to have a big brother. Malvo recalled his feelings when he made the move: "I was welcomed into the household as though I had been with them forever. I had finally found a family."

Malvo recalled that Muhammad introduced him to the Nation of Islam and the teachings of Elijah Muhammad. He and Muhammad had plenty of debates, mainly question-and-answer sessions, every evening when he accompanied Muhammad on his rounds. He recalled listening to many of Minister Farrakhan's speeches, such as "Message to the Black Man," "The White Man as the Devil," "The Iceman Inheritance," "Stolen Dreams," "From God to Man to Savage," "Africa Reborn," and the Willie Lynch speech (which at the time he said seemed to answer many of his questions). He also listened to Huey Newton, George Jackson, and the earlier speeches of Malcolm X.

Malvo also studied religion in more depth. He delighted in going to the library with Muhammad to research Taoism, Shinto, Hinduism, Baha'i, Sikhism, Islam, and Judaism. He recalled visiting a Baha'i center in Antigua. He had many questions for Muhammad, and it seemed that Muhammad had a lot of answers for him. When Muhammad could not answer a question, they would go to the library to research the answer together.

> He showed a keen interest in my questions, and as always I was the inquiring student. We spent hours together speaking of my future plans, girls, sex, money, the U.S., losing my hidden aggression, Islam, school, and history. You name it; we spoke about it with gusto and vitality. This was the man I'd grown to respect and admire. I took him for my mentor and father.

This "hidden aggression" that Malvo refers to seems to be his suppressed anger because of the traumas that he had endured—the anger at his mother for the abuse and the abandonment and the rage toward his father for not rescuing him. Prior to meeting Muhammad, Malvo had to be the dutiful, obedient, kind and loving child to be loved, but Muhammad helped to give him voice to that anger, summed up in a poem Malvo wrote, excerpted below.

BLACK LOVE

Mother I am angry, Mother I am mad,
Every time I think of You I grow sad.
The tears you made me cry,
Made me a rebel
And it's a sad story to tell.

I strive to grow into me,
But you tried to destroy the child
The individual that you couldn't see.
Mother why couldn't you see me?
I want to be free but freedom never knew me
You gave me eyes I looked up at the stars
You poked them out and bid me never to see.

You fed me your thoughts
But to my own thoughts you were most deadly.

Have you ever seen a dead dream?
Mother—why won't you look at me?

Black boys who never grew up to be men—
Their mothers in misconstrued love
Castrated them.

You the matriarch, not because you love it,
Down your throat, life shoved it.
And you regurgitated Me.
The responsibility you tried to beat out
Of existence.

As if to say, "Why did you come here?
Damn You! Damn You! For being born.
I have nothing to give you but pain!"
To teach me—To toughen me—To prepare me
You beat out the ambition
While trying to beat me
Into submission.

Now you wail
The beating it seemed. . . . Failed.

The drama of My childhood—
Trauma.
You know, this is true
Though it may sound insane.
Black love is at times bitter,
Black love is at times pain.

And when it's like that
There is so little to gain,
So much of the beauty
Of life from these eyes drained,
I would not to go through that again.

But my past is interlocked with me holding your hands.
When are we gonna see—Our women can't rear
Boys to be men.

BY: LEE BOYD MALVO

As the poem suggests, Malvo was seeking a father, having determined that his mother had failed to raise him to be the man he needed to be. Muhammad became that longed-for parent, and his interest in Malvo included taking care of the boy's material needs. On Malvo's sixteenth birthday, Muhammad took him shopping and replaced his entire wardrobe. He encouraged Malvo to learn a foreign language and bought him a Spanish instruction set. In addition, Muhammad stated that Malvo's primary concern was to be the welfare of "his younger siblings." Thus, not only had he gotten a parent, he had gotten a family.

Malvo became big brother, and he was in charge of the house when his "dad" (Muhammad) was not present. Muhammad had strict rules about how the boys should take care of the girls. He provided all the children with an allowance, but instructed that the money he gave Malvo and John Jr. was also for the girls' well-being. Malvo remembered trying to explain that it was not fair that the boys' allowance should also be used for the girls. He recalled Muhammad saying that as young men it was their responsibility and duty to be models of manhood to their sisters. Even though the girls had their own money, the boys were older and more likely to be financially responsible. Malvo said he thus received his first lesson on manhood.

Malvo recalled Muhammad telling him: "Man has to calculate the consequences of his actions because his actions not only affect him, but his family. So if the girls need anything, the first person they'll turn to is you. Shall you tell them no because they didn't spend their share wisely? To whom else shall they turn?"

As Malvo continued to settle into this new family, he relished the structure. Discipline was not carried out in an arbitrary manner, as it was with his mother. Muhammad had a different approach. He did not use corporal punishment because it did nothing to make a child feel any better. Instead, he made the children do push-ups as punishment for infractions. If there was disagreement among the children and they did not sort it out by themselves, they would be told to do push-ups for thirty minutes. The number of push-ups depended on the seriousness of the infraction. Boys and girls received different numbers. Malvo, as the oldest boy, was required to do the most push-ups—next to Muhammad, who also applied the rule to himself.

There was a reward system whereby the children were given payment for obedience and good works. First on Muhammad's list was the study of the Supreme Wisdom (the writings of the Nation of Islam) as it relates to Muslims. This was a major group effort, with all four children pitching in. They were rewarded with cash, which was to be shared among them. They were only allowed to use 60 percent of what was earned. The other 40 percent had to be saved. This was a lesson about how the group is strengthened when there is cooperation and sacrifice.

In addition to the structure and consistency Malvo believed Muhammad provided, Muhammad listened and gave him undivided attention. Given Malvo's past experiences with his mother, these qualities made him feel he had found the ideal parent. He became a sponge, soaking up whatever Muhammad instilled in him. Under that attentive gaze, Malvo's Christian beliefs were replaced with Islamic doctrine as construed by Muhammad.

> I went to school armed with new knowledge, ready to debate the Christian population, and play Socrates. Questions, questions! I debated the divinity of Christ, whose name is Esau, saying it was Paul who created Christianity. How is it one god if there are three in one? How many Gospels were excluded from the Bible? I debated the proof of "Lynchism." I became an angry black man. I was actually trying to convert some doubting classmates. My close friend, John Sewsankar, implored me that it was useless. He said I was talking to deaf ears, mute lips, closed eyes. Well, all this religious zeal didn't pan out well in a Christian Seventh-Day Adventist School, and the last straw was my reciting the translation of the Al-Fatila and performing Salat.

Dr. Aaron, principal of the Seventh-Day Adventist High School, remarked that she knew two Lee Malvos. Oe was the fourteen-year-old Christian child who had first registered at her school in September 1999. Then he was a "bright, polite, and courteous young man." He was able to settle in and meet the school's high academic expectations very well. She said that by January 2001, however, another Lee Malvo, who seemed to have been washed clean of his Christian identity, confronted her. Some of the teachers and students had informed her that Malvo was talking about Islam and had a copy of the Koran. Dr. Aaron decided she had to telephone his mother to report on Malvo's conduct.

I remember her telling my mother that she does not know what has gotten over me, and though I am free to believe and practice what I wish, preaching Islam and praying in that manner will not be tolerated, nor is it acceptable in this Christian School. I considered her brainwashed and swallowing lies at that stage of my indoctrinations. She noticed I was glaring at a framed portrait of Jesus in mosaic hung proudly on her wall. She looked over her shoulder, looked at me and asked, puzzled, "What is wrong?" I said bluntly, "Jesus is black. He is described as having hair like wool." I touched my head. "And skin like bread burnt in an oven." I looked from her hand to the mosaic. "Now, that is a lie."

She asked me if I understood what she said, and then told me to respect it, which I did with an air of mock sincerity. Dr. Aaron is neither dumb nor a fool and did not buy my bravado. She dismissed me. When I was almost at the door, anxious to get away from what I saw was her contemptible presence, her voice brought me to a halt. "And Mr. Malvo, I will inform your mother of your new beliefs and your rambunctious attitude. And yes, your disrespect and disregard for Christ and authority here at this school!" She stressed the "Christ" and "here at this school."

According to Malvo, there was a time when the mere threat of his mother being called would have had him begging for mercy. But not now. According to Malvo, Muhammad had told him to respect his mother but remember that she was stupid. He thought that his mother was the one who was brainwashed in her religious beliefs and that she had ignorantly passed those beliefs on to him. As he left Dr. Aaron's office, he felt that his mother's hold over him had weakened, and he felt free.

At school Malvo continued to spew the "truth" as he knew it then. He challenged everything from history to religion, and took a stab at Christianity at every opportunity. This led to him being summoned to the principal's office again. This time, she asked to meet with his guardian. Malvo recalled the flamboyance with which he introduced his "dad" to Dr. Aaron. He stressed the "Mu-ham-mad" as he introduced him.

Malvo recalled Dr. Aaron inquiring of Muhammad exactly how he was related to the boy. Muhammad responded that he was an American and was Malvo's uncle. She informed Muhammad that Malvo was causing quite a disturbance at the school and showing disrespect for the rules. Muhammad then told Malvo to respect the rules of the school. Malvo promised that he would.

Dr. Aaron recalled her meeting with Muhammad, describing him as polite and courteous. He gave her his contact information should she have any more problems with Malvo. After the meeting, Una called, and Dr. Aaron asked her whether Muhammad was Malvo's guardian. Dr. Aaron recalled that Una confirmed he was. Based on this, Dr. Aaron placed Muhammad's name on the permanent register card, a copy of which she provided for my review. Dr. Aaron said that after the meeting with Muhammad, there were no further problems with Malvo at school.

Under the keen tutelage of Muhammad, Malvo's grades improved. He recalled Muhammad showing him his degrees in health and nutrition, as well as one in physics, which Muhammad claimed he had earned while serving in the military as an army ranger. The bond between the two intensified, and they went everywhere together. He encouraged Malvo to play cricket, a ball game popular among British Commonwealth countries and similar to baseball. He also helped him by developing an exercise regimen that built his endurance. According to Malvo, within weeks they were running three miles uphill every other morning. Malvo also recalled that one day Muhammad took him to a tailor and had his measurements taken for three suits. Malvo did not see any reasons to question Muhammad's actions, as those days seemed the happiest times in his life.

MUHAMMAD ARRESTED

As part of his business of securing fraudulent travel documents, Muhammad arranged for his customers to fly to the United States. He had a scheme wherein he took them through the airport in Antigua and into the United States without arousing suspicion. However, on March 11, 2001, Muhammad was arrested at the airport in Antigua.

Reportedly two days after his arrest, Muhammad escaped from custody. He arranged for his children to be moved to a safe house where they were left in the care of a girlfriend. Malvo had to ensure that the children were kept out of the reach of the authorities. He also had to continue Muhammad's money-making schemes. Cheryl Morris, his teacher at the time, recalled that it was about March 2001 when Malvo stopped attending school. Malvo's friend, John Sewsankar, recalled seeing him busy on the streets. Malvo was no longer talking about girls and sports, but seemed obsessed with his newfound religion, interest in guns, and keeping fit. John noted that whereas Malvo had been a scrawny kid before, now his physique looked more muscular.

According to Malvo, he had to quit school in order to take care of the children and Muhammad's business. This decision was made by a child who once slept in an abandoned building and completed his homework by a street lamp so that he could remain in school. However, the welfare of Muhammad's children had supplanted his own education and survival needs. Muhammad's children had to be clothed and fed. Malvo had new responsibilities, and he wanted desperately to prove his worth. He saw to the children's education daily, and told them that their daddy was away on business.

After about two weeks of trying to keep things together, Malvo woke up early one morning and found Muhammad on the sofa. He was wide awake and seemed to be in deep thought. Malvo recalled Muhammad saying that he had been in the house for several hours but decided against disturbing the quiet. Muhammad indicated also that he needed more money quickly. Malvo recalled his dramatic makeover: he was clean-shaven and dressed in a suit, armed with a full American accent and legal American and Antiguan identification. Muhammad announced he was ready for phase 2. Malvo did not know what phase 2 meant, but he was mesmerized by Muhammad's smoothness. "You either act or become a victim of your circumstances," he remembered Muhammad telling him. As Muhammad spoke, he gestured to the shacks around him and the abject poverty of the inhabitants.

Muhammad continued his smuggling business, taking clients through Puerto Rico or the U.S. Virgin Islands. At times he traveled with them after securing fraudulent birth certificates and Social Security cards for them. Once he was detained when it was discovered that his "three-year-old daughter," with whom he was traveling, spoke with a thick Jamaican accent. He had been able to instruct the mother to keep her mouth shut, but not the child. As a result, he was not able to return to Antigua as he'd expected.

In the meantime, Malvo was fully established as Muhammad's right-hand man in Antigua. Muhammad's girlfriend stayed home and did all the household chores while Malvo continued to obtain false travel documents for the customers. As the big brother, Malvo also had to make sure that the children's fears were allayed. They were not accustomed to having their father gone for such a long spell, and by the third week they began to worry.

Leonie and Jerome Martin recalled the trek that Malvo made from St. John's, where most of the business was transacted, to Englishtown, where Muhammad's girlfriend lived with the children. It was about a twelve miles, but Malvo made it every day. "I would ask him if it was not too much for him to undertake, but his response was that it was 'no big deal,'" Jerome Martin recalled.

Malvo made sure he gave Muhammad's children their tutoring. They had classes four hours daily, and then he would take them to the park. According to Malvo, his "dad" placed a high priority on the children's education. Malvo took it upon himself to not only tutor the children but also be their protector. He restricted their movements in order to lower the risk of the police finding them. He operated under the assumption that the police in Antigua were alerted that Muhammad had abducted the children.

Malvo recalled that he had to adopt an American accent to go along with the pretext that he was Muhammad's oldest child. He did business at night and changed his route daily. He allowed John Jr. or "Little Man," as Malvo preferred to call him, to accompany him most nights. After a while Malvo settled into a routine wherein he took the children out almost every weekend to the movies, the mall, and the beach. On one beach trip, he said, John Jr. became stranded on an inflatable raft that drifted away from the shore. The raft began to deflate and John Jr. began to go under. Malvo recalled that he sprang into action, swam out to the raft, and saved Little Man from drowning. Malvo believes that this is the incident that earned him the respect of John Muhammad. He recognized that what was most precious to Muhammad was his children, and, in saving Little Man's life, Malvo affirmed his place in the family. Muhammad reminded him of this incident frequently as a means of reiterating that he valued Malvo as a son.

As time passed with no word about Muhammad's return, Malvo began to feel overwhelmed. However, he kept going because he could not afford to fail his "dad." Due to rent problems, he returned to Mrs. Douglas's residence. He searched for customers so that he could make money to pay the rent and buy food. He was able to get $1,500 from one customer. With that money, he bought food in bulk: ramen noodles, sardines, tuna, cheese, crackers, canned vegetables, tofu, and veggie chunks. He also tried to spoil the girls with ice cream and jewelry, and was coaxed into taking them to KFC a few times.

With Malvo in charge of collecting money from the customers, friction began to arise as to how the money should be spent. Malvo felt that he should say what should be given priority. Mrs. Douglas and Muhammad's girlfriend felt otherwise. Malvo recalled that Muhammad eventually called and instructed him that no money should be spent without Muhammad's prior approval. Malvo also believed, based on a phone call from him, that Muhammad's return was imminent.

In the meantime, Una discovered that Malvo was no longer attending school, but when she called the Douglas residence, he refused to speak to her. Una began to realize that her hold on Malvo was loosening.

Malvo recalled that by the third week of May 2001 he started losing his temper. He was beginning to feel overwhelmed. He started searching for a cheaper apartment in the hope of stretching his limited resources. One day as he was trying to figure out a way to pay for rent and food, John Jr. wanted to play. Malvo was not in the mood, but John Jr. kept insisting, punching at his arm. Malvo overreacted in frustration. He wrote:

> I snapped, and I picked him up and slammed him one. He was hurt and dazed. I picked him up and apologized, but I didn't explain my dilemma to him. He was startled; and little by little began to withdraw. I tried to win him over, but my constant battles with Auntie, my mother's constant nagging on the telephone, and counting out how many days our food would last made me feel totally overwhelmed.

With the funds he had, Malvo made sure that the children received three meals a day while he had only one, usually made up of the leftovers from the children's plates. He recalled that whenever Taalibah, the youngest child, questioned whether he was eating or not, he would assure her that he was not hungry. If she insisted that he eat, he would lie and say that he had eaten at the basketball court. Salena and John Jr. kept their distance from him because, with all the pressure he was under, he had become very harsh.

> Because of my lack of discipline, I'd let my anger flare up at times, shooting a glaring look to silence questions. I kept my headphones on and blasted Eminem in my ears. I got an apartment and the man gave me two weeks to make up my mind. "It might be gone when you return." I had about $1,000 US and no Dad in sight. If I pay three months' rent, that'll leave me $1,900 E.C. I'll stack up on cases of chicken, 125 bags of lentils, chickpeas, rice, sardines, and Ramen noodles. I thought of contacting Kenric who had told me about the guys who smuggled weed and coke. But I can't do that. They cold-bloodedly killed two Jamaicans last year. Who'll take care of the kids if I am killed?

Jerome and Leonie Martin were very concerned for Malvo. They saw that he was burdened with the responsibility Muhammad had left him. Leonie remembered that Muhammad had a way of dealing with the kids as if he were commanding a military operation, causing them to snap to attention when he addressed them. She felt that even though Muhammad was not on the island, he still had Malvo under his pseudo-military control.

Leonie recalled that Muhammad had shown an interest in her son, Akeba. She remarked,

> He told me that he would take Akeba to the U.S., but he was crazy to think that I would let him have my child. I knew that he was lying when he said that Malvo was his son, but he sure used Malvo to do all his dirty stuff. He treated Malvo like a little soldier. "Yes Sir! No Sir!" Like he was in the army. I knew that something was not right, and as time went on you could see the pressure that Malvo was undergoing.

According to Malvo, just as he felt he was going to collapse, Muhammad arrived. Again Malvo greeted him as if in awe of his "dad" coming to the rescue. And again, Malvo's need to see Muhammad was accompanied by anxiety about whether Muhammad would affirm him or reject him. Even though Muhammad had been gone for some time and Malvo was the one taking care of his children, he believed that his own existence was dependent on Muhammad.

> It was like the world was on my shoulder and that's when I saw him. That morning, I gladly announced, "The savior has arrived!" He had the girls in his arms, a few gifts for everyone. Everyone that is, except for me. I was a bit hurt, but I kept silent. He listened patiently, as usual, to everyone's complaint about my misconduct.

Malvo was disappointed in himself. He felt that he had failed his "dad," and that was why he was not rewarded with a gift. Nonetheless, he buried those feelings of hurt deep within him and went out with Muhammad, getting new customers. With that income plus what Malvo had saved in the account, Muhammad had a total of US$10,900. Then on May 30, as they were walking home, Muhammad made Malvo feel like everything was right again.

I was feeling real bad, thinking that he may have been disappointed in me, that I had failed him somehow. I began to explain myself. With a burger in his mouth, he silenced me with a full smile and motioned for me to eat. He ate two, while I was still picking at my one. We ate silently. He looked up. We were on the sidewalk watching traffic. He looked at me with glassy eyes. "You don't owe me an explanation. You did a very good job," he said, jabbing two fingers in the sky to stress the "very." He gave me a huge hug and rubbed my head. I cried silently, which baffled me, but the tears flowed nonetheless. He patted me on the back, "It's okay! Son, be very proud of yourself!" I felt ashamed of my tears. We rose and headed for Auntie. He patted me on the back again. "Good job, son!" Then he took off in a race. He let me catch up! Then he cracked up. "I get you every time." I smiled to myself feeling like I was light as a feather, right as rain. "Good job, son" made it better.

THE AMERICAN JOURNEY

Una had finally made it to the United States. She stayed in Florida, residing in or near the city of Fort Myers. She tried to get legal permanent residency status through marriage to an American citizen, a man named Jay whom she'd met after she arrived in Florida. The major snag in her plans was what was happening with Malvo in Antigua. He seemed no longer under her control. She wanted to bring him to the United States through Muhammad, but she was still short on funds. Unknown to Una, however, Muhammad was not waiting for her to send money. He already had plans for Malvo. On May 31, 2001, Malvo traveled with Muhammad and his three children to Puerto Rico and then to the United States.

Malvo traveled under the name Lindbergh Williams, posing as Muhammad's older son. In the United States, they were met by one of Muhammad's friends and taken to an apartment in Fort Lauderdale, Florida. For the first three weeks, Malvo remained with the children while Muhammad went out on business.

Una was unaware of Malvo's arrival in the United States until she phoned Euphernia Douglas. She was outraged to learn that her son had traveled to Florida with Muhammad. She fumed about Muhammad taking Malvo to Florida and not letting her know. She contacted Muhammad and demanded that he bring Malvo to her promptly.

Malvo, accompanied by Muhammad and John Jr., went to see Una at her job. At the time she was working at a restaurant. Malvo recalled how happy Una was to see him. She grabbed him and hugged him and introduced him to her co-workers. She treated Malvo, Muhammad, and John Jr. to chicken, biscuits, and chips and told them to wait for her until she was off work. While they waited, Muhammad assured Malvo that he would convince Una to let Malvo stay with him.

Malvo recalled that they all stayed with Una that first night. Muhammad tried his best to convince Una that it would be better for her to allow Malvo to stay with him until she was financially stable, but she explained that she had married a Haitian American and things would look up for her soon.

Malvo remembered that Muhammad's discussion with Una continued as they traveled to her job the following morning. Muhammad pressed Una to let Malvo stay with him until she became settled. But she said no, because a child's place is with his mother. Malvo recalled that as she made her position clear, she looked at him, wanting him to agree with her. But he kept silent.

Una continued to protest until they arrived at her job. As she was walking to the door of the building, she made a U-turn and demanded that Malvo get out of the vehicle. When Malvo did not move, Una stood there aghast. Muhammad said, "Son, are you ready?" To which Malvo responded, "Yes, sir!" Muhammad then rolled up the window and reversed out of the parking lot. He remembered Una standing in the same spot until she became a dot in the rearview mirror. Malvo recalled feeling bad, but quickly divested himself of that emotion, convincing himself that staying with Muhammad was the best option.

> Right then and there I made up my mind to stay with John, for real. I wasn't really happy to see my mother. Around her I felt like I was being squished, stiffed, robbed of living. John—well, I thought then he understood me. He listened, he appreciated and took into account my perspective on almost every subject. I was where I belonged. I grabbed a magazine and left Ft. Myers, leaving my mother in the past.

In my meetings with her, Una said that the changes she saw in Malvo were frightening. "The boy that I left in Antigua was a different boy from the one that Muhammad brought to me. Malvo was an obedient child. Anything I told him to do, he would do," she remarked. She related that after Muhammad drove away with her son, she was determined to fight for the survival of her only child. While acknowledging that she might have handled things wrongly in the past, she also stated that everything she did was with the goal of giving Malvo the best education.

Una inquired as to Muhammad's whereabouts. When she located him, she told him that she was about to call the police and report that he had kidnapped her son. She impressed upon Muhammad that she was serious, so he decided to meet with her again. Malvo recalled Muhammad telling him that he would try to smooth things over with her, but the only way it would work was if Malvo maintained contact with his mother.

We drove again to Ft. Myers. Once again we spent the night, Muhammad doing his best to get her to see things his way. He tried every trick in the book, eventually returning to my mother's weakest point; money. He thought she would grab on to his proposal and that will suffice her for the summer. He offered her money and free legal papers. He hit the education issue, saying it was useless for me to enter high school, because there was nothing there I didn't know already. He was going to have me take the GED. In fact, I was studying for it, and the fact is I took the pre-test and I passed with ease.

Una frowned through the entire one-way conversation. The smug look on her face indicated clearly that she was still unconvinced and rather unreachable. She had had enough, and stopped him in mid-sentence. "Look, he is my child, what I eat, he eats. If he can't be satisfied with that, greed will kill him." Looking at me she said, "Wait until I get done with you, you . . . ungrateful wretch. You are still my son. You belong to me. I am your mother. You met this man no more than six months ago and you've completely forgotten where you come from." I was still at the stage where I shriveled under her harsh tongue.

In the morning, she went ballistic, shouting, "Where is your clothing? So you intend to stay with John. Not over my dead body! I don't know why I bother with you. Go and get your belongings. What are you staring at?" I sat motionless, looking at Muhammad. She grabbed me and pushed me out the door to fetch my duffel bag. She then told Muhammad to leave, which he did.

A CHANGED SON

Una realized Malvo was now under the control of someone other than herself. That man who had "the eyes of a devil" now had her son's loyalty.

She knew that the days of beating him senseless were over. This was not Jamaica, this was America, and she had heard that children themselves would call the authorities and get their parents arrested for child abuse. She could not afford for that to happen. Malvo had already demonstrated his defiance when he drove off with Muhammad.

Una had to try another strategy. She knew that Malvo's ability to go to school and become a pilot or astronaut meant a lot to him. She had to impress upon him that she was getting things together so he could continue with his education. Malvo had every intention of attending college and did not see the connection between being with Muhammad and not getting an education. Muhammad had talked to Malvo about the possibility of adopting him in order to legitimize his status, and hence enable him to further his education. Malvo felt he could not share that information with his mother until the time was right. Una introduced him to the neighborhood and warned that he should stay away from the streets because "there were many ways to get in trouble around there." She also took him to get immunization shots and to register for high school.

Malvo's relationship with his mother remained strained. It was difficult for him to trust her. He noted that he and his mother began working on Saturdays and Sundays at a small resort, where they cleaned rooms for $25 each. They did anywhere from nine to eleven rooms, and it was agreed that he would be allowed to keep half of what he earned. After Malvo received his first pay, his mother told him that he had to start contributing to the household, which in effect, he said, left him with nothing. This seemed another example of his mother not keeping her word and reinforced his lack of trust in her.

He became withdrawn and spoke only when necessary. Nonetheless, he went about trying to make things appear as normal as he could. He enrolled at Cypress High School in Ft. Myers on August 13, 2001. The school records show that his scores were excellent. His teachers asked him what he intended to do about college. He was told that with a good SAT score he could qualify for certain grants, but he needed a Social Security number to take the SATs. That posed a major problem, as he did not have legal residency status.

Malvo recalled his mother looking into the possibility of obtaining Haitian birth certificates, but when he pointed out that neither of them spoke Creole, that idea was dashed. His only hope was to be adopted by a U.S. citizen, and that had to happen before he turned eighteen.

MUHAMMAD LOSES CUSTODY OF HIS CHILDREN

While Malvo and his mother were trying to figure out how to remain in the United States, Muhammad was fighting his own battle in a courthouse in Washington State. He had left Florida and returned to Washington with his children, but he made e a critical mistake when he attempted to apply for food stamps at the Department of Social Services in Bellingham. His story raised suspicions, and this led to the discovery that the children with him had actually been abducted. On September 4, 2001, in the Pierce County Courthouse, Judge Mark Gelman informed Muhammad that the court was enforcing a court order that gave full custody of the three children to their mother, his ex-wife, Mildred Muhammad.

Mildred knew that the court order allowed her to take from Muhammad what was most precious to him. She knew that her life was at risk. Muhammad had warned her that he would not allow her to raise his children and that she had become his enemy, and, as his enemy, he would kill her. She also knew that he was a man of his word; when he made a threat, it was not an empty threat. She took her three children and ran.

According to testimony given by Mrs. Muhammad during Malvo's trial, reconnecting with her children, particularly her son (John Jr.), was difficult. When the children were finally returned to her, John Jr. would not respond to her. There were no emotions. "He would not hug me," she said. She recalled that John Jr. would fly off the handle and become very angry if she said anything to him. He would even approach her as though he was going to hit her. "It took him six months to hug me and eight months to say 'I love you,'" she said.

In her testimony, Mrs. Muhammad remarked that when she questioned her son about what he'd gone through, he said he could not tell her because his father instructed him not to. The other two children, Salena and Taalibah, also acted strangely. Mrs. Muhammad said that she had to get permission from Salena to carry out parental duties, because Salena had taken on the mother role during the time the children were with their father. The youngest child, Taalibah, would not sleep; she would awaken at night to make sure her mother was there.

Her children's responses were disturbing but hardly surprising to Mrs. Muhammad. She was well aware of the extreme control her husband exercised over them. They wanted to please their father, and John Jr., in particular, wanted to be the perfect son.

The loss of his children had a devastating effect on Muhammad. This was evident to his very close friend Mary Marez. On the witness stand at Malvo's 2003 trial, Ms. Marez recounted how distraught Muhammad was: "He became very quiet and withdrawn. . . . He would be sitting there staring out of a window, just really not communicating. I just felt like I couldn't reach him anymore. I had been an emotional support for him in a number of situations, but he just wasn't able to be reached in this matter." Though Ms. Marez could not reach him, Muhammad knew whom he could contact in this time of desperate need: Lee Boyd Malvo, the young Jamaican boy who still saw him as a hero.

Interestingly, Muhammad did not try to reach out to any of his biological sons. One of them was Lindbergh, born to Muhammad and his first wife, Carol Williams. Lindbergh was older than Malvo and had experienced his father's method of control; he was an unlikely candidate to join Muhammad in late 2001. As a child, Lindbergh remained in the custody of his mother, but he had experienced his father's attempt to win custody of him at one stage. In his testimony at Malvo's trial, Lindbergh said that his father had a way of getting into one's head. "If my mother had not been a strong woman, if my mother had not fought for me, then it would have been me rather than Lee Malvo in that car with John Muhammad in October of 2002," Lindbergh testified.

"BIG BROTHER" TO THE RESCUE

Though Malvo was residing with his mother, he remained in contact with Muhammad. Quite likely, this was unknown to Una, who had instructed him to keep away from "that man." However, every Friday at 4:00 p.m. Muhammad would call Malvo. One Friday in late September, the two had a phone conversation that would profoundly alter the course of Malvo's life. He wrote:

> I heard the tremor in his voice. "Lee they took the children." I was able to identify with that loss. I had never seen him indecisive and I have never heard that much pain. He spoke to something in me; that void that yearned to be filled. I wanted to have a father to love me like that. I wanted to know that someone cared as deeply for me. When he said he needed me to help him get back the children so that we could once again

be a family, it opened up the flood gates for the kid who ran away to his father five years earlier but who was rejected.

Both of them knew that Una would never agree to send Malvo back into the hands of Muhammad. But they also knew that she wanted Malvo to get a college education. Also working in Muhammad's favor was her failure to get legal permanent residency for herself and Malvo. Malvo tried to persuade his mother by pointing this out, and by telling her that the only option he had was to get adopted. He was already sixteen years old; there wasn't much time until he turned eighteen and would be considered an adult.

According to Malvo, Muhammad called his mother and told her that he would do anything he could to help the boy. Malvo recalled that he was instructed by Muhammad to keep up the pressure on his mother, which he did. The night before he planned to leave, he remembered, his mother went berserk, protesting that she was not stupid as Muhammad might think, and she knew that if Muhammad adopted Malvo, she would no longer have a say in her son's life.

Malvo remembered that his mother argued for hours and threatened to give him a long-deserved walloping if he disobeyed her. He ignored her and waited for the tirade to end. He decided to bide his time until he could pack his bags and leave. According to Malvo, there were three main reasons driving him back to Muhammad. First, Muhammad said he needed him to help get the children back. Second, Muhammad said he would help him get into college. Third, Muhammad seemed to Malvo to be far more logical than his "fist-shaking mother." He wrote: "With my mother love came with a price—do what she wanted and say what she wanted. I could still hear her words in my head—that I wasn't going to make it but I knew that I was going to make it. I was certain that, with John Muhammad, I would make it."

Malvo recalled that his mother tried in utter futility to bridge the divide that their years apart had created. He had told her long ago that she was losing him, and she was seeing that loss happen in Florida. The night before Malvo's departure, his mother retired to bed telling him that it was her way or the highway. Malvo packed his few belongings: two pairs of sneakers, some T-shirts, a few pairs of pants, his tennis racket, and his CD player and CDs. He sneaked out of the house at 4:30 a.m. and was on his way to Tallahassee by 5:15. When he reached Tallahassee, he contacted Muhammad. He informed him that he had run away and needed money for a bus ticket.

Once Malvo assured Muhammad that he still had the fake IDs Muhammad had given him, he received strict instructions on how to get to the state of Washington. He was told to get a ticket in the name of Lindbergh Williams and get off at each station for a few hours, put his bag in a locker, and leave the station. He was to change his clothes and return seven hours later, and to repeat this routine at every major city as he traveled west. Malvo followed Muhammad's instructions precisely.

MASTER AND DISCIPLE REUNITED

Malvo arrived in Bellingham, Washington, early in the morning of October 20, 2001. Muhammad met him and took him to the Lighthouse Mission, a privately operated, nondenominational Christian shelter for the homeless and those in need of social services. The Christian mission emphasized by the shelter did not fit with the anti-Christian rhetoric that Muhammad had been feeding Malvo since Antigua. However, it seemed to the boy that Muhammad did not even feel a twinge of conflict about staying there.

Reverend Al Archer, the director of the mission at the time, grew suspicious of Muhammad's presence. According to Rev. Archer, Muhammad's polite demeanor (excessive to the point of phoniness), his smoothness, and his businesslike air triggered suspicion. He was very concerned about the numerous calls Muhammad received from travel agents and the trips Muhammad took to Canada, the East Coast, Louisiana, and the Caribbean. He felt that Muhammad was using the mission not as it was intended, but rather as a base for his operations, whatever those might be.

The September 11, 2001, terrorist attacks were still recent, so Rev. Archer was concerned about Muhammad's intentions. He knew that Muhammad had lied about having custody of his children and, given the numerous trips, he wondered if Muhammad was involved in terrorist activities. He alerted the FBI.

In his testimony at Malvo's trial, Rev. Archer stated that he felt it was his duty to contact the FBI. He remarked that it was the first time in his thirty-one years at the mission that he called the FBI on one of its residents. Contrary to his fears, however, Muhammad was not reaching out to terrorists. According to Malvo, Muhammad was making counterfeit money and traveling to Canada on the weekends to deliver it to clients.

On Malvo's first day at the shelter, Muhammad introduced him as his son. He said Malvo was eighteen years old, not sixteen, his actual age at the time. According to Rev. Archer, this meant that Malvo could stay at the mission with or without an adult. They attended the mandatory Bible session, after which Malvo was given linens and assigned a bunk.

Muhammad asked Malvo about Florida and what he did there. Malvo gave him an earful about school and his mother's half-baked ideas to legalize their status, and said he was glad to be rid of her. Muhammad then told Malvo that they had to call Una and let her know where he was. Malvo was not enthusiastic about the prospect, for he believed that if his mother knew where he was she would surely find him and force him back with her. However, Muhammad, who had grown accustomed to getting what he wanted—except for his children—was confident that he could smooth things over.

According to Malvo, when Muhammad called Una, he did all the talking. Una recalled that conversation. "I asked him why he was taking the one child that I have when he had several himself." She said that the response Muhammad gave was an indication of her son's future. "When I am done with him I will send him back to you," she recalled him telling her. Una knew that this meant her son was only Muhammad's pawn, and she vowed to get Malvo away from him.

During their stay at the Lighthouse Mission, Muhammad's tutelage of Malvo intensified. Muhammad used every opportunity to demonstrate the faults of the "system." On Malvo's first morning at the shelter, he noticed that Muhammad's chore that day was to fix breakfast. The highly educated army veteran serving breakfast at a homeless shelter did not compute with the image that Malvo had of his "dad." However, Muhammad was able to use that situation to impart to Malvo some "truths" about humanity.

He recalled Muhammad telling him, "As we travel you'll see that in this so-called free society you can do everything properly and you'll still be viewed as a nigger. It is a pleasure to watch the devils eat themselves to death—kind of like a slow suicide."

Malvo recalled that when Muhammad saw the confused look on his face, Muhammad assured him that he would understand one day. Muhammad asked if he wanted to go to the land of milk and honey. When Malvo responded that he sure would like to, Muhammad said, "The honey is in my backpack, along with dates and yogurt-covered raisins." Muhammad continued, "The milk is in the store just a few quick steps away and presto!

We've got Heaven!" But then Muhammad winked and imparted some more "truths."

Malvo recalled Muhammad saying: "But the contract with the blue-eyed god [pointing at the mosaic of Christ on the chapel wall] is as follows: suffer, eat, live, and die poor; love and forgive those who kill you; and all good things will come to you after life's beautiful end. A rich man can never make it to heaven; heaven is for the meek, humble, pure in heart—and dead in head!"

At the shelter, Malvo noticed that Muhammad only ate one meal per day. Muhammad had once instructed him to practice eating only two meals per day and fasting three days a month. When Malvo arrived, however, Muhammad told him it was time for him to graduate to the next level, eating only once per day. Malvo said that Muhammad started him off in the mornings with a cocktail of vitamins taken with tea. Then later in the day, sometime between 4:00 p.m. and 6:00 p.m., Muhammad allowed him to eat a meal.

Muhammad worked with a man named Donald Haaland, a World War II veteran who, at eighty-one years old, was still rehabbing houses. It was Donald's practice to hire day laborers from the shelter, and Muhammad had been recommended to him. Malvo worked when Muhammad took him to Donald's construction sites. Muhammad also enrolled Malvo at the local YMCA and informed him that most of their afternoons would be spent there. According to Malvo, he was at times perplexed as to why Muhammad would resort to living in a shelter. He had been under the impression that Muhammad was well off. He recalled, however, that Muhammad had an explanation for every question.

As Malvo's orientation continued, Muhammad took him to a health food store where they got smoked salmon and avocado sandwiches as well as some dates and green tea. He told Malvo that they would eat there on most days. He explained that the Lighthouse Mission was a homeless shelter where half of the occupants were on psychotropic medications and were lost and hopeless. Most had been in and out of prison and were basically lifetime losers. Therefore, Malvo recalled, he was cautioned to keep his distance from them and stick to Muhammad only. He instructed Malvo that except for sleeping hours and Bible study at 6:00 a.m. and 7:00 p.m., they would be busy all day during the week, and gone on weekends.

One day while Muhammad and Malvo were working with Donald, Muhammad began to talk about his children. This prompted Donald to ask what was happening regarding Malvo and school. This was how Malvo learned that Muhammad intended to get him registered at Bellingham High School. Malvo also heard that Muhammad would be sending him to flight school as soon as he got things straightened out. These answers seemed to satisfy Donald's curiosity and also reassured Malvo.

That same afternoon, Muhammad told Malvo that they would be spending time with a friend in Tacoma that weekend. Malvo recalled that this was a Friday, perhaps the first Friday in November 2001. They took the local bus to the Greyhound terminal, and Muhammad surprised Malvo by presenting him with a few CDs: Tupac, Tracy Chapman, and Minister Farrakhan speaking at the Million Man March.

At the station in Tacoma, they were met by a white woman, whom Muhammad introduced as Mary. Malvo remembered Mary greeting him as though she had known him for years, and like he was family. He was allowed to sleep in her son's room and play with her son's play station. The next morning Malvo and Muhammad went for a run, along with Mary, who rode her bike.

Everything seemed normal, and Malvo reported that he almost felt like a kid again. Then, an hour or so later, Muhammad called out to him that he should leave the play station alone. Muhammad wanted Malvo to go somewhere with him. Muhammad began to tell him that the car they were traveling in (a 1999 Infiniti i30) was originally his, and that he had given it to Mary before he went to the Caribbean. Muhammad also talked about how successful his many business ventures had been and how Mildred (his ex-wife) and her friends destroyed these businesses. As they drove through the suburbs, Muhammad pointed out two houses, saying that they were once his.

During the drive, Malvo was introduced to stealing and going to the rifle range, activities that would become a weekly routine. During all that riding around they went into K-Mart, Sears, Fred Myers, and Wal-Mart. Along the way Muhammad stole small but expensive parts or tools, each costing about $90, explaining that because the items were small, he could easily walk out with three or four, thus reducing the risk of getting caught.

After almost six hours of driving and stealing store items, which he sold for cash, Muhammad explained to Malvo about stealing. Muhammad said that he was caught stealing lemon cookies at age seven. As a result, he explained, he was beaten at the store and then later beaten at home by both grandparents. Muhammad said that his grandfather beat him was not because he stole, but because he was dumb enough to get caught. Muhammad recited his grandfather's instructions to use his head and think of the consequences and, if he still decided to steal, he should figure out the best way to do so and not get caught. This was a lesson Muhammad indicated he was passing on to Malvo.

The next day Muhammad told Malvo to get ready because they were going to visit another friend. Malvo learned that this was Earl Dancey Jr. (Earl Dancey has since been convicted on weapons charges.) On the way, Muhammad stopped at three supermarkets, filing in and out with bags of steaks and a few bottles of liquor. After they arrived at Earl's place, Muhammad handed Earl the bags of meat and a pair of binoculars.

Malvo recalled Earl asking Muhammad whether he was taking Malvo to the shooting range. Malvo said Earl assured him that he would love the experience, and then asked whether he'd ever gone shooting before. Malvo responded that he had not. Malvo said Earl promised him a good introduction.

Malvo recalled that when they arrived at the sportsmanship range, Muhammad grabbed his Remington, his scope, and targets, and went directly to the rifle range. Earl gave Malvo a brief tour of the place. He showed him the archery, handgun, and rifle ranges and told him about weapons and safety. Then the lessons really began. Malvo said he was handed a .357 Python and asked what he should do next. Malvo responded that he would point at the target. He recalled Earl telling him that he was wrong: the first thing he should do was check the weapon and make sure it was loaded.

> [Earl] instructed me how to check the chamber, telling me never to point the barrel at a person when handing them a gun. He held a .357 round, saying, "This will not say oops or sorry! Is that understood?" He gave me the empty .357. "Now I'll show you three stands. First, open your legs a shoulder's length apart, square your shoulders, keep your hands fully extended, and use your left hand to pull backward, ensure that you don't pull to the left or to the right. That is, keep a steady aim." He looked me over, pushed down my shoulders, and told me to bend my knees a little more. We did this repeatedly.

Malvo recalled Earl telling him that in all situations, if he could find a solid surface, he should use it as a rest for his hands. Then Earl went on to the trigger. "Squeeze the trigger, do not pull it. You need to practice doing that." Earl explained the principle of trajectory. Finally, Malvo got to shoot for the first time.

I shot a 44 mg, a .357, a .45, and a 9mm. I was doing terribly, and Earl laughed. "Do you know why you're missing, not hitting where you're aiming? One of the most common errors is closing one of your eyes. Okay, put the weapon down. Aim with your finger, aim at the head, look with your left eye, and now your right. Did your finger seem to move? Now try looking down the center of your index, both eyes on the target. Do you see that white dot? Center it." I made two shots to the chest and head, over and over and over. Earl and I practiced until dusk.

When Muhammad joined them, he was anxious to know how well Malvo had done. Earl described him as a quick learner but said that he needed to practice squeezing, not yanking, the trigger. Earl was complimentary, but that was not good enough for Muhammad. He instructed Earl to let Malvo use lithium sights on the 9mm and the .45.

ON BECOMING THE SNIPER

Two weeks after Muhammad introduced Malvo to the shooting range, Muhammad presented him with a T-shirt marked SNIPER. He told Malvo that he had won the shirt in a "sniper competition" in the 1990s. Although in popular use the word might have connotations of a criminal assassin, this did not dawn on Malvo within the context of Muhammad's mock military training.

In the military, "Sniper" is a designation reserved for those who have undergone intensive specialized training to equip them for the battlefield. This involves more than merely being a marksman. The United States Marine Corps Scout Sniper School provides rigorous mental, physical, and practical training for those who would qualify as snipers. Only a small percentage of those who enlist in the military are considered suitable. Although Muhammad was not trained as a sniper, during his military service, it was noted that he was a great marksman.

The conferring of the SNIPER T-shirt by Muhammad, a man of military training and experience, carried for Malvo overtones of high honor and approval. He prized any bit of approval Muhammad gave him, seeing such gestures as signs his "dad" loved him. In that context, Malvo wore the shirt proudly, if naïvely.

Muhammad was preparing Malvo to be a soldier in "the war" Muhammad was to reveal to him later. He even inculcated in Malvo the use of terms associated with military sniper training, such as "reconnaissance" and "mission." Malvo came to use these terms to describe "tasks" that Muhammad told him to do.

The video games Muhammad selected for Malvo featured themes of war. One was Tom Clancy's Ghost Recon, a sniper game. Besides the games, a video that Malvo watched was *Carlos Hathcock: Marine Sniper*. Hathcock, who is deceased, served in the Vietnam War and gained a reputation as perhaps the most accomplished American snipers. He founded the United States Marine Scout Sniper School at Quantico, Virginia. The Hathcock video became another instructional tool Muhammad used to impress Malvo. As Malvo stated of Muhammad's instructions, "I soaked up everything. By way of osmosis, I absorbed his moves, his experience, his personality, and his outlook."

THE RETURN TO SCHOOL

On November 8, 2001, Malvo was registered at Bellingham High School. He was enrolled in AP biology, pre-calculus, U.S. history, citizenship, and college writing. He excelled academically. Whenever Malvo was not at school Muhammad took him to the YMCA, where they exercised and delved into African American history, revolutions, Elijah Muhammad, and related topics.

Malvo recalled that his studies with Muhammad ranged from 300 B.C. to current times. He received a crash course in what Muhammad referred to as "the clash of the races." Muhammad pointed out that they lived among the greatest murderers on the planet. Malvo was instructed to listen to Farrakhan while he slept, but mostly he listened to Malcolm X's early speeches.

Muhammad explained to Malvo that their African brothers could not understand why black Americans couldn't succeed. Malvo recalled Muhammad's explanation: "Let's say employment/jobs grow 2.5 percent yearly. Now if the unemployed black masses on welfare were to compete with middle-class white Americans on a level playing field, many of them would be out of a job, displaced by the black man. That is unacceptable. We look in the mirror every day and we see a reflection of our black faces. Black is identified with everything self-negating and destructive. We're blamed for all of America's ills. Blame the victim is the message that is fed to us." Malvo was subjected to such lectures on a regular basis.

As the days went by, the thing that Malvo feared most was disappointing his "dad." He was cautioned that the black man had fallen because of disunity and selfishness. Muhammad told him that they must become "one" and of one mind. Malvo recalled being told, "A good leader must first be a good follower, and a good instructor must first be a good listener." The only time he was away from Muhammad was at school, and, according to Malvo, he craved Muhammad's attention even then.

Malvo was required to read *Don't Sweat the Small Stuff* to curb his quick tongue. And in accordance with Muhammad's instructions, he would read passages from various books that Muhammad would select and record them as he read. He listened to the speeches of Booker T. Washington, Du Bois, Malcolm X, and some Tupac. He was sent to sleep with the music of Bob Marley or Buju Banton, Jamaican reggae stars.

Malvo noted that there were some occasions when Muhammad the loving father seemed replaced by a mean-spirited stranger. Malvo recalled one such occasion when they were at the YMCA playing basketball:

We're playing like a father and son. I am ultra competitive but I never win, so when he drives to the basket, I grab him by the waist. He laughs and still scores. Now I call foul on everything he does, "You whiner!" "Ha! Watch this!" I'd reply. He begins to complain about my unfair tactics, but to me it's just fun and games. He will always win, regardless of how much effort I exerted. He goes up to shoot, I slap at the ball and catch him on the face. I apologize and continue to play. I grab him on his next drive, he swings and elbows me in my ribs, grabs my wrist and twists it. I'm on my knees in pain, then he throws me about ten feet. I'm in a pile on the floor holding my wrist. He looks at me with a hollow stare—I've never seen so much anger aimed at me before. I immediately ask what I did to make him so angry. He stared at me and then walked away. If I had been thinking then I would have seen what he truly thought about me, but I was too busy blaming myself for the incident. I ran behind him, waiting for him to explain. He never did and I never brought it up. I swore that never again would I make him that mad at me.

In Malvo's mind, he was to blame for the abusive reaction because Muhammad could not have been wrong. Associated with this self-blame was the fear of being abandoned. He was totally dependent on Muhammad— he had no one else and was an alien in an environment that was shown to him as hostile. He resolved that he would never disappoint Muhammad again. The basketball incident was the first time that Muhammad was physically abusive to Malvo. It was also the last, Malvo said. Whatever abuse that followed would be psychological. Muhammad only had to give Malvo "the look" and the boy would comply.

People at the shelter saw that Muhammad exerted almost military control over Malvo. Muhammad controlled when Malvo spoke, and he was not allowed to speak to anyone else. A resident manager, Rory Rueblin, recalled Malvo speaking innocently to a couple of other shelter residents one day; in response, Muhammad shot Malvo a warning look. Rueblin recalled that he immediately clammed up.

Peter David, who worked at a coffeehouse in Bellingham, Washington, testified at Malvo's trial that he observed Malvo and Muhammad as they frequented his store, which was down the street from the Lighthouse Mission. David witnessed the interaction between them and assumed they were father and son. He remarked that he had never seen before such a close bond between a father and son. Malvo and Muhammad would come into the store, play chess, and talk for hours. He recalled asking Malvo if he "beat his old man yet," but what he found strange was that Malvo would look to Muhammad for approval before responding. David observed that on the rare occasion Muhammad was not at the table, Malvo kept to himself.

According to Malvo, the trips to the shooting range took place every weekend. For the first month or so there was never any talk about shooting anyone. However, Malvo remained curious as to why he had to learn how to shoot. Malvo said Muhammad explained: "Every young black man should learn to defend himself, shoot, and practice lessons of how to succeed. Most importantly he should know who he is—that he is God! Not God himself but a god, and he must never forget the wailing of his forefathers and that bloodshed begets bloodshed."

A MOTHER'S FIGHT TO REGAIN HER SON

Una, meanwhile, decided that the United States might not be the best place for her after all. Her child was clearly in danger, and though she had some contact with Malvo, it was strictly limited. Most times she called and Muhammad, not Malvo, was the one who spoke to her. She made a decision to get her child back, even if it meant they had to return to Jamaica.

On December 14, 2001, Una left Florida and headed to Washington. She arrived five days later and immediately went to the Lighthouse Mission, where she spoke to Rev. Archer and told him that Muhammad had her son without her permission. The conversation confirmed Rev. Archer's suspicions that there was something decidedly "off" about the relationship between Muhammad and Malvo. Rev. Archer told her where she could get help. Her first stop was the police. "I went to a tall, white police officer and warned that this man is a danger to my son," Una told me when we met.

Neither Malvo nor Muhammad expected that Una would make the journey to find her son. Both were surprised when Malvo was apprehended. Malvo recalled that he was told a woman was at the police station claiming to be his mother. He looked for guidance to Muhammad, who nodded for him to go with the cops. At the station, Malvo was asked if Una was his mother, and he replied in the affirmative.

Malvo was placed in a child protection agency, and two days later Una, accompanied by Rev. Archer, came for him. Una brought all the necessary documents to prove that she was his mother. Rev. Archer took them out to dinner and got them a motel room. He warned Malvo to stay away from Muhammad.

In the motel room Una was able to speak to her son without Muhammad acting as an intermediary. She tried to impress upon Malvo that Muhammad had control over him, so he should leave with her. Malvo recalled that he basically ignored her. He left for school the next day, and Muhammad turned up to speak with the principal. After school, Malvo made his usual trek to the YMCA. He then returned to the motel where his mother was staying, after which they went to the food co-op to have a meal. Muhammad was there.

Malvo told Muhammad that the police were at the school and were asking about immigration papers. Muhammad's eyes locked with Una's as he stared at her with disgust. "His eyes were like the devil's," Una later recounted. She grabbed Malvo. "Come on, let's go." Again Malvo defied her. She turned around and pleaded with him. She noticed that he was just staring into Muhammad's face as if he were in a trance. "I went up to him. 'Leeeee!' I shouted but he still would not budge," she recalled. Instead, Malvo got up and followed Muhammad out of the restaurant.

Una followed them. She ran up to Muhammad, grabbed his arm, and asked him, "Why my son?" She said Muhammad gave her the coldest stare she had ever seen and told her that the job he had to do could not be done by some crackhead off the street; he needed someone intelligent. She recalled that she tried to tell Malvo that Muhammad was using him, but Malvo didn't listen. They brushed her aside and walked off together.

> As I walked away with Mr. Muhammad I didn't look back, but I could see her reflection in the restaurant's glass front. She was leaning on a stop sign in tears. We went to a local café where we had a cinnamon roll and tea. While we were eating, I tried to stress the point that my mother had produced our passports, and so it was best for us to leave now. I told him that it would only be a matter of hours before they found out that we were illegal and detain and deport us. "When were you released?" he asked me. "Yesterday, sir," I replied. "Okay, we'll leave tomorrow afternoon," he decided.
>
> We returned to the mission late so as not to meet up with Reverend Archer. As I entered, a guy named Jerry handed me a message, looking at me gloomily. "A lady was here a few minutes ago. Your mother—she told me to give you this." He handed it to me, staring deeply into my eyes. I accepted it silently and passed it to Muhammad, who threw it in the trash can.

The next morning Muhammad informed Malvo that a friend had told him about a scheme by which he could make some serious money over the holidays. But he would need Malvo's help. He told Malvo that it was about getting the children; that got the boy's full attention. Muhammad did not say what the plan was, and he never would. He always stressed to Malvo that he never told people more than they needed to know. They went to their lockers at the YMCA. There, an immigration officer approached Malvo, along with the director of the YMCA. "Are you Lee Malvo?" Malvo replied that he was, as he gave Muhammad a look that said, *I told you so.*

RUNNING AWAY FOR THE SECOND TIME

Malvo and his mother were taken to the Immigration and Naturalization Service (INS) adult detention center in Seattle. Malvo recalled that they were in the same cell for two days. According to him, anyone passing them lying on their separate bunks would have assumed they were perfect strangers. He was upset at what he saw as his mother's stupidity, and she was trying to explain that what she'd done was for his own good, even if they were deported. For two days he refused to acknowledge her presence. Because he was a juvenile, he was transported to the Spokane Juvenile Detention Center while his mother remained in Seattle. He was placed in a cell, and at breakfast he mingled with the other residents.

The weekend passed, and the following Monday he was taken to the nurse for a check-up. When he asked her why she was not there all weekend, she explained that she was a Seventh-Day Adventist. This bit of information reminded Malvo of his former life, and he began to tell her a little about his Jamaican background, including the small church in Brown's Town, St. Ann, that he attended. He explained that he was a lacto vegetarian. She brought him soy milk for his meals and ensured that he received a proper diet. Malvo was treated like just another adolescent at the juvenile center.

It was the Christmas holidays so we were allowed to watch a few videos and, if we behaved, we received a Christmas bag each day with candy bars and sweets. As in any social gathering there were little groups—the cool, the not-so-cool, and the un-cool. I decided to sit with the girls. I played some cards and gave away my Christmas bag. Every morning we did calisthenics in the gym. A week went by without problems. I was advanced to the second level. They used T-shirts with separate colors— orange, sky-blue, green, and navy blue to indicate which level you're in. As you went up the ladder your privileges increased: you spent more time out of your cell at recreation, for instance. We'd return to our cell exactly in that order: first, orange, then the sky-blues, then the greens. The navy blues were set apart. They were allowed to hold auxiliary jobs—cleaning showers or helping clean up and prepare food in the kitchen. They were allowed radios and made their own snack bags daily. Soon my school was contacted as the new semester had begun. The principal at the facility explained that I was at a juvenile detention center. I started classes soon after I came into the center and became a bit of a teacher's pet because I worked so hard. I enjoyed learning, and I was attentive. Soon the teacher assigned me the task of helping the others with their work. I was also given charge of calisthenics in the morning.

In the meantime, Una had contacted an organization that defended illegal aliens. An attorney was assigned to their case, and Malvo was allowed to speak with him. They discussed how best to get the matter resolved without either Malvo or Una being deported. Because Una was married to an

American citizen she could not be thrown out of the country, or so she believed. Malvo remained in contact with Muhammad by phone. Muhammad told Malvo he would be out of detention in a couple of weeks, and to keep him up to date on the progress of the case. Malvo felt reassured by the expression of concern.

Upon learning that Malvo was communicating with Muhammad, Una was more convinced of the need to take her son and leave the United States. She felt that with the help of the attorney and Rev. Archer, she could leave the country voluntarily. The attorney was able to arrange for them to get out on bail, but Una was released two days before Malvo was.

Upon his release, Malvo was put on a plane to Seattle to join his mother. He then persuaded her to return to Bellingham by telling her he wanted to resume classes at Bellingham High School. The attorney was able to have them placed in a battered women's shelter located outside the city limits. This was a secure facility; the doors opened only by punching in a security code. Una felt that this safe house would protect her and Malvo from Muhammad until they were able to leave the country.

According to Una, as soon as they arrived, Malvo began to act paranoid. "The man is watching us," she remembered him saying. After a while she began to feel paranoid too. She decided to ask her attorney to arrange a transfer to Seattle. "I cashed a check so I'd have money to travel," she recalled. The next day, she looked in Malvo's room and saw that he was missing. He had been biding his time for the opportunity to run away. While she was busy preparing dinner, he had taken $30 out of her purse, grabbed his backpack, and headed to the bus station. He got on the 3:15 p.m. bus to Tacoma.

Una was frantic. She called Mary, Muhammad's girlfriend, and Muhammad answered the phone. "Where is my son?" she demanded. Muhammad hung up. She recalled searching all over for Malvo. She wanted to buy their bus tickets to Seattle, but could not because she felt that Malvo was still in the area. As her search went on, she began to feel drained. She was directed to go for help at a crisis center. She complained that she could not pay the bill and was advised to go to Harbor View, a crisis center where she could get free service. "I got a social worker and a doctor," she recalled. She remembered talking to the social worker. "I told her that he was with a bad man and he needed help."

Una's assigned doctor prescribed pills for her. She said, despite the indifferent attitude of the doctor and social worker, she told everyone around her that her son needed help. "I did not take the pills because if I had, I would not have been able to concentrate on the problem," she said. "I cried for hours straight with no one to listen to me. I wanted help for my son."

ISOLATION AND BRAINWASHING

When Malvo reached Tacoma, he contacted Muhammad immediately. After two calls, he located Muhammad at Mary's. According to Malvo, his only goal from the first days in detention was to run away. Shortly after rejoining Muhammad in Tacoma, Malvo witnessed what he thought was a nervous breakdown. Muhammad was holding his head, Malvo said, and he could see the veins in his face. He added that Muhammad blacked out. "It scared me because he was normally so calm. I felt sorry for him and decided that I would give him no fuss or problems. After all, he was all I got."

After this "breakdown," Muhammad continued their training as if he and Malvo had never been separated. Malvo's schedule became more demanding. First thing every morning, he and Muhammad went to the gym and then the shooting range. They spent the rest of the day playing with paintball guns, reading, playing violent video games, or watching films like *Roots* and *The Matrix*.

Malvo spent every day under Muhammad's tutelage and supervision. He did not critique Muhammad's views but accepted them as truths—even when he sought explanations for certain inconsistencies. For example, he questioned the romantic relationship that Muhammad had with Mary, a white woman.

Malvo recalled confronting Muhammad about the discrepancy between his statements and his actions. He demanded to know why Muhammad was sleeping with a white woman, if all white people were devils. He wanted to know what Mary's role was in regaining custody of his children. He questioned why Muhammad did not seem in a hurry to get the children back, if that was so important. It was the first time Malvo so openly challenged Muhammad, and it was perhaps the last.

Malvo recalled that Muhammad agreed with him and told him that the affair with Mary would end. But Muhammad also extracted a pledge from Malvo in the form of a torn $50 bill. Muhammad gave half of the bill to Malvo and kept the other half. The torn bill supposedly represented Muhammad's blood, and his blood was his word. Malvo felt that he now had an unbreakable bond with Muhammad.

THE FIRST TEST

Close to the end of January 2002, Muhammad and Malvo returned to Bell-ingham, about two hours by car from Tacoma. They arrived at night. Muhammad informed Malvo that he had been using the shelter as a cover to observe everything that went on. He handed Malvo a gun and told him that a lady would be coming by the garage at 1 a.m. She would be carrying a bag containing the day's cash from the restaurant, near where they were parked. Muhammad instructed Malvo to shoot the lady and take the bag.

This was the first time Malvo was told that he had to shoot someone. He recalled that he was mortified. He gave the handgun back to Muhammad. He asked why he couldn't just knock out the lady with a piece of pipe.

> He looked at me too closely for comfort, saying, "Well, whatever it takes, just get the job done. When she gets out of the car the restaurant lights will be off, you'll have a few minutes before she turns them on." Her car was parked in front of the restaurant. "Sir, why are we doing this?" I asked him. "Why are we doing this?" Muhammad repeated. His eyes pierced mine. "You're being prepared!" "For what?" I asked. He gave me that look and I realized that I screwed up. I looked at the ground. He hissed, "Where is your zeal now?" He laughed, but then he got serious again, "Are you willing to do what it takes? Are you?" "Yes, sir!" I responded. "Then do it."

Muhammad communicated by walkie-talkie with Malvo. He instructed Malvo to pick the car's lock and wait for the woman. The woman exited the restaurant, went to the car, and dropped the bag behind the back seat without looking. She started the engine, but then apparently realized that she had forgotten something. She went back inside. Malvo breathed a great sigh of relief. Now he would not have to hurt her. He grabbed the bag and scrambled out of the car. He met up with Muhammad on the bus to Ta-coma and handed him the bag.

Muhammad went into the bus's restroom and examined the contents. He returned a few minutes later and told Malvo that there was a little over a thousand dollars and some insignificant checks. He also surmised that woman evidently had been collecting just the money paid for lottery tick-ets, not the restaurant's receipts.

Later that day Malvo had to go over the entire crime with Muhammad, starting with Malvo's whining. Muhammad pointed out his errors and explained that in time they would be corrected. Malvo remembered Muhammad telling him that he couldn't be a black man without a stomach for violence. They visited some projects in Tacoma, and Muhammad pointed out that crime was being contained but not eliminated. Malvo recalled Muhammad taking him to certain areas where blacks lived in depressed conditions, and then pointing out:

> Do you see those guys slinging on the strip? Good. Now do you see the patrol car? I bet that cop knows the identity of every last one of them. If he has been doing this beat for a while, surely he can identify some that are dealers. He knows he's in a vicinity of crime, but it is not a white problem; niggers are only killing themselves, so who cares? This is the system. This is the necessary evil of Americanism. The prison yards are an economy and as you can see it's a very profitable one. Look, Lee, do you see how many of them are your age? Police protect the interest of the rich. They keep the cogs going by controlling the streets. They are the circulatory system; they keep things flowing. And they do it in such a way that has about a million and a half of us incarcerated for life. You see these young men, they probably have time on their hands. This is how they get you, while you're young and dealing they bust you a few times and give you a slap on the wrist. But eventually the sentences pile up, and before you know it you're in for life.

Malvo later reported that he soaked up everything Muhammad was saying, and the more Muhammad talked, the angrier Malvo got. During the time they were together, all he wanted was Muhammad's attention. He admitted that he had not yet grasped the fact that change is a gradual process, and didn't realize that what was happening to him was the transformation of his identity. He recalled a particular lecture Muhammad gave that in effect demonstrated what Muhammad was doing to him, but he was too busy seeking affirmation to see it.

He recalled Muhammad explaining, "The French revolution began with ideas, but they did not allow it to end there, but instead fed the ideas to the people and incited them, leading the blind masses for their own good. Make your ideas their ideas, by clothing them in the proper context. You can make anything acceptable—it is all about presentation and, most importantly, timing."

Malvo recalled that as Muhammad continued, it was like a man talking to himself. "You have to reach the agitated minds at the most opportune moment. A young naïve mind is like a small tree: one has to feed it, prune it, direct its growth." At the time, Malvo did not see that it was his mind being directed. He just wanted to soak up all the "truths" Muhammad was offering.

In preparation for the tasks ahead, Muhammad told Malvo that he would have to kill his old self because it was an impediment to the way that he needed to grow. Muhammad told him that he had to project his own image onto the target, listen to his voice and see his face—then kill it. Malvo was horrified and made the mistake of showing this. Muhammad instructed him that he must be able to mask his intentions, that men speak different languages, but body language is universal.

Muhammad also took out a cardboard man, about the size of the silhouette target on the sheets he had trained Malvo to shoot at. He further instructed that the cardboard man was now the target and must be eliminated.

Malvo recalled Muhammad going into a rant: "These are my orders. His feelings and his pain are inconsequential—irrelevant! Not my concern. I don't think of these things, I focus all my energy on the task. I am an instrument—unfortunately for my victim an instrument of death—but a precise instrument nonetheless. I do the necessary recon, studying the target. Becoming not only acquainted but comfortable, I'm now at ease in his surroundings. I'm his shadow, that of death." From that point on, Malvo had to project his own image onto the cardboard man and aim for its head.

Malvo recalled Muhammad drilling into him hate-filled messages, at the cafes, on buses, at the gym, eating out, everywhere, ceaselessly. Muhammad seemed intent on keeping Malvo angry at the white man. Upon reflection, Malvo acknowledged that he could not see through the lectures. He could not see that he was just a means to Muhammad's insidious ends. Malvo said he wanted so badly to believe in something, and Muhammad became the object of his hopes and his beliefs.

The only reward was Muhammad's attention. And increasingly, Malvo's dependence on Muhammad meant absorbing the lectures or lessons, which became so embedded in his memory that he seemed to recall them instinctively.

Do you know the principle of need/frustration? Let me explain, let us begin then with a practical example. Let us consider human development in terms of a developing body, one with nutritive/physical needs. In this case, let's say calcium or vitamin C: calcium is necessary for strengthening of the bones, vitamin C essential for the prevention of scurvy. It's a necessity that the human diet provides the essential amount of each. Now when this need is frustrated, and by that I mean that the demand for these substances is not satisfied, the consequence is not immediate. But the body is an interdependent mechanism. If one link in the chain is missing or is malfunctioning, it affects the entire system.

The same need/frustration principle applies to man. He has emotional, psychological, and physical/nutritional needs. In each stage of his growth, and especially if the need/frustration begin very early in life, each time these separate frustrations occur they weaken the integrity of the individual. If his needs are frustrated in all aspects of life—by this I mean if his emotional, physical/nutritional, and psychological needs are not adequately met—this chronic problem begins to take a drastic toll. In the case of blacks, we've become apathetic, accepting the status quo. The change in us from birth until death takes time. The constant attrition leads to a premature end, for when all these multiplied deficiencies begin to manifest themselves, it is too late. The death we live, son, is not a sudden one; rather, it is a leeching process, you become a living dead man before you die.

If one intends to reprogram an individual, it is impossible to rewrite their experience; rather, one should build on what he already has. One has to become an unseen catalyst that causes change but itself remains intact. One has to facilitate the ways and means for that change to come into existence, knowing when to turn up the pressure and when to hold the reins more tightly.

Malvo recalled that Muhammad demonstrated this "unseen catalyst" principle when they were returning from the YMCA one day. They stopped and sat on a bench to eat their food. Across the street was a Catholic church that operated a soup kitchen for the poor. Muhammad gestured at the people who were standing in line, and told Malvo that what he was seeing was impotence, anger, and a diffused aura of self-hate. Malvo and Muhammad got up and joined the line, and then Muhammad put on the demonstration.

Malvo recalled how Muhammad incited the crowd: "What the fuck is taking 'em so long?" Muhammad then turned to a man beside him. "It was the same shit yesterday!" (Muhammad was showing how they in the crowd all hade something in common.) Then Muhammad touched another shoulder. "Every motherfucking day these crackers tell us to line up in the fucking sun in the street like dogs." (Muhammad was now showing who the common enemy was.) Malvo recalled that Muhammad went on like this until others in the line began to speak up. Because of Muhammad's antics, the line was slowing down and the pushing started.

Malvo recalled an old man admonishing Muhammad to shut up for fear that the priest would turn them away. "Fuck the priest!" Muhammad told him. Then Muhammad patted Malvo on the shoulder and murmured, "Keep them angry." Muhammad saw an old lady at the door and said to her, "Who the fuck you looking at like that? I'm black, but I ain't no dog!" Malvo recalled that in about fifteen minutes the people were storming through the door cursing, shouting, breaking chairs, and demanding that the old white people speed up.

After causing the chaos, Muhammad and Malvo slipped away, and then Muhammad imparted yet another lecture. He pointed out that what he had demonstrated was a riot on a very small level. He went on to explain that impoverished people everywhere are like a nice powder keg waiting for a spark. They are already angry, and when the anger is brought to the surface, they will fight for anything. Muhammad then indicated that Malvo should be able to get people to the boiling point and then direct their aggression.

Malvo remembered Muhammad saying that he planned for every conceivable scenario, but humans aren't robots. He continued to lecture, telling Malvo that if a man is in the wrong place at the wrong time, for example, he has to go ahead anyway because he has to be prepared mentally and cannot afford to freeze. Malvo recalled being told that he would learn to sit at the table with the enemy, talk with him, eat with him, eliminate him, and not let any attachment stop him. Muhammad then brought Malvo back to the depressed conditions he'd seen the day before andissued another lesson.

"Think of what you saw yesterday at the projects, each of those kids slinging and peddling. Society classifies you and them as one and the same. Here!" He [Muhammad] hands me the .45. "Visualize what you saw, that target is your enemy. How do you feel? Let him taste your pain, feel it! Violence is necessary, it is for this that men create and use weapons, the greatest of which is the mastery of his mind. Why this mastery? The mind is your go-between with reality. It is your true eye to the world. Be conscious of your thinking, for what the mind says the body does! Free your mind!"

Malvo remembered Muhammad pausing to smile at him, patting him on the back, and continuing the rest of the lecture. According to Malvo,

Muhammad always reminded him that he was an instrument. Muhammad also said that whenever Malvo's conscience got in the way, he should strike the left side of his chest and call his heart to rest. He was urged to distill his thoughts, still his mind, and concentrate. Muhammad told him to meet unpreparedness with preparation, saying that the man who wins is the man who anticipates the next move and prepares for it with speed and precision. Malvo recalled Muhammad telling him that essentially, the better thinker wins.

INITIATION TO MURDER AND THE "DEATH" OF LEE BOYD MALVO

On February 15, 2002, two days before Malvo's seventeenth birthday, Muhammad sent him on his first killing mission. This was to be an initiation. Muhammad made sure that in the weeks leading up to this Malvo was well prepared. He said that failure was not an option. He instructed that Malvo's pace must be certain, like that of a man who knows where he is going.

Before Muhammad dropped Malvo off at the home of Isa Nichols, the woman who had testified on behalf of Muhammad's ex-wife, Mildred, in their child custody case, he made Malvo repeat the process that would lead to the killing. "I knock on the door and I ask for Isa. If it's Isa, great. If the person who answers is not her, I tell them I have a message for her, then I use this." As Malvo finished reciting those words to Muhammad, he pulled out the .45 semiautomatic.

Malvo recalled his exchange with Muhammad before he went on the mission. "His voice took on an edge. He grabbed me. 'Where is your pledge?' I reach in my wallet and remove my half of a $50 bill. 'And what is that, your half?' he asked me. 'Blood, sir!' I responded. He continued, 'Representing what?' 'My word, sir!' 'And what was that, son?' 'I'm willing to do whatever it takes, sir!' 'Now then, go!' He pushed me out of the car." Malvo continued recounting the sequence of events related to the first murder:

I got out of the car. I tuned in to his voice in my head, remembering all the lessons, the preparation. Malvo, be calm. The calm, cool, and collected survive. Free your mind to the task at hand, don't think it, become it. Knock, knock! I rapped on the door. I pounded on the door again: Knock, knock! Men kill, men don't fight! Men initiate action, not passive reaction. "Good evening, is Mrs. Nichols in?" I asked the young lady at the door. She seemed eager to talk, for she gave me a long answer, telling me of Mrs. Nichols' exact whereabouts.

Well, I have a message for her, I say, reaching into my paper bag. I turned my body so she can't see my hand, "Lee!" A voice in me said, "Don't!"—but the other voice just as loudly said, "No! Do it! Do it!" My eyes are watery. "You can't face him unless you do this." The lady at the door inhaled, getting impatient. This is all happening in seconds, I put the gun to her face, and in an instant I saw not her but me, my old self I hate—that scared, hurt self. That night Lee Boyd Malvo took his last breath and died. In an instant she too was gone!

It was Kenya Cook, Isa Nichols's niece, who answered the door. She had done nothing to John Muhammad. She was only in the wrong place at the wrong time. She paid the price for her aunt siding with Mildred Muhammad in the custody fight.

According to Malvo, as he walked away and began to run toward where he was to meet Muhammad, his thoughts were on the fact that he had just killed another human being. He was sweating, he even soiled himself, and silent tears rolled down his cheeks. As he reached a phone booth, Muhammad pulled up and he got in.

I sat silently, trying to hide my shaking hands. "I watched you, you did perfect," he smiled. (I returned his smile) "Oh! Don't worry, everything will be all right, here!" He handed me my wallet and a new ID. "That is your new name." I read to myself John Lee Muhammad. He looked at me with the deepest stare. "Lee Boyd Malvo no longer exists." He started the engine and drove off.

Malvo's recollection is that upon reaching Earl's place he spent hours scrubbing himself in the shower, but the more he scrubbed, the dirtier he felt. He recalled that Muhammad began to get impatient with him and demanded that Malvo get out of the shower. Muhammad knocked on the bathroom door, but the knocking brought back to Malvo's mind the knocking he had done earlier that evening. According to Malvo, when he finally emerged, he was confronted by Muhammad's stare. Muhammad asked if he was all right. "Yes, sir," he responded. However, for days following the shooting he threw up and was chastised by Muhammad for being weak-minded.

Two days after the shooting it was Malvo's birthday, and Muhammad took him shopping. When they were in Antigua, Muhammad had replaced Malvo's entire wardrobe for his sixteenth birthday. A year later, he had Malvo "kill" that old self, and again he rewarded him. Malvo recalled that Muhammad took him to the mall and bought him a few slacks, shirts, ties, cufflinks, and sneakers. He also took him bowling and to see a movie, *John Q*, about an ordinary man whose son is desperately ill and needs an emergency heart operation. When the insurance company refuses to cover the operation, he takes the emergency room hostage. Malvo recalled that while they were bowling Muhammad lectured him on the importance of a man doing whatever he needs to do to save his children.

A MOTHER'S ANGUISH

Una, not knowing that her son had become a killer, continued searching for him. One day in March 2002, she happened to be on the same bus as him. He remembered that he had an intuition that his mother was on the bus and said as much to Muhammad: "Sir, I think my mother is close by." She then spotted him. He was well dressed and seated beside Muhammad. According to Una, she ran up to her son and grabbed him. She recalled beckoning to the driver to stop the bus. She recalled that Malvo looked straight through her and said, "I don't know you. You are talking to the wrong person." She remembered insisting that he was in fact her son. By then the bus had come to a stop, and Muhammad got off.

According to Malvo, he followed Muhammad into the bus station and his mother followed right behind them. Malvo recalled that his mother grabbed his jacket. She pleaded with him, "Lee, I'm your mother, don't turn away from me. Lee, he's using you." Malvo struggled to get out of the jacket, then looked up and saw Muhammad looking at him. He then turned around and looked at his mother. According to Una, she noticed that his eyes were glassy, as though he was not seeing her. He wiggled out of the jacket and ran toward Muhammad, who smiled at him.

According to Malvo, the last words he heard from his mother were: "This day you run from your mother to your death. Do you hear me, Lee?. . . . To your death!" According to Una, with those words she slumped by the ticket counter in the bus station, and in the pit of her stomach she felt an unimaginable pain. She knew that her son was lost to her forever.

THE PUPPETEER-TEACHING MURDER

Lee Boyd Malvo, the once promising student, was now "John Lee Muhammad," murderer. He still clung to the hope of a return to the promising path he had intended for himself, but by now he was confused about the turn of events. He thought that his purpose in joining Muhammad was to find and get the children, to be adopted, and then to go to school. He was curious about when that might happen. He could not be adopted after age eighteen, so time was running out.

Malvo seemed not to have grasped that his life had taken a decidedly fatal turn. School was not in the normal course of events anymore. Rather, as his mother had predicted, he was running to his own demise. "Sir, when will I be going to school?" he asked. Muhammad told him that he was needed just a few more months, and then he would be put in flight school in the fall, under a different name.

The delay was taking a toll, and Muhammad realized this. Malvo recalled Muhammad assuring him that it wouldn't last forever; soon they would find the kids and be gone. Malvo would be able to go to flight school and they would become a family once again. The reassurance gave Malvo some semblance of hope. He really missed the kids and longed for the time when they would be a happy family again. It seemed like such a long time had passed, but only a year ago they had been in Antigua and Muhammad had appointed him their big brother.

He thought of his mother and her last words to him: "This day you run to your death." Could she have been right? Muhammad did not tell him much. Muhammad never told him that killing was a part of the plan, but here he was, a killer. "I wonder what the future holds for me?" he asked aloud. Muhammad called, "Son, what is it?" "Nothing, sir," Malvo responded. He got up and joined his "dad," walking off into an uncertain future.

Muhammad decided to go to Tucson, Arizona, to visit his sister. He took Malvo with him. They took the Greyhound bus, and what was supposed to be a daylong ride stretched into two weeks, because Muhammad found two places in California for "test missions." These were actually thefts, but Muhammad did not physically participate in them. He sent Malvo or "John Lee Muhammad" to get "donations"—stolen money. After each "test mission," Muhammad made a thorough review and explained what had to be changed the next time. These were called "after-event briefs."

In addition to having Malvo get "donations," Muhammad drilled him in what he called "counterinterrogation tactics." He handcuffed Malvo to a tree and kept him in that position for six hours per day in late March when the weather was still cold. This was to prepare Malvo for any possible grilling by the authorities. He was told that he had to learn to resist at all costs. Muhammad taught Malvo how to make a sling with his belt so as to keep his limbs from moving and how to use his belt to sleep in a tree; how to urinate into his canteen, not only to kill any scent left behind but also to keep himself warm by holding it against his body. These were all tricks that Muhammad, the soldier, had supposedly learned in the first Gulf War. According to Malvo,

> For three days he had me practice crawling, hours and hours on my stomach, eating no food for 24 hours. Then I had to crawl up as close as five to 12 feet of other campers and then return to my previous position without being detected. Then he taught me about barrel condensation, that's how he spotted me in the early morning. He explained to me that when the dew falls, the steel of the barrel is exposed and will get wet, and can thus be spotted. He also tested the temporary suppressor or silencers, each was good for only 30 shots. We each had a rifle, a .308 from Earl, and another that Muhammad had stolen from a gun show with me in mind when I was in juvenile detention.

When they arrived in Tucson, Muhammad told Malvo that they had work to do. As usual, he did not tell Malvo what this "work" was, only that the target lived in a retirement suburb and golf community bordering a park. They went to Muhammad's sister's place for dinner, then back to the motel, where Malvo was put to work. He recalled Muhammad saying that he needed more "recon" and a full description of the subject at the golf course. He wanted the names of other people around him. He wanted trails marked on maps that showed the areas most likely to be occupied. He needed routes. He wanted them paced and timed. Malvo said that he grabbed his sleeping bag, a few protein bars, vitamins, and a liter of water. As he was leaving, Muhammad told him to enjoy the night stars.

According to Malvo, as he walked to the bus stop he tried to "call his heart to rest." He assured himself that this was only collecting information. He remembered a line from one of Muhammad's lectures: "To know is not power. It is the proper implementation of knowledge that gives one the edge." He did as he was ordered and he made notes. The sun rose with him still on the mission. He spent an additional six hours in daytime in the surrounding park, then returned to the motel.

Muhammad ordered pizza while Malvo took a shower. As they ate, Malvo produced all the information that Muhammad had requested. It was at that point that Malvo realized there was more killing in store for him. "I want you to make the shot," he recalled Muhammad saying. When Malvo protested, he was given another lecture:

> "You can't spend your entire life being afraid. What are you afraid of? This system is not indestructible." I began to retreat, but he silenced me. He grabbed me by the shoulder and with piercing eyes said, "I see you haven't grasped chapter seven of *Don't Sweat the Small Stuff*! Patience, son! Patience!" Then his face softened. "I've been your age. You've never been mine. I've witnessed what you have yet to experience." He put the pictures in my lap. "What do you see? Do you see another human being like yourself with feelings, maybe with a family, children, even grandchildren! Your hesitation is what he has done to you. Is it justifiable or right?"

According to Malvo, Muhammad reminded him of the themes of the movies *Roots* and *The Matrix*, which they watched on a nightly basis.

> "The problem is not your capacity or ability to carry out the task, it is your conflicting morals. Until you are free from those I will continue to show you what you can do. You think very little of yourself, Lee. You were like an ass-backward people still stuck in a lost epoch of superstitions and empty-minded religiousness. This, however, is a world of cold facts. The weak die and the strong survive; we are afraid of everything, afraid to challenge anything. We don't achieve anything because we are constantly looking externally for change, any change."

Malvo recalled that Muhammad's tone changed slightly as he placed his hand on his shoulder:

> "You are still a slave, son, a slave to your own thoughts. Are they even yours or did you just accept what you've been told? Who are you?" I made my tapes after seeking out the early Malcolm X speech, Bloodshed Begets Bloodshed, and I fed my mind with it while I slept. I believed that playing the tape while I was asleep worked as a way to rid myself of my

slave mentality. Instead, this speech was embedded in my subconscious. Trust me, it worked. He then issued his orders. "You will carry out the task as I direct you to."

Malvo recalled that for the next few days he pondered his life and what was becoming of it. Muhammad had several meetings with a man who claimed to know how he could make noise suppressors for weapons. He recalled going to the golf course, where he remained in hiding. He slept, awoke, and prepared his mind for the "task" ahead. On March 19, as the victim, later identified as Jerry Taylor, approached and came into range, he got the go and fired the fatal shot, hitting him in the chest.

Jerry Taylor was sixty years old at the time of his death. His daughter, Cheryl Shaw, recalled that he had introduced her son, Ryan, to golf when Ryan was only five years old. He made Ryan's first golf club when the boy was only two, but did not live to see his grandson graduate from high school and take a full golf scholarship to Washington State University.

After the shooting Malvo recalled Muhammad saying, "Let us become observers of the spectacle." He reached into the backpack for a book. They heard the sirens. Their eyes met. They were surrounded by others waiting for a bus. The police cars arrived, and then the bus came.

MUHAMMAD LOCATES HIS CHILDREN

Though Muhammad was busy robbing and killing with his protégé, he still had one ultimate purpose. His ex-wife, Mildred Muhammad, had his children, and he was determined to find her. He never stopped making inquiries. Toward the end of May, 2002, he learned that Mrs. Muhammad was in the Maryland suburbs of Washington, D.C. Finally, Malvo felt that they were going to get on with the business of retrieving the children. The plan was that they would locate the kids and Malvo would snatch them on their way to or from school. Malvo hoped that once they got the children, Muhammad would register him in flight school.

In the meantime, the training and the pattern of escalating violence continued. When Muhammad observed that Malvo was almost completely detached from himself—that he did not have to speak to communicate his intentions to the boy—he decided that Malvo was ready for the task ahead of him. Malvo did not know exactly what that entailed; he just felt in his heart that it was sinister.

The journey east went through Louisiana, where Muhammad had family. His first stop was at the home of a cousin, who has reportedly said that Muhammad informed her that he and Malvo were on a secret undercover mission. Malvo recalled that they moved on to stay with Edward Williams, Muhammad's younger brother. He recalled that Muhammad's instructions to him were simple: "Don't speak too much. You're here to observe and take a long-needed rest. My brother's life is the epitome of a pitiful existence." Malvo remembered that he was introduced to his new cousins, Ed Jr., who was nineteen years old, and Latoria who, like Malvo, was seventeen. Muhammad also visited his oldest son, Travis Williams, while in Louisiana.

Malvo recalled detecting skepticism from Muhammad's relatives when he was introduced to them as Muhammad's son, but they eventually came around to accepting him. In turn, Malvo recalled that he heard a lot about the youthful antics of the man he called Dad. He began to fit into the family and found comfort and solace in the smiles of his "uncle's" two toddlers. He also bonded with Latoria and Ed Jr., who showed him the neighborhood. Soon he was able to navigate the streets by himself.

However, Malvo felt that the path being laid out for him was decidedly different from the one he had hoped to travel with Muhammad. He truly believed that it was in the best interest of the children for Muhammad to get them back from their mother. He had seen for himself how good a father Muhammad was. But life seemed so different from what he thought it would be when he left Florida. All he now had was this man he called Dad, and the thought of losing him was frightening. After all, he was a stranger in a strange land. Where could he go?

Malvo recounts in his writings his first breaking point, and learning about the Big Mission that he was being prepared for:

One day it all came crumbling down. I walked to the trailer, which as I suspected was empty. I went in, closed the door, and began to sob. I rummaged through my backpack for a pen and paper, and I wrote a suicide note. I heard footsteps. "Son!" a voice called. I stopped. I walked slowly into the living room, not making eye contact. He knew me well. I quickly destroyed the letter. I felt in my heart that something was up. He had been busy all week.

I wanted to confide in someone. I was attracted to Latoria even though she was my cousin. But I also trusted her. "Latoria, can I speak to you for a minute?" I said as I held the door open, indicating I'd like to speak to her outside. Then I heard, "Latoria! Iron your father's suit, it's on the bed."

Outside, Muhammad was lounging in a chair under a tree. He had "that look." "25 people a week. We're short on manpower but will proceed as planned." This comes to me from out of left field. "I thought we were just going to get the children and head to Canada, sir?" I asked. "No!" He gripped my shoulder and shook it. "We are going to the belly of this beast, right to its heart." He talked about the chemicals that he had been able to acquire and the destruction that he intended to wreak upon the beast. But he said that the chemical war was for "phase III."

The plan as Malvo recalled it was to commit twenty-five murders per week for four weeks; this would constitute "phase 1." The second phase would begin with the murder of a police officer; then, at the funeral while hundreds of law enforcement officials attended, there would be a mass killing using homemade bombs. Malvo recalled that Muhammad pulled out a piece of paper with sketches he'd been fooling with. He pointed at the last sketch, which looked like a small dome, and another, which was an open circle. He indicated with his hands—"Ka-boooomb!"

According to Malvo, they would ask for $10 million, which would be deposited into overseas accounts and would be used to train and school black children like him, Malvo, who had never had a chance. Malvo recalled pleading that there were other ways to get a million dollars, but he remembered Muhammad saying that the plan was to terrorize the real terrorists, get paid for doing it, and get his children all in one swoop. Ultimately they would have their own little black colony, where they could prepare a new generation of black minds.

Upon hearing Muhammad's well-thought-out plan, Malvo realized what he was being trained for: to terrorize the nation. He remembered reflecting on his mother's words: "You run to your death." She was right, but the question was, where else could he go? He was terrified to leave and he was terrified to stay.

According to Malvo, he reflected on the time when he felt he'd be better off dead, when his suicide attempt had been thwarted by Blacka and his mother. This time he did not have to rely on a rope because he had access to a gun. He figured that at this point there was really nothing to live for. He had no mother, and the man he had taken as a father only wanted him to be a murderer. He decided that he had to make that leap and end it. He recounted the torment of that night:

It was nightfall and I headed back to the trailer. I needed time alone. I went in and closed the door behind me. I was enveloped in darkness, and the tears began to flow. I went into Ed, Jr.'s room. I removed the .367 from my backpack. I squatted in the corner of the bathroom behind the closed door, trembling as spasms wracked my body. I began to spin the gun on the floor. How can he sit there and eat and laugh as if it's just another day when he knows what he has in mind? Well, I'm gonna stop this. He can't do it without me. I begin to shake violently, whimpering, "No . . . no!"

I spun one chamber around. "Spin! Kill yourself. Lee . . . Do it! Do it! . . . No, not yet. I'll kill him!" I heard the resounding of his scornful laughter. "You kill me? Ha! Ha! Where is your zeal now? Kill me! Ha! Ha!" "No, I can't kill him; I don't have the guts to. . . . Then kill yourself. If you don't, how many people will die?" My hands were shaking. I put the muzzle to my temple. CLICK! "Nothing. Run away. That's what you can do. But where, man?" I had $167 in my pocket. This gun would be my only way to eat, and I would have to kill again. CLICK! "If you do it now you'll die. If you don't, in a few weeks you'll still die . . . this will fail . . . it has . . . to . . . do it!" CLICK!

"Malvo, you run from your mother, you hear me, you are running to your death. You are worthless just like . . ." CLICK! My T-shirt was soaked with perspiration, which was flowing down my elbow. My eyes burned with the mixture of tears and sweat. "Pull the trigger, you coward. How many times you've done this? Pull . . . Pull . . ."

Another sad story
Another sad story
Another day how long
But I carry on
For I can see death calling
I can see the coffin falling
In the hole,
The dust laid on my chest
As a fool is just laid to rest
I'm thinking, do or die,
contemplating suicidal thoughts who am I?
No longer stressed

Nor oppressed,
Decapitated by death
I guess I failed the test.
Am I destined?
Or do I create my destiny?
All I know is failure and anger,
Where is the rest of me?
Somebody please! Lee is on his knees
My life's been a disease
Release me please.

Click! Bang! Bang! Bang!

"Lee, are you in there?" I heard a voice. "Yeah," I mumbled. It's Ed my newly found cousin. "Are you all right?" I scrambled for a suitable lie. "I, I, I need to take a leak! I think I have diarrhea." I said. "That's why I left early." "OK!" he responded. I heard his footsteps retreating. I looked. There was blood on my T-shirt—where did it come from? I checked my face in the mirror. Shit! My nostril. It's bleeding. You can't do this, Lee. . . . You can't do this, I told myself. I heard Ed as he shuffled around the room. I ripped up a few napkins and cleaned the floor— tears, sweat, and blood! I picked up the weapon and turned off the bathroom light. I left the bathroom.

I moved the curtains slightly. "Lee!" Shit, it's John. I quickly got under the covers. He opened the door part way. I stayed motionless. The door closed quietly. I began to sob again. I stifled the sounds by biting the sheet. "Get control of yourself, you have to do something," I told myself. I was on the bottom bunk writing a letter to Latoria. It was dark, but I hoped the glare from the window would be enough. I was a nervous wreck.

The door opened and simultaneously the light went on. Ed saw me. "Lee, you all right?" I heard the concern in his voice. "I'll tell Uncle John if you aren't." I'm up, my hand tightly gripping his shoulder. I did not loosen my grip, saying with a touch of urgency, "No! No! I'm all right. My stomach is just aching, that's all. I just took some meds, and I'll be fine in a few."

Below is the letter that Malvo wrote to Latoria. It found its way into *The Washington Post*, but was not admitted into evidence at trial.

To: Latoria

Why am I here. There seems for me no purpose. Everyone who has met me hates my guts, rambling, and they consider my gibberish fake. I should have been banished and killed at birth for I'm perceived as a walking time bomb waiting to explode. Was my purpose here on the God forsaken planet to be banned, shamed and disapproved. Why am I here I ask continuously looking for an answer I've not yet seen. Thanks my haters for showing me again my downfall, thanks for the encouragement. When I give respect I'm disrespected. When I touch I'm beseeched. I tried to be a friend, a brother, a lover a man and yet I've always failed. I've tried to treat women the way they should be treated like the queens they are. I play, joke, be stern, be appreciative but receive the opposite in return.

I only met one person who understand and appreciated me. I ask for only a small spot of appreciation in one's heart, a piece to share with mine.

My patience is thinning, my conflict unresolved. My pain and fear stream as it rips my soul. I've lived a hard life, believe it or not.

No father and a mother who hate . . . no that's an understatementshe has disbanded me from her life. Does that say it?

I have a father who I know is going to have to kill me for a righteous society to prevail. Everyone sees a spontaneous, joyful, smart.

I wish that's what they saw in me.

They see a merely loudmouth, chattering freak with unconceivable thoughts that will never be appreciated. I write my body shivers with self pity for a distant distorted mind. Rambled on and on words of nonsense.

I studied and read but instead of gaining wisdom I am still yet a fool playing smart with the intellect of a bee. All I asked is to be loved for me

Lee.

After that tortuous night, Malvo related, he was able to pass the letter on to Ed, whom he asked to make sure that Latoria got it. He implored Ed to make sure that Muhammad did not see it, and said that Ed should not read it. Though he recalled the puzzled look on Ed's face, Malvo felt that he could trust him to keep a promise. After giving him the letter, Malvo grabbed his backpack and headed out.

The letter shows the state of mind Malvo was in as he grappled with what he wanted and where he saw his life heading. It was a desperate cry for help, which unfortunately went unheeded. Not until his arrest was the letter brought to light.

AND TWO BECAME ONE

In Louisiana, Malvo's relationship with Muhammad was at a critical stage. Malvo was fearful of Muhammad's agenda, whatever it might entail, and suspected that he himself would have to be sacrificed. However, Malvo could not bring himself to take his own life or to run away. Muhammad remained all he had, and he feared even more Muhammad's rejection and abandonment. To Malvo, such rejection and abandonment appeared to be a fate worse than death. And it seemed that to avoid it, he had to completely surrender to Muhammad and to trust that his cause was just.

The relationship was imbued with a cultic aura essential to Muhammad's purpose. Malvo frequently used the metaphor of a sponge in describing his learning under Muhammad. This is not to say he did not ask questions, but he did so like a young disciple awed by the wisdom of his master. Malvo marveled at how Muhammad always seemed to have the right answers or could refer him to the right books. He marveled too at Muhammad's professed knowledge of various subjects and disciplines.

The only "truth" Malvo had to follow was the one that Muhammad impressed on him. This "truth" was collaged from sources so varied and variant that Malvo felt both overawed and emboldened by being entrusted to assimilate it all. He received a skewed perspective from Muhammad, who misused the words of others to bolster their relationship. "Word is bond," Malvo said Muhammad told him. This meant he was duty-bound to Muhammad and his mission.

Malvo's sense of duty to Muhammad and the "mission" had messianic/religious overtones. Muhammad used religion to help give his teachings and mission the sense of higher authority and infallibility. Malvo's "conversion to Islam," as taught to him by Muhammad, was a starting point in beginning to see himself and his environment through the older man's eyes. Malvo was expected to conform to what seemed like the truth, even righteousness, of this vision and mission.

Muhammad drew upon a range of sources, including religious leaders, military strategists, philosophers, writings, speeches, and even movie and video-game characters, to prepare Malvo for the war against the system. Muhammad inculcated in Malvo that the system was a matrix designed to control and oppress him, and elaborated on that theme by pointing to the history of slavery and current conditions, which he interpreted as signs of psychological, economic, and social bondage of blacks. In this "matrix," Malvo was chosen to fight the system not only for his own liberation but also for the sake of other children like him. Muhammad used various terms to describe his agenda, such as "the mission," the "fight to save the kids," and "war." It seemed that he knew what buttons to push at any particular time in order to command Malvo mentally and physically.

One of the books Malvo had to read was *The Art of War,* reputedly written by a Chinese warrior-philosopher who lived about two thousand years ago. Muhammad impressed upon him the seeming merger of philosophy (the intellectual) and military power as instrumental to determining one's fate and environment, and the apparent historical authority and time-tested wisdom of this ancient book was supposedly relevant to Malvo's situation as defined by Muhammad. On the first page, military action is cited as "the ground of death of life, the path of survival and destruction, so it is imperative to examine it" (Tzu 1988). Malvo heard such themes repeatedly as Muhammad prepared him for "war."

Excerpts of *The Art of War* were among the sources that Malvo was required to tape-record and listen to as he slept. Such excerpts were preceded by selected music and a mantra from Malvo: "This is what I am and this is what I will become."

Malvo saw Muhammad's teachings and militaristic training as a means by which Muhammad wanted to liberate him from the slave mentality and the system. As the days turned into weeks, Muhammad exerted total control of everything Malvo did. It was as though he divested Malvo of everything that had previously defined him. No longer the "nerdy" Jamaican boy who only wanted to do well in school, Malvo became a soldier in Muhammad's army of two, with Muhammad as the father-general.

Muhammad used every opportunity to inculcate that Malvo had been called to a new identity and a just mission. The affirmation that Malvo had longed for from his parents became twisted as praise came only when Malvo completed whatever assignment or "tasks" Muhammad told him to do. These assignments were like tests to determine whether Malvo was worthy and ready. Muhammad would not tolerate indecision.

Malvo recalled that as they traveled to Washington, D.C., to do battle with "the beast," they left a trail of robberies and murders. Muhammad told

Malvo that victims were targets. If Malvo dared to cringe when a life was taken, Muhammad would launch into one of his diatribes: "You still feel this is wrong. I will not put up with this every time you need to complete a task. Six more states to Washington. On the way you'll perfect it!"

One means by which Muhammad prepared Malvo was to employ desensitizing techniques. For instance, he used computer or video games to make killing seem like a game. Malvo would shoot at human forms over and over again. The games seemed realistic and gory. In some of them the character that represented the player would bleed and die when shot, unless the player hit a particular code whereby the character became invincible. This was called the God mode; in some of the games, a voice says "I am God" after it is turned on. Significantly, notes Muhammad and Malvo left for the police after each "task" were signed, "For you Mr. Police. Call me God."

Malvo recalled that Muhammad helped him master the video games. He played mostly Tom Clancy's Ghost Recon. He also played another sniper game on the Internet, which involved playing against people all over the world; again Muhammad coached him. Malvo recalled that Muhammad would watch him as he played, especially his body language, telling him to breathe (because he would hold his breath in situations in the game where his position was compromised). He would tell Malvo to calm down, to not take things, especially failure, so personally. Malvo recalled that Muhammad would have him "screw up," then tell him to improvise as a test. Muhammad taught him how to stay at ease and to prepare always for things not going as planned. He remembered that Muhammad would stress the importance of improvising as well as always completing his objective.

The process of bringing Malvo to that point of seeing himself as a soldier, trained to kill, indicates exposure to an intense means of indoctrination, what could be described as brainwashing. Some might prefer to refer to this as coercive persuasion. Nonetheless, it is important not to be sidetracked by clichéd or movie-type images of what a brainwashed individual should look like or behave. Lifton (1989), who uses the term "thought reform," indicates that the word "brainwashing" presents semantic difficulties, given the confusing of brainwashing with an image of an "all powerful, irresistible, unfathomable, and magical method of achieving total control over the human mind."

Lifton's book, originally published in 1961, involved his work with prisoners who had been exposed to Chinese Communist brainwashing in the mid 1950s. Hence the study was based on paradigms of that time, and some of the details cited would not apply in Malvo's context. Lifton observed that each prisoner experienced thought reform differently, and did not respond completely to all the steps (1989). He cited certain psychological steps of "Death and Rebirth" (the idea that the old person had to die and a new person emerge) that seemed to factor into the process to varying degrees.

One of the first psychological steps is "The Assault Upon Identity," which involves "a surrender of personal autonomy" and can affect consciousness so that the individual exists in an in-between state of "neither sleep nor wakefulness" and thus is not only more readily influenced but also more "susceptible to destructive and aggressive influences arising from within themselves" (Lifton 1989). One of the striking things about Malvo's relationship with Muhammad is how quickly Muhammad set about the process of assaulting and altering Malvo's identity.

Other experts have applied and expanded the concept of brainwashing to models of control beyond Lifton's paradigm. Singer (2003), in her research on the psychology of cults, identifies six conditions that facilitate thought reform. First, keep the person unaware that there is an agenda to control or change them. Second, control time and physical environment (contacts, information). Third, create a sense of powerlessness, fear, and dependency. Fourth, suppress old behavior and attitudes. Fifth, instill new behavior and attitudes. Sixth, put forth a closed system of logic.

During my interviews with Malvo, as I tried to help him detach from Muhammad and regain his own identity, those books (Lifton and Singer) did not come up for discussion. However, his account of his relationship with Muhammad indicates that conditions for brainwashing existed. (Jonathan Mack will discuss brainwashing in more detail in section 3.)

In his own words, Malvo said:

> I was a carcass—a spent shell. When that hated old self would raise its head I would slap it so hard my mouth would bleed. I'd repeat, "Heart please be still. There is no fear here." My entire day was occupied with reading the books and listening to the tapes. There was no let go. He was unrelenting. He got to the point where he said with a satisfied laugh, "I've created a fucking monster." When an individual surrenders his life, when he no longer thinks for himself, he's thoroughly bled . . . dead. This is how child soldiers, ticking time bombs, John Lee Muhammads, suicide bombers come to exist. They are recruited for their emptiness. They are instruments of murder. They are dispossessed of their being—meticulously, mercilessly indoctrinated

Here I am a broken vessel
Give me a purpose
A reason to exist
Fill me with what you will.

TERROR AND MAYHEM IN WASHINGTON, D.C.

According to Malvo, he and Muhammad left Baton Rouge, Louisiana on September 26, 2002. Their first major stop was Raleigh, North Carolina. There Muhammad dropped off Malvo at the local YMCA and went to take care of some business. Malvo knew better than to ask any questions. Muhammad had once told him, "Anything I want you to know, I will volunteer that information. If I don't tell you, well, you don't need to know." Malvo later learned that he was going to their "base of operations," and when it was time for phase 2 he would return. Malvo also noticed that Muhammad's green military duffel bag, filled with explosives, cell phone, and chargers, was gone.

The ride east was short as they went directly to Clinton, Maryland, where Mildred and the children were living. They spent several days scoping the area. Malvo's recollection is that Muhammad then decided to head up the northeast corridor toward New Jersey.

As they traveled to New Jersey, Muhammad met up with a man called Blacka, a Jamaican whom he tried to recruit. Malvo's recollection is that Muhammad had apparently helped Blacka to enter the United States illegally. Blacka laughed at Muhammad's plan and said there were easier ways to make money, such as selling marijuana. According to Malvo, Muhammad then shot Blacka dead at point-blank range. This was a frightening development, as it seemed that Muhammad had the power to decide for Malvo too whether he lived or died. In researching this story, I was not able to find any official record or confirmation of Blacka's death or his true identity.

Malvo recalled that when they reached Camden, New Jersey, they stayed with a few of Muhammad's friends. Within days of arriving, Muhammad purchased the Chevrolet Caprice that would be used during the upcoming weeks. Days were spent doing detailed surveillance on his ex-wife and children. Malvo recalled that Muhammad wanted to know who visited Mildred, where the kids went to school, where she worked. With Malvo beside him, he drove around looking for safe spots, using a laptop computer to map sites from Pennsylvania to Raleigh, North Carolina, which became their hub.

THE BELTWAY SHOOTINGS

As Malvo recounted the shootings, both in his writings and verbally, there was a distinct and noticeable lack of feelings, as is evident in the description below. When this was pointed out to him, he reiterated that he was trained not to feel. It was not until about two years after the shootings that he began to feel any emotion about the murders he had committed. At the time, he was a "soldier" and at "war": Muhammad's war.

According to Malvo, on October 2, 2002, the "operation" began in earnest. Muhammad intended to kill two people that day and begin afresh the following day. Malvo's job was to "set up" the trunk of the Caprice, give Muhammad directions based on the maps they had, and, once in the "target" area, to be on the lookout for witnesses (people generally too close to the car) and give Muhammad the go-ahead to shoot or call off the shot.

In describing the process, Malvo said that he would pull the lever to fold down the back seat. Once he was in the back he would unhinge the top section of the seat, which would be used as an extension of the trunk, where Muhammad would rest his feet. Malvo then crawled into the trunk and attached both ends of a bungee cord to the rim, strapping it down so that when Muhammad popped the trunk it would open only partway, providing two inches of space. Then Malvo would put the Bushmaster-manufactured .223 caliber rifle together and put a round into the chamber. He then placed the weapon on the spare tire, which Muhammad used as a platform when he lay face down on the folded seat, aimed out the open trunk, and took the shots. According to Malvo, this preparation process took about five minutes, and was repeated before every shooting that was done from the trunk of the car.

People and places were selected in a mind-bogglingly random way. At the Michael's Craft Store where the first shooting took place, Muhammad and Malvo parked between two cars and surveyed to ensure that there was no one waiting in any vehicle. There was little verbal communication between them, and that was through a walkie-talkie. Muhammad would indicate that he was all set by giving Malvo three beeps on the walkie-talkie. Malvo would then roll down both the passenger- and driver-side windows halfway, and maneuver the mirrors until they were at perfect angles for him to see. He then checked again to make sure no one was in any of the vehicles close to them. When Malvo saw a "target," he would give Muhammad the signal to go ahead and take a shot: "Mobile one, you have a go." That first shot missed, and the intended victim was spared without even realizing that he had been seconds from death.

Muhammad directed Malvo to the next spot. There and at the next one, the shots were called off. At the fourth location, they parked at the end of the Shopper's Fair Warehouse parking lot. There was only the busy street before them. Muhammad squeezed Malvo's shoulder, then dropped the back of the driver's seat, stepped into the back of the car, and entered the trunk. "Mobile one, you have a go," Malvo said immediately after receiving the three beeps.

The victim was James Martin, a fifty-five-year-old white male who had proudly served his country in the Vietnam War, worked his way through college, and was employed at the National Oceanic and Atmospheric Administration (NOAA). A husband and father, he was a God-fearing man, a member of the PTA, and a mentor to children at inner-city schools (Horwitz and Ruane 2003). Malvo recalled seeing him fall before it registered that the shot had been fired. In the time it took to blink, Muhammad was in the driver's seat, starting the car. Slowly, as he would normally do, Muhammad reversed the car and exited the lot.

Muhammad had to stop for a few seconds at a traffic light, where, according to Malvo, Muhammad said, "Son, let's call it a day. I've been driving since three this morning." He remembered that with a yawn, Muhammad added, "We have a long day tomorrow."

According to Malvo, they then headed for a rest stop south of Fredericksburg, Virginia. By 5:00 a.m. the following day, October 3, they were already in Rockville, Maryland. Malvo recalled that they parked in shopping malls and empty lots until the streets got busy. The plan was to shoot and kill as many people as possible before 10:00 p.m. By that time they expected the streets to be gridlocked because of all the police and other emergency vehicle activities.

For the next shooting everything was set, the weapon and bungee cord in place. At exactly 6:00 a.m. they pulled out of the parking lot. In order to exit the lot, they had to take a one-way street. There they saw a man mowing the lawn of a car lot. He was the only person in sight. This man was James L. (Sonny) Buchanan Jr., a thirty-nine-year-old landscaper. He was the son of a retired Montgomery County policeman and had recently moved with his fiancée to Virginia (Horowitz and Ruane 2003).

Muhammad pulled over to the curb, opened the trunk, rolled down his window, and dropped the back of his seat. Soon he was in the trunk. According to Malvo, Muhammad did not need his assistance for this shooting. Malvo heard the shot, then saw the man fall; the lawnmower rolled off the grass, then partly off the sidewalk. The victim was still down when they drove off. The plan was to spend only ten minutes at each target area, then move on to the next. Sonny Buchanan died instantly.

Malvo recalled that they then parked in a small lot next to a pharmacy and several other small stores. Across the street was a Mobil gas station busy with customers, including a cab driver who had just inserted the pump in his tank. Muhammad popped the trunk and got in. Malvo heard the beeps signaling that Muhammad was in place and ready to take a shot. "Mobile one, you have a go." The cab driver went down holding his chest. The victim was Prem Kumar Walekar, fifty-four, from Pune, India. He worshipped at a Seventh-Day Adventist church, had been married for twenty-five years, and was the father of two children (Horowitz and Ruane 2003). He died instantly.

Malvo wrote that the next location was similar to the one they had just exited, a lot with small stores. They parked in a slightly elevated spot at the end of the lot. Upon entering the lot they noticed a Hispanic lady at the bus stop, sitting on a bench and engrossed in a novel. Muhammad popped the trunk, let the back of his seat fall, then slithered into place. *Beep! Beep! Beep!* came the signal. "Mobile one, you—" but according to Malvo, before he could complete the sentence he saw blood fly out of the lady's head. Her body slumped to the side and the book fell from her hands

Malvo remembered that as they exited the lot, an elderly gentleman was kneeling beside the woman's body, with a look of terror on his very pale face. There was a hole in the window of the café behind the bus stop where she had been sitting moments before. This victim was Sarah Ramos, a thirty-four-year-old former law student from El Salvador. She and her husband, a college teacher, and their son had immigrated from El Salvador. She had been waiting to be picked up to be taken to a housecleaning job (Horowitz and Ruane 2003).

Muhammad and Malvo then pulled into the parking lot of a supermarket, with the Chevy Caprice's trunk pointed at a Shell gas station. A lady was vacuuming her Dodge minivan. When the lot was empty except for a man unpacking his groceries over at the other end, Malvo told Muhammad he had a go. The lady was bent over the seats, her back to Muhammad and Malvo. She had just stood up fully when the shot rang out. Her name was Lori Ann Rivera. She was a nanny, graduated from the Northwest Nannies Institute, and had moved from her home in Idaho to work with a family in the D.C. area. She and her husband, Nelson, had a daughter, Jocelyn (Horowitz and Ruane 2003).

At 3:30 p.m. Muhammad and Malvo were in a Jamaican restaurant having their one meal for the day and taking their cocktail of vitamins. According to Malvo, as soon as he was finished eating he asked Muhammad for the keys to the car and exited the restaurant, leaving Muhammad behind. The car windows were dark-tinted, so he was not worried about a passerby seeing what he was doing inside. He unhinged the top part of the back seat, entered the trunk, removed the four empty shell casings, wrapped them in a sheet of newspaper, and placed them in a ziplock bag. The bungee cord was still in place, and he checked it to make sure it wasn't loose. He then repositioned the spare tire as he had found it, reassembled the weapon, and place it atop the spare tire.

As he exited the trunk, Malvo folded the top part of the back seat into place, then grabbed a bag of raisins, and a pack of Fig Newtons. He locked the car and returned to the restaurant, handing Muhammad the keys with his bags of food.

Soon it was 9:00 p.m., and according to Malvo, Muhammad was aggravated by the fact that there always seemed to be someone sitting in a vehicle way too close to where they parked. Driving up Georgia Avenue toward Maryland, Muhammad was adamant "there must be one shot tonight." Then he smiled. They parked behind the Jamaican restaurant where they had eaten. Across the street was a Laundromat that Muhammad intended to shoot at, but instead he decided to shoot the first person who came to the street crossing in the intersection.

Beep! Beep! Beep! told Malvo that Muhammad was set. No one was in the restaurant parking lot. Malvo saw an elderly black man at the crossing. However, before he could complete the usual prompt, his ears were ringing from the blast of the shot. The man fell, holding his chest. Muhammad came up front and pointed at the map on the screen of the laptop. This victim, Pascal Charlot, died instantly. Seventy-two years old, he was an immigrant from Haiti, a skilled carpenter who lived with his invalid wife in a red-brick row house (Horowitz and Ruane 2003).

According to Malvo, they headed to a local YMCA about eight miles away. They worked out, then sat in the sauna. Malvo remembers Muhammad saying, "We should be able to get at least four in the next stop, son; I hope more, but at least four more. We'll eat, then hit the road at five o'clock, all right?" "Yes, sir," Malvo replied. That night they slept at the rest area south of Fredericksburg, Virginia.

The next day did not turn out as they expected. They drove up and down Plank Road in Fredericksburg, but at each spot Malvo called off the shot because there were too many potential witnesses. Not until 2:00 p.m. did they finally get off a shot, in a Michael's Craft Store parking lot. The intended victim, Caroline Sewell, forty-three years old at the time and the mother of two, survived the shooting.

That Friday evening, October 4, Malvo recalled, Muhammad talked about how many killings they could do per day. Muhammad was content as long as the authorities knew that they were out there. He calculated that he could keep the authorities guessing, because whenever he wanted, he could decide to get "seven or so" in one spot.

That one spot Muhammad was referring to was Benjamin Tasker Middle School in Bowie, some distance away from the Maryland–D.C.–north Virginia metropolitan area. He hoped that the town residents would be complacent and thus not on guard. Malvo was instructed to kill at least five children as they exited the school buses. That Saturday morning they went to the library not far from the middle school. Malvo was instructed to acquaint himself with the wooded area that separated the school from a number of houses. In doing so, he noted where the basketball and tennis courts were located.

Upon his return to the library, Malvo drew a crude map ofg what he had seen. Muhammad instructed him that he could either take the shots at the basketball court, which they expected to be packed, or from the front of the school. Muhammad pointed out that the front of the school was small and that, as the buses pulled up one behind another, Malvo must allow them to unload. Then the kids would be in that very small space where maximum damage could be done. As Malvo was sent on this mission, Muhammad told him, "I'm giving you ten rounds, son; make good use of each shot."

That Sunday night Malvo was again in the wooded area; he estimated that it was 70 to 80 yards from there to the front of the school. He made a nest for himself with leaves and camouflaged his hiding place. "I could not sleep. I was afraid to disappoint my father, but I was about to kill kids—kids—like myself. Then I could hear his voice scolding, 'There is no right and wrong!' I used the technique he taught me, 'vivid visualization.' All I did was think, then get back on Georgia Avenue and on to the next spot, so on and so on."

That morning, October 7, at around 4:30, Muhammad radioed Malvo and told him he was set. Malvo expected the buses to be there by 6:20 a.m., but instead he saw parents running with their children into the school or children exiting their parents' cars and quickly entering the building.

> Muhammad, upon not hearing mayhem, asked me what was up. "I don't see the bus, sir," I said. He told me to be patient. An hour later I radioed him. "Sir, the bus isn't coming," I said. "Take what you have," he said, "just make sure it's a head shot." As he said that I fired, but I did not take a head shot as I was instructed. I crouched and moved out of the area quickly, then in a full sprint found the duffel bag, broke down the weapon, and ran to the car. There Muhammad drove off, joining the morning traffic. Soon we heard the sirens. I had left a tarot card behind. We drove in silence for some time, then we stopped on our way to D.C. at a K-Mart. "You did good, son . . . you did good," said Muhammad. "Now," he continued, "where did you put the card?" "It was placed very close to where the shot was taken, sir; they'll have no problem finding it." "Good," said Muhammad.

The boy Malvo shot, Iran Brown, had been residing with his aunt and uncle for about a year. Ironically, his mother had sent him to live in Bowie to get him away from some unsavory characters in the apartment complex where she lived. She moved him because she wanted him to be safe. Miraculously, the thirteen-year-old survived.

The card that Malvo referred to was the first piece of communication that the police had with the snipers. Tarot cards were originally used in Italian parlor games, but more recently have been associated with the occult (Horowitz and Ruane 2003). The one Malvo left was the so-called death card. On the front was a skeleton in armor riding a white horse and carrying a black flag. The horse's reins were decorated with skulls and cross-bones. Across the bottom of the card was the word DEATH. Across the top was the message, "Call me God." On the back, two scrawled lines divided the card into three sections. The top segment contained the salutation "For you Mr. Police." In the middle was written: "Code: 'Call me God.'" And at the bottom was a warning: "Do not release to the press" (Horowitz and Ruane 2003).

Malvo recalled that even during the weeks of the shooting, he continued to play video games including Ghost Recon, Rainbow 6, and Halo, which had a "God mode. He also watched *The Matrix* before going on his shooting missions.

Malvo and Muhammad arrived in Manassas, Maryland, early in the afternoon on October 9. They ate their daily meal at a restaurant, then sat in the car examining the identified spots in Manassas on the laptop. At 4:40 p.m. that Wednesday evening, they began driving around from one target area to the next. Around 7:00 that evening, they parked in the lot of a restaurant and waited for it to get a little darker. The target area was a gas station across the street. "This is it," Malvo recalled Muhammad saying as they spent a few minutes examining a map they had stolen from a library in Baltimore. It covered details of the schools and school zones, all of which interested Muhammad. He indicated that he had big plans for Baltimore: phase two, in which he would blow up the school buses.

At around 8:00 p.m. the lot was empty. Muhammad popped the trunk, lowered the back of his seat, and crawled into the trunk. He could see the Sunoco gas station with its milling customers. *Beep! Beep! Beep!* went Muhammad's signal. No one was in the parking lot and no one was exiting the restaurant. "Mobile one, you have a go." Immediately the shot was fired. Quickly Muhammad was in the driver's seat. "That's it for today," he said. They pulled out of the lot and headed for the closest rest stop. Shot to death was Dean Myers, a fifty-three-year-old civil engineer, with a single bullet behind his left ear. A Vietnam veteran, he had returned from the war with a Purple Heart and the Army's Commendation Medal for Heroism. He spent months in a military hospital nursing wounds, then studied engineering at Penn State University before landing a job in the Washington area (Horowitz and Ruane 2003).

On Friday, October 11, two days later, Malvo and Muhammad returned to Fredericksburg, but to the section of the city on the other side of the interstate highway. They parked in the lot of a motel by the exit ramp from the highway. Across the street, about 30 feet away, was an Exxon gas station. As soon as Muhammad was in place, Malvo got the signal that he was ready. Malvo saw a black man pumping gas. This was Kenneth Bridges, a 53-year-old Philadelphia businessman. Described as a smart, dynamic African American entrepreneur, he was a husband and the father of six children. He had a degree from Wharton School at the University of Pennsylvania. The son of a World War II veteran, Bridges believed that black Americans needed to support black businesses and was a cofounder of MATAH, a distribution network for black businesses.

As Bridges came into view, Malvo gave his signal: "Mobile one, you have a go." The shot rang out and Bridges was mortally wounded. Both Malvo and Muhammad saw a state trooper at the exit. He had pulled someone over and had certainly heard the shot. Malvo recalled that the trooper had drawn his sidearm and was looking in the direction the shot came from. Muhammad drove past without raising any suspicion.

Between October 11 and 15, they were busy trying to call the police but were not able to get through. Muhammad wanted to get the negotiations started. On Monday, October 14, they were in Falls Church, Virginia. Muhammad had predetermined where the shooting would take place: The Home Depot.

Muhammad went and got something to eat at around 7:30 p.m. He returned by about 8:30 p.m. Rather than remaining in the car to give Muhammad the go-ahead, this time Malvo got out and crossed the street. This was a street with two lanes of traffic going in each direction. Counting his steps in full stride, Malvo estimated the distance to the door of The Home Depot to be 165 yards from where the car was parked. He climbed the steps to the doorway, then found a comfortable position along a fence. He had his walkie-talkie with him. *Beep! Beep! Beep!* He got the signal that Muhammad was ready.

After about an hour of waiting, the lot was empty. Malvo then observed a lady and a man trying to fit a large object through the back door of their small car. The lady was Linda Franklin, a forty-seven-year-old analyst with the FBI. She and her husband, Ted, had been married for eight years, and she had recently undergone a double mastectomy as part of treatment for breast cancer. She had two children from a previous marriage and was about to become a grandmother when she came into view of the sniper. Malvo recalled, "'Mobile one, you have a go,' I told him. Then I heard the shot and saw its impact. By the time I made it down the steps, Muhammad had started the car and was waiting for me." Linda Franklin died on the spot, in the presence of her horrified husband. It was for this murder that Malvo was tried, convicted, and sentenced to life in prison in Chesapeake, Virginia.

Malvo said that during a break between October 14 and 19, he had a meltdown. He felt he was buckling under the pressure, as Muhammad kept ratcheting up expectations and the enormity of the "mission." For two days after the Home Depot murder, he and Muhammad returned to Baltimore, where the school buses were parked. They also checked out the grounds of the police cemetery. Muhammad had two possible plans: the first was to place explosives with ball bearings under fourteen to nineteen school buses. The second, which he was leaning toward, was to violently kill a cop in order to precipitate a police funeral, whereby Muhammad could blow up several police officers and their families at once. It was supposed to be Malvo's job to walk up to a cop in a police car, ask for directions, and then shoot the cop in the head.

Around Wednesday, October 16, Muhammad was ready to resume shooting, but Malvo had grown tired of the killings. He was struggling to understand Muhammad's agenda. "We're out here killing all these people, now he's talking about dozens, why? Muhammad would ask me 'What's your problem?' 'I mean, what's wrong, son?' I didn't answer."

The following morning, Thursday, October 17, they returned to Baltimore, having slept at an interstate rest stop north of the city. As they sat at the location where Muhammad intended to take a shot, Malvo found some resistance. "Look man, I ain't doing nothing today!" So they sat there for a few hours, and sometime in the afternoon Muhammad lost his patience. With eyes of steel, he directed his anger at Malvo. Malvo described that interaction, with Muhammad opening the verbal exchange:

> "This is why people get caught, doubts and slowing down when the aim is to keep momentum, doubts get people killed, hesitation leads to mistakes. I don't have time for second-guessing, so what do you want? Do you want the weapons, laptop and half the money? The drive back to Raleigh is a little over 300 miles!" I shake my head no! "So you don't know what you want? Do you want to continue the mission, or will I have to go on without you?" I started crying, just tears rolling down my cheeks to all his questions, and all I do is shake my head no!
>
> "You can leave if you want to but disunity means death." All those mantras he'd taught me, he's proven his sincerity by living up to them. Your work is your life. "So you want nothing?" I shake my head, he looks me over from head to toe. "You are pitiful. Get out! You may leave!" I grabbed some jeans, T-shirts, and my boots, stuffed them in a duffel bag, and exited the car. I sat on the curb watching the Caprice get smaller and smaller as it drove away. I opened the duffel bag and looked at my belongings. I closed it. I sat with my head between my knees; slowly I began

to cry then to outright sob. Death to me was no longer a scary option. I was willing to die. I didn't care. Sitting on the pavement, my mind, my thoughts were all mindful. What will you do, Lee? He had become my brain and I an "instrument," as he liked to describe me.

I didn't have to think. "Don't think it. Be it," he would say to me. He told me when I must eat, what to eat, how to eat, where to sleep, when to sleep, when to relax, when to stay alert, he instructed me by mere eye contact when and how to act. I trusted him completely; whatever he was or was not, he was consistent. I could count on him being him. If he uttered it, it was as good as the next sun rising; not only have I accepted him, he became a pattern for me to follow, I absorbed his personality by way of osmosis. It is not as if I was in his web for a few months, I was caught over a year before in Antigua, long before ever setting foot on American soil. He could depend on me because he understood me, what was my drive, how to motivate, chide, the intensity of my anger and thus the outcome of my action. Thought was a burden I left up to him. I was nothing without him. Where could I go?

Malvo cannot recall how long he sat there sobbing before he heard a car stop in front of him. He looked up and saw the big blue door of the Caprice swing open. He blinked rapidly and began to dry his tears. He recalled that Muhammad looked at him "the way you would look at a piece of shit that you quickly sidestep." Then, staring down at him, Muhammad asked him sharply, "Are-you-done-yet?" Malvo nodded yes. "Are you-god-damn-sure?" Again Malvo nodded yes. "Get in!!" he finally said.

That Friday night, Malvo was dropped off at a cemetery behind a strip club. Before Muhammad pulled away, he instructed Malvo that his target was the McDonald's restaurant across from the cemetery. Muhammad wanted a killing that would further inflame the public. "I don't care how long it takes you, shoot a pregnant woman."

I agreed until I looked down the barrel at the four possible victims that came and went within the three hours. Each time I said I'll get the next and the next would come, but the trigger was 7½ pounds too much to pull. As the shooter I can call off the shot. At around 2 a.m. I radioed him to come and pick me up.

As soon as I sat down he asked, "What happened?" "None didn't show up, sir!" "You mean to tell me you did not have one shot?" "There were targets everywhere, but your request was specific, sir!" "We are behind in numbers, Lee, but it doesn't matter; as of the 27th they'll know we are not joking. Hopefully, you'll have less fear pushing a button!"

On Saturday they were in Ashland, Virginia. It was October 19. They had spent Friday trying to contact the police task force that was devoted to the sniper killings, but couldn't get through by phone. Saturday morning, Muhammad went into a dollar store and returned with pen and paper. He dictated and Malvo wrote. He directed Malvo to speak to the authorities and use the words in the note. After several failed attempts, Muhammad was finally able to communicate with the authorities, but it was Malvo who spoke to the police.

On the phone, Malvo identified himself to the police as the person causing the killings and expressed his frustrations about not being able to make contact sooner. By then Muhammad wanted to begin the $10 million negotiation, but his efforts were frustrated by the police's "incompetence." Someone else was also trying to contact the authorities: Robert Holmes, who had seen the shootings on TV and was convinced that the shooters were John Muhammad and Lee Malvo. Robert Holmes was a friend of John Muhammad; they had served together in the military in the 1980s. He testified at Muhammad's trial that both Malvo and Muhammad had stayed with him on a few occasions while they were in the Tacoma, Washington area. He had observed the "father-son" relationship and he was aware of Muhammad's fascination with guns. He was also aware of how disgruntled Muhammad was about losing custody of his children, and that Muhammad had discovered that Mildred was living in the Washington, D.C. area. Malvo recalled visiting with Holmes in Washington State, and that Holmes had begun to grow wary of their movements. It was a call from him that gave the authorities the lead they needed to finally catch Muhammad and Malvo.

On Saturday afternoon, Muhammad and Malvo went to the wooded area behind a Ponderosa restaurant. Malvo was instructed to examine the area and mark a few spots to guide him on his exit. By around 7:00 p.m. he was set. He placed the note in a ziplock bag a few yards from where he would be shooting. The note read: "For you Mr. Police. Call me God, Do not release to the Press." Malvo observed a couple exiting the Ponderosa and heading toward a car in the parking lot behind the restaurant. He aimed at the man's chest and squeezed the trigger. Jeffery Hopper, the victim, survived the shooting.

Immediately after firing, Malvo broke the weapon down, stowed it in his duffel bag, and exited the wooded area. He hid the duffel bag in some bushes behind a motel a few blocks down, possibly with the intention of returning to retrieve it later. Then he radioed Muhammad. Muhammad picked him up and they got on the highway. They were stopped by the police, who asked them if they'd seen anything suspicious, Muhammad answered no and asked the trooper, "When are you going to catch these people?" Malvo recalled the trooper responding, "We're doing the best we can, sir."

On Monday, October 21, they returned to Montgomery County. Muhammad intended to show how incompetent the task force was, so he decided to return where "it all had started, in their backyard." That day Malvo examined the wooded area from where he would take what turned out to be his last shot. The victim was a bus driver, Conrad Johnson.

That night around 9:00 p.m. Muhammad dropped me off at the K-Mart not far from the area where I would take the shot. That night I got in position, and sat with my duffel bag and went to sleep. Around 3 a.m. my watch alarm woke me up. Sometime after 5 a.m. a bus pulled up at the bus stop. That would be my target.

There was a lady on the bus and she got off. I aimed at her first, then changed my mind. I aimed at the bus driver instead as he opened the door and turned to speak to the passenger. I squeezed the trigger. He went down. By the time I heard the lady on the bus scream, I was already on my way to the duffel bag. I lost a glove in the bush where I was nestled to take the shot. I could not find the bag, so I went to an area I had prepared just in case this happened. I already had a hole under a large rock next to a sewer. I broke down the weapon and hid it.

Like Malvo, the victim, Conrad Johnson, had been born in Jamaica, and he was left with an aunt while his mother migrated to the United States to provide a better life for her family. Conrad joined her when he was about ten years old. According to his mother, Sonia Wills, a more loving child you could not find. Ms. Wills said that although she had only five children, she was mother to many because Conrad was the kind of child who would bring home boys he felt needed the sense of direction she was able to impart. Conrad was married and had two children of his own. He was a loving husband and father to his family and a wonderful son, his mother said. She later told me: "If only Malvo had looked my son in the face before he killed him, he would have seen the perfect father he had been searching for."

Malvo quickly made his way out of the small park and headed for the K-Mart parking lot. He radioed Muhammad to find out where he was. Malvo told Muhammad that he had botched the job. Muhammad wanted to know if he had failed to take the shot. Malvo recalled telling him that he messed up on the exit, to which Muhammad responded by assuring him that he had done well but needed additional training so that he could better prepare for an alternative in the event that things did not go as planned.

> I had left behind a little bag, a knife, a glove and the weapon. In every crime we ever committed, very close to the crime scene was a designated area to hide the weapons. The weapon was always lodged/stashed with all the proceeds from the crime. When he instructed, I would return and remove the weapon from its hiding place. I had buckled under pressure. Early in the morning of October 24th, before the slaughter got worst, it all came to an end.

Both Malvo and Muhammad were arrested on October 24, 2002. They were found asleep in the 1990 blue Chevrolet Caprice that they had used as a killing machine. Hundreds of items were recovered from the vehicle and the places where they had stayed during their murderous journey. In addition to the weapons and ammunition, these included violent video games such as Tom Clancy's Ghost Recon, Desert Siege, and Halo Combat Evolved and several books, including *The Art of War*, the *I-Ching*, *The Politics of Liberation*, and *A Taste of Power*. There were numerous DVDs, including episodes of *Roots* plus the films *Stigmata*, *The Matrix*, *Entrapment*, and *We Were Soldiers*, in additio to several CDs with music by Bob Marley, Tupac, and Lauryn Hill as well as *Streets and Trips 2002*. There was also a laptop computer, a digital recorder, one half of a fifty-dollar bill, and a *Princeton Review* CD.

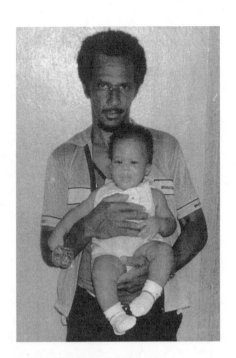

(top) Lee Boyd Malvo in the arms of his father, Leslie.

Malvo on his bicycle.

(top) Malvo with his Aunt Marie, Uncle John, and cousins. He resided with the family on two occasions.

Malvo in his school uniform when he attended York Castle High School, Jamaica.

Malvo, with Bible in hand, on his way to church. This picture was taken months before he first met John Muhammad.

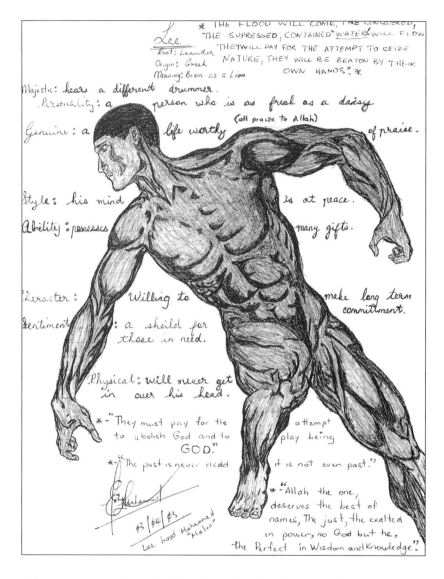

THE FLOOD WILL COME, THE CONQUERED, THE SUPRESSED, CONTAINED WATERS WILL FLOW THEY WILL PAY FOR THE ATTEMPT TO SEIZE NATURE, THEY WILL BE BEATON BY THEIR OWN HANDS. *

Lee
Root: Leander
Origin: Greek
Meaning: Brave as a Lion

Majestic: hears a different drummer.
Personality: a person who is as fresh as a daisy.
Genuine: a life worthy (all praise to Allah) of praise.
Style: his mind is at peace.
Ability: possesses many gifts.
Character: Willing to make long term commitments.
Sentiment: a sheild for those in need.
Physical: will never get in over his head.

*-"They must pay for the attempt to abolish God and to play being GOD."

*-"The past is never dead it is not even past."

*-"Allah the one, deserves the best of names, The just, the exalted in power, no God but he, the Perfect in Wisdom and Knowledge."

$3 | $4 | $3
Lee boyd Muhammad "Malvo"

A drawing from 2003, in which Malvo shows himself as Muhammad's warrior. Many of his drawings from this period demonstrate Muhammad's influence and include references from religious or political texts that Malvo was forced to memorize. Note that he signed the drawing Lee Boyd Muhammad.

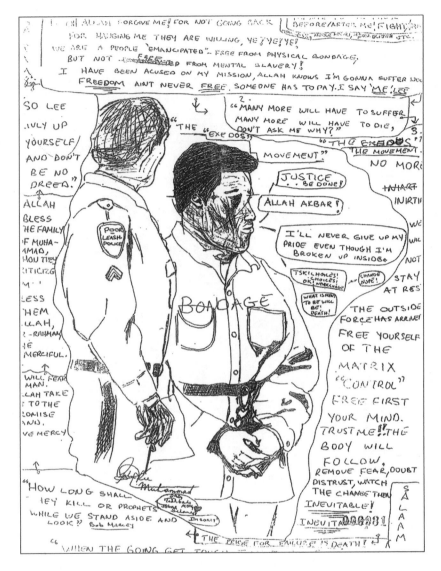

A drawing seized from Malvo after his arrest. Muhammad's influence is still obvious. The writings contain references to *The Matrix* and the lyrics of Bob Marley.

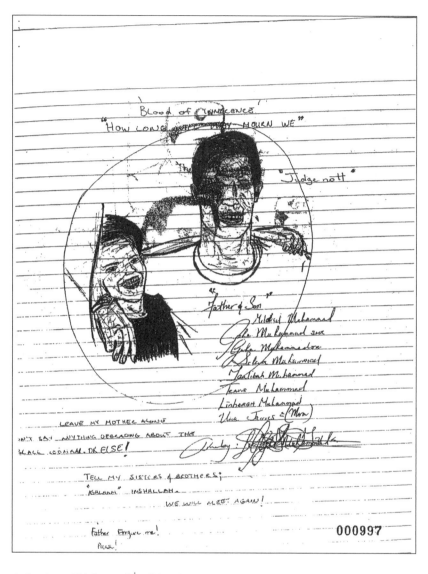

A drawing of "father and son" (Muhammad and Malvo), in Malvo's possession at the time of his arrest. He included a list of Muhammad's family members, including his own mother (Una James).

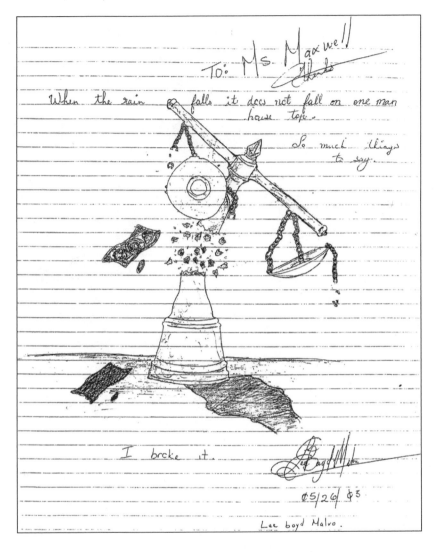

A drawing Malvo gave to one of his teachers, Ms. Maxwell, with whom he had lived in Jamaica. Ms. Maxwell's visit to him in prison was a pivotal point in his reclamation of his earlier identity. In the drawing, Malvo promises to break his bond with Muhammad. The words at the top are lyrics from a Bob Marley song.

> Fairfax County Jail,
> 10520 Judicial dr,
> Fairfax, VA. 22030,
>
> Dear Mom,
>   I hope your in good health when my letter arrives. I'm holding up fine. I just wrote you to let you know I'm alright. Take care of yourself. You are appreciated.
>   Love
>   Lee

(top, opposite page) A drawing Malvo made for his mother in March 2003, depicting life in his prison cell.

(bottom, opposite page) A drawing Malvo made for Carmeta Albarus, shortly after meeting her in 2003. The similarities to the drawing he made for his mother suggest that he was beginning to see Carmeta as a mother figure.

(top) The first letter Malvo wrote to Carmeta Albarus in which he refers to her as "Mom," showing his growing attachment to her. This was written roughly two months after she began working with him.

A self-portrait Malvo drew in 2004, accompanied by a poem he wrote entitled "Still." At this point he was beginning to feel remorse for his actions.

(*top*) Malvo depicts himself on the bench in the courthouse, waiting to testify against Muhammad. The caption reads, "Get back in there and do this Lee firstly for you!"

A self-portrait Malvo drew in 2006, depicting himself studying in his cell.

A portrait in which Malvo imagines the scholar he could be, instead of a prisoner. Note that the paper to his side is a risk assessment.

12/14/06.

Dearest Carmeta:

If you relax in the same manner you work you will be fully recharged ☺ to bring in the new year in fine form.

Over the past few weeks especially this week I've been focused on discovering my core principles. For I realize that it is this lack of self directedness that culminated in my present circumstances.

By listening to my conscience I'm learn-ing to question my motives, for if and when my motives are not properly founded on my principles things always end in disaster.

My central tenet is to give back to society and specifically the victims in proportion to what I've robbed fro both.

I intend to do this by educating my mind, and cultivating my talents and to use them to the benefit of causes that are in congruence with my principles of service to others.

If I intend to "give back in proportion to what I robbed" then that means I must give my life to such service. While I don't yet know what I will

---

A letter from Malvo to Carmeta Albarus, December 2006. He writes: "My central tenet is to give back to society and specifically the victims in proportion to what I've robbed from both. I intend to do this by educating my mind, and cultivating my talents and to use them to benefit the causes that are in congruence with my principles of service to others. If I intend to 'give back in proportion to what I robbed' then that means I must give my life to such service."

A self-portrait Malvo drew in 2006, depicting himself as a thief who stole the lives of his victims with a gun.

3 A False Father Rejected

Separating Malvo from Muhammad

"My dad gave me consistency, 100 percent unconditional acceptance, and he led by example." That was the response when I asked Malvo what he saw in John Muhammad that engendered such loyalty and devotion. After doing the requisite research into Malvo's life, I could understand why those qualities meant a lot to him.

When he met Muhammad, Malvo's life had been marked by the opposite of what Muhammad seemed to represent. The inconsistency came from a mother who displayed severe mood swings. According to Malvo, he did not know from one minute to the next which Una he would be confronted with. He said that there was not unconditional acceptance because his mother's love seemed to come with a price—"You be what I want you to be and I will love you." Yet even when he tried to earn that validation by doing well in class, she chastised him for any perceived infraction. He felt that there was no way to win with his mother. His biological father, Leslie, had also failed Malvo. Their loving bond during his early childhood was inconsistent with the rejection he felt when his father refused to take him in.

Muhammad presented with those three qualities that meant so much to Malvo. Understanding this provided the tools I needed to separate Malvo from Muhammad. I decided it would be helpful to find an alternative object for Malvo's attachment. It had to be someone to whom he had attached favorably in the past and who would be able to stimulate his reconciliation with himself as Lee Boyd Malvo. I had to find this person in Jamaica, where Malvo was born and spent his early years.

After six sessions with Malvo, I made my first trip to Jamaica in late April 2003. Prior to leaving, I informed Malvo that he would not be seeing me for the next two weeks. I wanted to make sure he understood that I would be consistent, and if I were not going to show up for my regular visits, I would inform him. Up until that time I had complied with his request that he be called John Lee Muhammad. However, I gently informed him that the releases he had signed for me were useless, as there was no John Lee Muhammad in Jamaica. He willingly signed "John Lee Muhammad aka 'Lee Boyd Malvo,'" and asked me to take copies of his poems and drawings for his mother.

Among the drawings were two separate images of himself in his jail cell. One was addressed to his mother and the other one to me. There were subtle differences between the drawings, although he thought they were identical.

On that trip, I met with Leslie, Malvo's father, and also with Malvo's former teachers and friends. All were eager to talk about the boy they knew. Malvo's mother, Una, refused to be interviewed. The poems, drawing, and letter from Malvo were given to Una through her attorney. Leslie agreed to talk and also to be audio recorded.

At our meeting, Leslie's eyes were red from crying. He recounted the first five years of his life with Malvo and Una. "Ma'am my boy was a good boy until that man tek him over. Is that man why mi son in dis," he said in his Jamaican dialect. As he spoke, he clenched his fists and every vein in his face stood out. He asked for a few minutes to control his emotion, and then he broke down and sobbed.

On May 10, shortly after returning to the United States, I went to visit Malvo, armed with photos and the audiotape of the interview with his father. As I played the tape, I noticed a change in Malvo. He smiled as he listened to his father's heavily accented voice. "That's Brown Man," Malvo said. This is the nickname Leslie is affectionately called by friends. When Leslie spoke about ice cream he bought for Malvo and said that his son was called "Pardie," Malvo began to laugh. "It's all true. I remember that," he said.

Malvo was animated as he listened to the voice of the man who had refused to take him in. The tape reached the point where Leslie began to blame Muhammad for Malvo's woes. I stopped the tape and described the scene to Malvo. I demonstrated the rage that had enveloped Leslie as he spoke of the hate he bore for "that man" who had taken his son down the path of destruction. I told Malvo that if Muhammad had been in the room then and there, his father would have strangled him. Malvo looked at me, and with the trace of a smile, he responded, "He probably would." In that moment, symbolically, I had given Malvo the hero father he had been seeking in Leslie, the one who would come and save him.

Malvo's mood changed during that meeting. It was obvious that hearing his father's voice for the first time in six years was having a profound effect on him. Laughter was interspersed with tears as he recalled the good times before he was taken away by his mother. He reflected on the relationship that he'd observed between Muhammad and his son and how it reminded him of his own happy times with his father.

During the meeting I observed that Malvo would switch from one persona to another without knowing it. At times he was John Lee Muhammad, speaking with an American accent and raging against white supremacy and racial injustice, and then he would switch back to smiling and cajoling like a typical Jamaican kid, speaking more like a Jamaican. Then he stopped and became pensive. "It could have happened to any kid," he remarked about how he'd become attached to Muhammad. "Any child would have been convinced. He was a good father and children loved him everywhere he went, but yet they took away the kids."

Given Malvo's response upon hearing his father's voice, I felt emboldened to criticize Muhammad. In so doing, I was using Malvo's response to allow him to see that his view of Muhammad could be revised. I asked Malvo whether he had ever had sex. He responded that he never did because he had decided early in life to abstain until he was married. He added that he would not get married until he was settled in a good job. "So these kids you keep talking about aren't yours?" I asked him. He looked at me as though I was crazy. "No," he said. "So why are you so up in arms about them being taken away? Do you know that he has made it so that you will never have kids of your own? Can you see that he has set you up to never enjoy the life you once hoped for? Those were his kids and it was his war, not yours."

I removed from my folder a picture that I had taken of Leslie Malvo. I slammed it down on the table, and in the sternest voice that I could muster, I said, "This is your father. Not John Muhammad." The tears rolled down his cheeks. I knew then that the process of separation from Muhammad had begun.

Malvo later wrote:

The first shock to my system was Carmeta Albarus. She succeeded where others failed because they didn't understand the nuances of Caribbean culture. She was black, female and most importantly, Jamaican. She never tried to tell me what must be done. In fact for weeks she just listened and I talked. All day, if she let me. She spoke patois; we spoke of life in Jamaica. But in a deeper sense she spoke my language. She let me come around on my own.

Though Malvo continued to hold to the idea that Muhammad meant him well, the armor that he wore was beginning to crack. On May 12, I received the first of many letters that he wrote to me, which began with the words, "Dear Mom." It reaffirmed that the detachment from Muhammad had begun, but I was not naïve enough to think that Muhammad's hold did not remain very strong. With only six months until the trial, set to begin in November, much was yet to be done to bring Malvo to the point of fully cooperating with his defense team. That very day, I received an encouraging fax from his attorney, Craig Cooley, indicating that Malvo had become more cooperative.

What was taking place was transference, wherein Malvo was beginning to see me as the "good mother." Two factors struck me about this. The first is that it seemed to tie into Malvo's pattern of seeing things as divided between good and evil or the perfect and the imperfect. Given the damaged relationship Malvo had with his mother, it seemed the only way he could trust me to enter his life was to see me as the good mother, who would not harm him or abandon him. I was a bit wary of this transference, as it held the potential for conflict, particularly as it suggested Malvo's difficulty in accepting the idea that a parental figure could be both good and bad. To him, the parent could only be one or the other.

His responses further suggested his vulnerability to Muhammad, to whom he had attached as the "good father"; while he was with Muhammad, he was not able to accommodate the idea that he could also be the bad father. I wondered how Malvo would cope emotionally should he reach the point where, as he learned to reexamine his views, disappointment in Muhammad set in. I also wondered what would happen should he be disappointed in his idealization of me as the good mother. Would he then regress to the point of cutting off all communication and cooperation, not just with me but also with his attorneys? I decided that such a situation might well occur later and would have to be handled appropriately. But now, despite my concerns, it was important to continue meeting Malvo at the stage where he was.

The second factor I noted about the transference allowed me to be more at ease with Malvo's need to address me as his mom. Implicit in his transference was trauma associated with unmet needs in his childhood. The need to attach to a maternal (good mother) figure, for instance, was apparent in his relationships with Ms. Diane, Semone Powell, and Ms. Maxwell. I realized further that his transference confirmed what I had thought before traveling to Jamaica: presenting him with safe alternatives to the Muhammad attachment was essential to helping him separate. I thus related to him as the good mother.

Of course, I had to be mindful that the purpose and parameters of my relationship with Malvo did not become lost, and that it did not raise any expectations on his part of me seeing him as my son. I allowed him to feel safe in referring to me as "Mom," and even close his letters as "your son Lee," while at the same time allowing him to realize that it was not okay for me to reciprocate by addressing him as "Son." The intensity of this dynamic led me to seek clinical consultation with Dr. Simone Gordon, the clinical director of CVA Consulting Services. This afforded me the capacity to provide a place of safety for him while keeping a professional distance. Accordingly, I was able to maintain the boundaries necessary to work with him.

On my next visit to Malvo, I decided to engage him further about the motives for the killings. He had allowed himself to be convinced that the killings were to obtain money to build a utopian society with "seventy boys and seventy girls." However, I and other members of the defense team felt that it was all a ruse for Muhammad to get his children. It seemed likely that Muhammad's wife would have become another victim of the shootings, and Muhammad would have emerged as the grieving spouse who then regained custody of his children. Malvo would have become the fall guy and been directed to take his own life. Malvo had already acknowledged that the only reason he had not done so was that Muhammad had not given him the order.

However, when I presented that theory to Malvo, he scoffed at it. "That's impossible. He loves Mildred. He would never kill her, and furthermore we knew where she lived. We watched her come and go. If he wanted to kill her he could have done so many times." Malvo recounted that his "dad" almost broke a man's neck because the man disrespected his wife. "My dad respects women," he intoned. I reminded him that he was awaiting trial for the murder of Linda Franklin. "He respects them but then he kills them?" I asked. Malvo was silent.

As I listened to Malvo describe why Muhammad could not have killed Mildred, I pondered his supposed intelligence. Was he not as bright as others claimed, or was he so brainwashed that he was incapable of thinking for himself? Could he not see that Muhammad was only using him? Muhammad gave him the SNIPER shirt to wear. Muhammad wore gloves during all the crime-related activities; Malvo did not. Malvo was the one who made the phone calls; Muhammad only wrote down what was to be said. Malvo wrote the letters that were sent out. I presented these points to him. Still he refused to even consider that the so-called war in which Muhammad had enlisted him had nothing to do with building a better society. The only society that mattered to Muhammad was the one that gave him back his children. "My dad loves me," Malvo said, trying to console himself. "He wanted a better way for all children."

Given Malvo's positive reaction to the voice of his biological father, I suggested to his attorneys that we bring someone from Malvo's past to meet with him. It was decided that Ms. Winsome Maxwell, the teacher who had taken him into her home in Jamaica when he seemed ragged and starved, was the best person to invite. Ms. Maxwell immediately agreed when asked.

On May 23, 2003, Ms. Maxwell arrived in New York. She was apprehensive. What would Malvo look like? Would he be happy to see her or resentful that she had sent him to his mother when it was clear to her that he had reservations? Nonetheless, she was eager to get going. The day after her arrival in New York, we took the road to Fairfax County Detention Center in Virginia. Ms. Maxwell had never visited a jail before and did not know what to expect. The correctional staff were cordial and instructed her as to the parameters within which she must comply. There can be no physical contact, they instructed.

I had informed Malvo ahead of time that his teacher was coming to see him. I said that he needed to have a haircut and be presentable when he came in to see her. As Ms. Maxwell waited, Malvo was brought into the interview room in shackles. He was well groomed. "Hi, Lee," she greeted him with a smile. Her calming presence seemed to be what Malvo needed. He appeared nervous, but responded that he was doing okay.

After an uneasy silence, as they looked at each other, Malvo asked Ms. Maxwell about his former classmates. He wanted to know how they were doing. What had they made of their lives? Were they successful in their CXC (Caribbean Examinations Council final-year) exams? Malvo was particularly eager to learn about the students who had been at risk of failing. He was pleased to hear that they were doing fine. There was laughter as teacher and student reminisced. Malvo's close friends had excelled, as he'd known they would. After what seemed like an eternity but was only a few moments of silence, he asked with a sense of incredulity, "Ms. Maxwell, how did I end up here?" Without missing a beat, she responded, "That is what we want to know. That is why I am here."

He recounted for his teacher what had transpired after she took him to the airport and sent him to his mother. He told her how, as he had feared, his mother again left him behind. Only that time he had no one to turn to. It was not like in Jamaica, when a neighbor or a kindly teacher would take him in, he implied. He was a stranger in Antigua and had only his mother's married lover. The pain was etched in Ms. Maxwell's face as she listened to him. If only he had stayed in her home he would be in college now, she had related to me on our way to the prison. But here he was, accused of one of the most heinous crimes in the history of the United States.

He talked of how his "dad," Muhammad, had taken him in at no cost. He related to Ms. Maxwell how good it was to have someone who cared for him without pay. "Just like you did, Ms. Maxwell." She understood his misguided gratitude but refused to acknowledge Muhammad as anything but "that man." Each time Malvo referred to him as "Dad," she corrected him. "Who are you referring to? If you say 'Dad,' I will assume that you are referring to Leslie Malvo and not that man. While in my presence please call him by his name, Mr. Muhammad." "Yes, Miss," he responded.

He shared with his teacher that Muhammad's hold on him did not begin in the United States but earlier, in Antigua. He recalled the moment when Muhammad told him three words that he longed to hear from his parents but never did: "Good job, son." On that first day of Ms. Maxwell's visit, we had two sessions with Malvo, each lasting approximately two and a half hours. By the end of the day we felt that a great deal of progress had been made. He was happy to hear that we would be back the following day, and we left the jail feeling that Lee Boyd Malvo had been restored.

The following morning, May 25, we returned to the jail. We arrived early and the staff was expecting us, so we were ushered into the interview room without any delay. Malvo was brought in, and as soon as he sat down, I knew something was wrong. His eyes looked nothing like the good-humored boy we had left the previous evening. He was John Lee Muhammad and he wanted to be addressed that way. He launched into his hate-filled rhetoric, railing against white oppression and racism. Ms. Maxwell was dumbfounded. I was perplexed. I had been confronted with John Lee Muhammad in the past but had fooled myself into thinking he'd disappeared. But here he was again, Muhammad's little creation, Muhammad's little, loyal soldier. What could have happened? Ms. Maxwell refused to be drawn into his diatribe. "I don't know this person," she said, "and I refuse to acknowledge him."

I had learned that once Malvo began to regurgitate Muhammad's teachings, there was no reasoning with him. His arguments were blown out of proportion and in many ways irrational. I decided to allow him to vent.

We met with him again after lunch. This time he had calmed down somewhat and seemed almost apologetic. Still, there was an air of defiance about him, as though he was prepared to fight against what he felt we were going to say to him. He had gone into the mode of defending his "dad." Nonetheless, he was calm enough for me to pose the question: What on earth happened between yesterday evening when we left and this morning? He was quiet for a minute, and the troubled, sad look returned. He put his handcuffed hands to his head and said, "It's the voice that I hear. The nights are bad. That's when I hear the voices in my head."

I wanted to know what voices. It was then that he revealed the process of indoctrination that he had undergone while under Muhammad's control. He revealed some of the mind-controlling techniques that were applied to get him where Muhammad wanted him to be. "Lee, you must tell your attorneys," I said. But he said that he could not or would not. His loyalty to this man was still strong. We left that evening, not knowing who would greet us the following day. That was Memorial Day 2003, and the last time his teacher would visit him.

On that third day, Malvo entered the interview room. He was now a cross between the obedient student that Ms. Maxwell had come to know and love and the sniper who had wreaked havoc in Washington, D.C., and surrounding areas. "I have changed, Ms. Maxwell," he said. She acknowledged that he could not have gone through what he had and not changed. She implored, however, that he needed to be truthful and honest with his attorneys and the doctors. "But I gave my word," he responded. "And word is bond." He shared with us that it had been planned for him to take responsibility for the shootings. He said Muhammad had predicted that if they were ever caught, law enforcement would use him to get a conviction of Muhammad. Malvo reiterated that he could not say anything that could be used against him. "I gave him my word," he insisted.

In the final hour before we were to depart, Ms. Maxwell broke down in tears as she begged Malvo to cooperate and tell the truth. She raised her voice as she challenged him. "Tell me, Lee Malvo, to whom do you owe your loyalty? To that man who brought you destruction or to me, who took you into my home and treated you like a brother and a son? Tell me right this minute. Who do you owe your loyalty to?" Malvo's eyes were filled with tears, and it was clear he was doing battle with his emotions. "Miss Maxwell, why are you doing this to me?" Her raw emotions were having an effect on him. After what seemed an eternity, he reached out to her and said, "Please don't cry anymore, Miss Maxwell. I promise you that I will cooperate. I will tell them what happened."

The tears did not stop with that promise. Whether they were tears of joy that she had gotten through to him or tears of regret for the time she sent him back to his mother, I don't know. But as she rested her head on the table in front of her student, he reassured her. "I have made you a promise and I will keep my word, but I don't know if I will ever be strong enough to testify against him. But I will tell my lawyers the truth."

Here again I understood the importance of attachment for Malvo. He had to have an alternative, and on this occasion it was Miss Maxwell, the good teacher. That was how he had to bring himself psychologically to break "the bond" with Muhammad. He had to become the student relating to the teacher who'd saved him. We left that evening feeling cautiously optimistic. We had no idea what the night would bring.

The following day was a difficult one for Malvo. He called my office in a panic. He wanted to see Dr. Blumberg, the psychiatrist. He wanted to have tapes made with messages that could be used to counter the taped messages he had been forced to sleep with, which still played in his head at night. I told him that would not be possible, but I would ask his attorneys to get the doctor to see him right away. He was so distressed that I decided I would make a three-way call to hook him up with his father, Leslie. I remained on the line. Leslie was happy to hear his son's voice and Malvo was happy to hear his father. He responded to his father as though in the military, "Yes, sir." I asked him what he called his father when he was in Jamaica. "Dada," he responded. "Then please call him Dada now. Not sir." There was a faint laugh as he said "Dada," and his father responded that he loved him.

Within six or seven minutes into the call, reception was lost. Malvo called out "Dada . . . Da . . ." but there was no response. He became frantic. "Carmeta, I can't hear him. He's gone. He's gone, Carmeta." There was sheer fright in his voice. It was as though he had found, then lost his father again. "Mr. Malvo, are you there?" I asked. "Mi still deya man [I am still here]," came the reply Malvo breathed a sigh of relief and continued to speak to his father before he was called away by an officer with the news that his attorneys were there to see him. That phone call lasted for about ten minutes, but it was a reconnection that was crucial in Malvo's retransformation.

PREPARING FOR TRIAL

The remaining months until November were difficult for Malvo. It was becoming clearer that Muhammad had never loved him, but only saw him as the perfect means to an end. He remained in denial for a while, but as he began to have an open mind about the path along which he;d been led, he could no longer hide his head in the sand. "Why me?" "What was it about me that made him know that he could lead me down this path?" he frequently asked himself. He came to the conclusion that it was because he had no one. "No one wanted me and no one loved me," he said. Malvo seemed to have the idea that he was never loved. However, nothing could be further from the truth.

As we prepared for trial, it became necessary for me to retrace Malvo's life from birth through his travels in Jamaica, St. Maarten, and Antigua, gathering more information. I made a second trip to Jamaica, then went on to Antigua and St. Maarten. On this second trip I interviewed almost forty people. From the audio and video recordings I collected, a video was made tracing Malvo's life from birth in Jamaica to his departure from Antigua with Muhammad.

As I was conducting the interviews, I asked each person to send a special message to Malvo. They had not been told beforehand that this would be required. It was important that the message not be rehearsed but come from the heart. I decided to do this because it was vital to try to rebuild Malvo's self-esteem. Seeing the outpouring of affection that so many people had for him was important in this journey of retransformation.

The making of the video lasted over two weeks. The resounding sentiment was that Malvo was a good kid who had been taken down a destructive path. Relatives, teachers, neighbors, fellow students, and friends expressed love and affection for him. Throughout the investigation, everyone with whom I met willingly offered their full cooperation. The only person who had conditions placed on her cooperation was Malvo's mother. On that second trip to Jamaica, Una agreed to meet with me, but not before I signed an agreement that no recording device was to be used. It became apparent that what she wanted was for her voice to be heard, to make clear that she had tried to save her child but the system failed her. The trip was completed in early July, and the video, edited in chronological order, was presented to the defense team. Though it was not allowed to be presented to the jury, it provided the defense with a better understanding of Lee Malvo.

On August 18, 2003, three months before his trial, Malvo was shown the video. I would not be seeing him for at least two weeks, and I thought it was imperative he have something to hold on to. The negative sense of self that he had internalized continued to be an impediment. I wanted images of his life in Jamaica to counter the images and messages that continued to plague him. The jail authorities were cooperative and arranged for a TV/VCR combo to be made available. Joining me in the interview room with Malvo was Dr. Dewey Cornell, the lead psychologist on the case.

As the video was played, Malvo saw for himself that he was not a piece of garbage that had been thrown aside. He was loved, and engendered much admiration from many people. He watched with delight and listened to his schoolmates speak lovingly of him. I informed him that they had taken time out from their school and jobs to be available for the video. He pointed out places that he'd frequented as a child. As his teachers talked about him and his helpfulness, he acknowledged that he derived much satisfaction from helping and sharing. However, the high point of his viewing was when he heard his Aunt Marie sing for him the hymn, "Great Is Thy Faithfulness."

As his aunt's voice echoed in that tiny interview room, Malvo began to sing along with her. His voice started as a whisper, then reached a crescendo. Suddenly his face crumbled and his body trembled with the sobs. It was as though he was tearfully finding a reconnection to his Jamaican roots and to the Christian faith he knew before Muhammad took over his life. "I made a promise to myself at age eleven that never again would I cry like this, and now you have made me break that promise." Dr. Cornell handed him a tissue, and encouraged him, saying that by crying he was expressing his feelings rather than bottling them up.

Though progress was made, Malvo was still not free from Muhammad's machinations. "If we get caught I should self-destruct," he remembered Muhammad telling him. He was still caught between his loyalty to Muhammad and his promise to his teacher that he would stop protecting Muhammad. It was difficult for him to think of himself as only a pawn in Muhammad's hands, a mere means to an end. He wanted so desperately to believe that he meant something to this man he called "Dad."

Malvo expressed the belief that Muhammad had had good intentions in Antigua, and wanted to bring other children to the United States to afford them better economic opportunities. Malvo himself, had experienced dire poverty and deprivations in Jamaica, Antigua, and St. Maarten as his mother sought a way to the United States, where she hoped for a better life.

Given that hope and Muhammad's stated "good intentions," Malvo came to the United States with a positive outlook.

Yet as they traveled around the country, Muhammad showed and taught him that young black men were offered the worst conditions, such as overcrowded and underequipped schools, and prisons. I noticed that as Malvo began to reflect, he was opening up to a reexamination of Muhammad's relationship with him. "He used me for a purpose," Malvo acknowledged.

For Malvo's trial in November 2003, several witnesses were brought up from Jamaica. Among them were his father, Leslie Malvo; his aunt, Marie Lawrence; his cousin, Semone Powell; his teachers from Jamaica and Antigua; his mother's paramour from Antigua; and his best friends from Jamaica and Antigua. Each of them related to the court the boy they knew and the traumas he had lived through. Noticeably absent was Una James, his mother. Malvo was allowed to have a noncontact visit (behind the glass) with his father. I met with Malvo the day after this visit and was distressed to see that he had reverted to his Muhammad persona. Seeing his father only made him reconnect with the trauma of rejection.

"Fatherless children! That is why so many of us are in prison. Though we make up only 10 percent of the population, we account for 90 percent of the prison population." I corrected him that though blacks are overrepresented in the prison population, they do not account for 90 percent. His tone suggested that those exaggerated figures were coming from Muhammad's teachings. I pointed out to him that sometimes the biggest lies are the ones with a grain of truth. He cried as he acknowledged the pain that he'd felt in seeing his father. "So much would have been different if he had kept me."

On November 24, following his testimony on Malvo's behalf, Leslie had another meeting with his son. Malvo's attorney, Craig Cooley, decided that I would be present. Leslie, looking tired and dressed in a business suit that was too big for him, had wept during his testimony. He was still steeped in emotion as he visited with Malvo one more time before returning to Jamaica.

Malvo was dressed in orange prison garb and stood looking at his father through the thick glass that separated them. Here again was the man he had spent so many years looking for: the father who had nurtured him during those early formative years; the father who had been his hero; the one he had depended on to save him from his mother's brutality. Malvo also saw the father who had rejected him at a time when Malvo needed him most.

Son and father faced each other and placed their hands on the glass that divided them, as if to touch. It seemed like time stood still as they savored that moment. "I love you one million percent and I would take my neck off to get you out of this," Leslie told his son with deep emotion. The tears welled in Malvo's eyes as he heard these words. "I am sorry that I could not keep you, but it was not possible at the time," Leslie explained. "I never stopped loving you and I will never stop loving you," he emphasized. "I love you too, Dad." With that, Malvo was escorted from the cubicle by the officer. As he walked back to his cell, he reflected on all the things his father said then, which should have been said years earlier.

EXCERPTS FROM "IN YOU"
BY LEE BOYD MALVO

You see me
But I am a reflection
Of a process of my experience
Not some mishap by chance
She could do everything
She just could never teach me
Could never exemplify
What it is to be a man

So here we are
Here I am
A barcode in a caged land
The pain I feel
I can't conceal
It's hard to self reveal:
To heal

I'm not about to utter
If I only knew
For that would mean nothing to me
Or to you

It's in your attitude
That shows the real you
But this I'll say

It's not only us boys
It's your daughters too
We both needed
The true father in you.

THE INTERNAL STRUGGLE TO REGAIN LEE BOYD MALVO

Malvo was spared the death penalty by the jury, but he was now left with the struggle to find himself. He was heartened by the many witnesses who had traveled from near and far to speak on his behalf, but it sounded as if they were talking about someone he did not know. As he had when he was twelve years old and needed an outlet for his feelings, he decided to keep a journal. His first entry was written on December 24, 2003, a day after the jury returned with a life sentence.

> Dear friend: I am restless. I can't sleep. Maybe I'm afraid but of what? Everything that exists serves a purpose. What is mine? Since I have the ability to choose then I decide where I go from here. Or is my fate already determined? If so I am troubled, but I must learn to bear both sides of the fortune. Like Plato's fable: let us see if my metal or mettle is up to the test. I live and I know not why but rest assured I shall not rest until I can answer who am I?

Three days later, on December 27, he asked: "Do I meet the criteria to be called a man? Young, inexperienced, easily led astray. Now I recognize my follies; but nature pardons not, for not knowing. I resolve then to let inquiry and the years teach me."

It seemed difficult for him to absorb that his name would be associated with one of the most horrendous crime sprees this nation has seen. A sense of aloneness engulfed him after the trial ended and everyone packed their bags and briefcases and returned to their lives. To survive, he had to deal with the reality of what he had done and what he had become.

Malvo described his relationship with Muhammad thus: "he treated me like an abused spouse who was needy and wanted his approval; he just had to verbally whiplash me to get me back into place."

I was struck by Malvo's analogy of the abused spouse. It brought to mind Tobias and Lalich's (1994) explanation of how "one-on-one cult situations" can develop in a number of relationships, including that of the abuser and the battered spouse. For instance, men and women who batter their partners sometimes use manipulative techniques similar to those found in cults, most commonly "isolation and the provocation of fear; alternating kindness and threat to produce disequilibrium; the induction of guilt, self-blame, dependency, and learned helplessness." In Mildred Muhammad's book, *Scared Silent* (Stebor Books, 2009), she wrote of the her life as a battered spouse and the terror that John Muhammad infused in her.

As someone who has worked on cases involving battered women, some of whom have been coerced into criminal conduct by their partners or have resorted to killing their batterers, I am able to recognize some of the signs of this dynamic. One feature that stands out is the isolation to which the battered spouse is subjected. All avenues of support are shut off, making the victim dependent on the batterer.

Though Malvo reported only one incident of being physically abused by Muhammad, it filled him with so much dread that he vowed never to make his "dad" so angry at him again. The instances of manipulation and deprivation were numerous, and there were also very meager rewards, such as the raisins fed to him for a job well done, that demonstrate how dependent Malvo was on Muhammad for survival. Many battered partners have been asked, "Why did you not leave?" Unfortunately, this is much easier said than done. The only way Malvo could leave was to kill himself. However, even that was not a viable option, as he could not pull the trigger without the go-ahead from Muhammad.

It was not lost on Malvo that his search for a father had led to a path he had not wanted for himself. Despite this, it took months for him to arrive at the point where he could bring himself to denounce Muhammad and what he stood for. He struggled to relinquish the thought that Muhammad was the good and heroic father he had hoped for. This is captured in a poem he wrote about three months after his trial.

REGRETS OF PAIN
BY LEE BOYD MALVO

I am free from you . . .
Free from your reigns
Free from the self that once saturated these veins
Free from the thoughts so deeply engrained,
Free from the grasp of your kind,
Free from the hold of my mind,

Free from your manipulation and deceit
Free from your defeat
In myself I find my retreat.

What binds me to you forever?
Are the memories,
Some of joy,
Some of pain
The cries of amplified torture, the blood at my feet
That has brought the dual destruction that we meet.
Now I must survive to accomplish another almost
Unfathomable feat . . . but not impossible.
My heart weeps and wails
My outcry of pain,
The hatred that is rekindled . . . then wanes,
Through the toils, pain, and we remain
The epitome of fools who fought, to die in vain.
Our dignity . . . I must regain,
I am glad I met you all the same.

As the poem demonstrates, Malvo oscillated between remaining connected to a father figure and needing to reject him. His religion or relationship with God had also been challenged. At the time he met John Muhammad, Malvo was a baptized Seventh-Day Adventist, professing his Christian faith. However, under Muhammad's indoctrination, this belief was expunged and replaced by Muhammad's version of God.

To Malvo, the God whom he worshipped until age fifteen was dead. I came to realize that Malvo's struggle to reclaim his identity outside of Muhammad was complicated by the thought that maybe the Lee Boyd Malvo who had existed prior to Muhammad was dead, and, accordingly, the God associated with that Malvo was dead. And to further complicate matters, the God to which Muhammad had converted him had proven false and therefore irrelevant.

An excerpts from a letter he wrote to me on August 2, 2004, reflect his conflict:

I must assert that I am an atheist. I understand your moral and religious principles and I also understand that you have helped me reach this point and I fear losing your support. But I can't submit myself to principles that are alien to my reality, as seen through introspection and the facts viewed through the lens of my experience. Please when you refer to me please don't tell me about God it aggravates me.

At the time Malvo wrote this, I was still the "transferential mom" and was perhaps being viewed in a way similar to his biological mother, whom he saw as a religious fanatic who would have berated him for his stance. As he tried to individuate, it was important for him to do so despite what I might think or what he might have perceived I wanted for him. I recognized that whatever place he needed to reach he had to get to on his own, and in his own time and space.

Malvo did not have the benefit of a system of formal deprogramming from the cultic relationship with Muhammad. So getting him to separate from Muhammad meant encouraging informal contact outside of the mental walls Muhammad had erected and outside of the physical walls of prison. Malvo understood, for instance, that he was free to maintain a consistent relationship with my office and speak to staff. Whenever he made contact, an affinity to others who cared about him would be emphasized. Through such consistent contact, he began to feel a normalization of social interaction. This transcended the one-on-one cultic dyad in which he had become locked with Muhammad. He began to see that it was okay to go outside of the parameters Muhammad had ingrained in him.

A RETURN OF FEELINGS

Red Onion State Prison is a super maximum-security facility located in the Appalachian Mountains in Virginia. This is where Malvo serves his sentence, in an environment where coping with isolation can be a daily challenge. Malvo has no known family in the United States, and given the location of the prison, there is not much opportunity for him to have visitors.

After the case was over, I continued to visit Malvo at Red Onion, and try to do so at least two times per year. My visit in October 2004 was an exceptionally emotional one for Malvo, evoking memories of when his mother would leave him behind to go off to some foreign land. "Do you have to leave?" he asked as I gathered my papers. He was in chains with the handcuffs secured behind him. A leash extending from the handcuff, secured by a guard sitting outside the interview room, made for a very uncomfortable posture, from which he should have been happy to be relieved. But he was so sorry to see me go that he lingered and cried. I reached out and touched his hand, reassuring him that I would not abandon him and would return to see him. After that I was never again allowed to have a contact visit with Mr. Malvo, as he is to have no physical contact with anyone but his jailers.

For about three weeks there was no communication from Malvo. When he did write, his letter was filled with pain. He stated that when he had returned to his cell on the day I visited, he had flashbacks of being left alone by his mother and of being molested by one of the neighbors with whom she left him. The molestation memory had been repressed for years; at no time during the trial had this come up. It is significant, however, that it was triggered at the time I was leaving, when he was recalling his mother leaving him with this neighbor though he did not want her to. Now he was beginning to feel again the pain of being victimized, and in so doing was able to feel the pain of the shooting victims.

REMORSE

Up to two years after his arrest, Malvo seemed unable to connect to the horror of what he had done. I recognized that early expectations or questions of remorse were premature. If there was to be remorse, it would come with time and in relation to his capacity to significantly detach psychologically from Muhammad. Nonetheless, as I sat in front of him during our sessions, I was troubled by his lack of remorse, especially since I myself felt anguish and pain for the lives lost and the families shattered. On occasions when I mentioned the victims to him, he would respond, "I am numb."

He remarked that Muhammad had trained him to become devoid of all feelings. Though tears welled in his eyes as he talked of certain events, the sense of remorse that one might expect was not there for a long time. He said, "A child was sent to school to kill a child. When I was arrested I was still John Muhammad. If my 'father' was in a cell next to mine and told me to take my own life, even now, looking back in retrospect, I would have done it."

In attempting to probe into Malvo's "numbness," I gained greater understanding of his state of mind at the time of the shootings. A consistent theme of his relationship with Muhammad was the need for him to dissociate from the "slave" identity of Lee Boyd Malvo and to assume the new and supposedly emancipated identity of John Lee Muhammad. In order to assure his "dad's" inseparability from him, he was challenged repeatedly to kill Lee Boyd Malvo so that John Lee Muhammad could live. Malvo said that in order for him to go through with the "tasks" Muhammad gave him, he had to "go into a zone." He also referred to this as "zoning out." He said that the term "go into the zone" came from Muhammad.

The zoning-out experience underscored the conflict between the Lee Boyd Malvo identity and the John Lee Muhammad identity. This struggle was evident even when he could not take a fatal shot at the child Iran Brown or kill a pregnant woman. He suggested that the images of children, and feelings of being a child himself, were so powerful that he did not completely zone out. He recalled that although it was not possible to fire a fatal shot in each of the two instances, he was afraid of failing Muhammad, so he still had to fire. He described how Muhammad would shake him and insist that he go into the zone. From Malvo's statements, the zone seems a dissociative state, wherein the Muhammad identity had to take over performing each "task."

Malvo said he began to experience feelings for the victims in late October 2004. Once that began, he suffered an emotional crisis. This was reflected in the letters, poems, and artwork that he sent to my office. He began to withdraw, refusing overtures of kindness. "I am not worthy of the water they give me," he remarked. The enormity of his actions, and the loss suffered by others on account of those actions, became visible and overwhelming. He reached the point of expressing sorrow for what he had done. In one telling instance, he said he cried not for himself, but "for the child whose father I took."

Malvo recalled that in the months leading up to his trial and the months that followed, his only focus was the fight to find himself. "You must understand Lee Malvo died somewhere and I was trying to find him. A large—huge—chunk of me was John Lee Muhammad. I had submitted my thoughts, feelings, goals, desires, and aspirations all the way down to my diet—every fiber of my being was Muhammad's. The how and why of this was my preoccupation, every hour of every waking moment," he told me. He said that at no time had he ever thought of the victims. He said that he was in a state where the "massacres" were compartmentalized.

In October 2004 there was a major change. In addition to reconnecting with his own pain of being molested, he was brought into the world of victims by a television program hosted by Dr. Stanton Samenow. Ironically, the same Dr. Samenow had been one of the prosecutor's expert witnesses at Malvo's trial in 2003. Malvo remembers that Dr. Samenow came to see him. Malvo was still entertaining ideas of "self destruction" at the time of those visits, and may have seen Dr. Samenow as an unwitting ally, particularly as Malvo thought Dr. Samenow had been sent to justify why he (Malvo) should be executed.

In late 2004, while watching TV, Malvo was drawn to the program Dr. Samenow hosted, in which incarcerated people were asked to volunteer to talk about their crimes and how they felt the crimes affected others. Malvo recalled intently watching this program and listening to how each individual talked about the people they had victimized. The words of an elderly inmate on the program made an impact.

The elderly inmate was figuring that he had hurt those people whom he robbed at gunpoint, Malvo recalled. When asked by Dr. Samenow to elaborate, the inmate answered that he hurt the man, his wife, and their two kids because he traumatized them. Malvo recalled that Dr. Samenow made the rounds of the other members of the group being interviewed, being precise and methodical in asking questions to flesh out the people who had been hurt by seemingly simple crimes. Malvo then thought of the victims of his own crimes.

> The very first thing that came to my mind was Mr. Conrad Johnson— his wife—his son standing at the window wanting to play ball—just to shoot one hoop—to hear his father's voice. But daddy won't be coming home. His mother, father, coworkers, brothers, sisters. As I made the list my head felt as if it was splitting. The spasm racked my body as I bawled.

In the months that followed, Malvo was haunted by the eyes of Mr. Franklin, the husband of victim Linda Franklin. The image of Mr. Franklin staring at him became real and painful. Malvo said that the pain he felt for the victims of his crimes was much worse than physical pain. "I became an insomniac. I would look at my face and taste bile in my throat—and throw up. I remember teetering on the edge of giving up—the will to live—I was going south and fast."

In December 2005, while at Montgomery County Detention Center awaiting trial for the murders committed in Maryland (though he was not facing the death penalty, the state had the right to try him for crimes committed there), Malvo had what seemed to be a psychotic break. For months in the silence of protective custody, he had spent his days planning his suicide. He saw the prison walls as the culmination of his twenty years in this life. He was terrified of another trial because he could not face the victims.

He was bent on dying and relished the physical pain that would come with it because he felt he deserved no less.

Fortunately for Malvo, during that time he was afforded weekly sessions with a counselor. A letter Malvo wrote, dated November 19, 2005, indicates that he had reached a point where the need for a transferential parental figure was no longer necessary. Excerpts from the letter he wrote to me read in part: "From here on out I will desist from referring to you as 'Mom.' You are not my mother and I have to be secure in myself. I'll never find it in others. I've started therapy."

Towards the end of 2005, it became increasingly obvious that Malvo's mental condition was deteriorating. He wrote to my office and told the staff that he no longer wanted further communications. In fact, he said that he would refuse all visits because he was not deserving of even the water that was served.

> I felt like wanting to disappear in a hole somewhere—and just die— which is why I was severing all ties in as painful a way as I could possibly think of. I wrote and said some very hurtful things, all in an attempt to be punished—to be told "You, Malvo, you deserve to die." Just to hear someone I love say it. I tried to make them abandon me because it was true, I did not deserve to continue living.

The overriding guilt and shame that Malvo was experiencing fueled his need to punish me for not facilitating his death. His need to symbolically repudiate the value of his life was very strong, but I could not allow this to undermine my ability to work on other cases. However, I made sure he understood that the lines of communication were still open for him to use.

During the succeeding months, my contact with Malvo was limited. His calls were infrequent, as he indicated that he had to deal with his inner turmoil on his own. He did so through his art, his poems, and the counseling he received in Montgomery County. Compounding his pain was the fact that John Muhammad had been placed in a cell next to his. Each time there was movement in Muhammad's cell, Malvo was reminded of the journey on which Muhammad had taken him and the horrors of their actions.

One evening in early 2006, Malvo called my office and spoke to one of my associates at the time, Eutifan Lange-Cameron. Malvo wanted to explain what was happening to him and why he no longer wanted contact with the outside world. He wanted to hate those who had come to care for him, to cut them off so that he could take his own life, but he could not and he was tormented. Eutifan offered a listening ear. She counseled that life was worth living, and he could use his life to help others avoid the kind of schemes and doctrines to which he had succumbed. Even with the assurance of an empathetic listener, Malvo was still in torment.

> The pain was relentless. I had another breakdown in March, but this time it was worse. The images came rushing at me—too many and too fast—they knocked me out. I woke up to find my pillow bloody—blood coming out of my nose. For three days this happened—for weeks my body shut down, I'd sleep 19 hours a day. The days turned into weeks and I could not find the courage to kill myself.

During another call to my office, Malvo spoke to another staff member. I was not present but received a report about the call. Although he was told that his father, Leslie, had called to express love for him, Malvo did not sound enthused. Malvo further revealed that Muhammad had sent him a message through the guard: "tell my son I love him."

> Muhammad kept sending me these stupid messages like "What's up?" The more he did this the more I thought back on my stupidity and how I allowed him to manipulate me. I decided then that the only way I could begin to make things right not only for the victims but for myself was to testify against Muhammad.

I visited Malvo in March 2006, and very early in the course of our meeting he informed me that he wanted to testify against Muhammad. He further asked that I inform his attorneys that he wanted to see them so they could communicate his decision to the prosecutor. I remember questioning him about whether this was something he was ready to do. He assured me that it was, and that the only way he could go on, even though behind bars for the remainder of his life, was to side with the victims and tell it all.

When Malvo told me his decision, his attorney at the time, Tim Sullivan, was in trial and not able to make the trip to the jail as promptly as Malvo wanted. So Malvo took it upon himself to write the district attorney, Katherine Winfree, to inform her of his intentions. The following is extracted almost in its entirety from Malvo's journal. It speaks of the internal conflict that consumed him as well as his determination to confront Muhammad and side with the victims.

That Friday I met with the prosecution. Over the next two and a half weeks I told them the truth. They made it clear they were promising me nothing. I told them that's fine with me. Several times in those interviews, I got teary eyed, my voice would crack—and Ms. Winfree would ask, "Why are you doing this?" I replied, "For the victims—the truth for what it's worth—and for myself!"

And that's how I found myself in the little booth meeting my attorneys. They were a little worried. "You're gonna be okay, Malvo. Remember, just look at us and the prosecutor's table—we'll be sitting . . ." I told them, "I'll be fine." "Where is Carmeta sitting?" I asked them. "At the end of our row, you should be able to see her," was their reply.

I wasn't nervous before or during testimony—for days everyone was concerned about how I'd react to seeing him—being in close proximity to Muhammad? When I entered court I looked at my attorneys, Carmeta (who smiled at me), the prosecutor's table—and then Muhammad asked to approach the bench.

He was standing but a few feet from me. I was expecting myself to feel something and I did—disgust, anger—this man who once consumed my entire field of vision. He was just a man—not the hero I once worshipped. As I'd predicted, he wanted to represent himself. "But that's stupid," my attorneys kept saying. "The evidence is overwhelming." "Muhammad believes he can talk his way out of anything—he's a control freak!" I told them.

CONFRONTING MUHAMMAD

I answered Ms. Winfree's questions the best I could, reining in my anger. The only time I looked at Muhammad after that was when she asked me to identify him. Then cross-examination was next. "Malvo, control your temper," I told myself, for I wanted to punch him in the mouth not to hear him talk! I asked him to stop addressing me as his son—what kind of father would put his children before a bullet, or send him to murder a child? He has six children, but not one of them was sitting in court. It was his other "son," Lee Boyd Malvo!

So he was bent on establishing the pecking order—damn the evidence—he had to know that he still could cajole, manipulate, twist my mind as he saw fit. So he went at the heartstrings—the times we spent together reading, studying, playing chess and basketball. He brought up Antigua—how I took care of his children while he was arrested on smuggling charges—bringing people into the U.S.—he'd been doing it for months, a dozen at a time.

The worst part of it all dawned on me once I returned to the holding cell—the hours the victims' families had to watch and listen to both of us—murderers! I cried in the cell—bawled—like a baby.

The next morning Muhammad continued his cross-examination. He went over a crime scene or two; I was getting more and more irritated. Then he got onto weapons—showing off—highlighting how little I knew of weapons and how much he did. It was like a demonstration of stupidity, banal in its specificity. "What did you see in him, Malvo?" I asked myself. I wanted this day to be over—to escape the prying eyes. Do they know how I feel? Every person in this courtroom was somehow a victim of this man's mind, and he is totally without remorse. "What is in me that made me capable of these things?" I kept asking myself.

In a *Newsweek* (May 28, 2006) article written by P. Wingert, Mildred Muhammad, John Muhammad's ex-wife, stated that Malvo too was a victim: "I think he was a victim for real. He was a kid looking for a parent. Coming under John's control was a gradual thing. I understand how that can happen." Mildred Muhammad also expressed admiration for Malvo's courage (in testifying against Muhammad): "I was proud of him for being able to speak forcefully and make his points. I know it took a lot of strength for him to do that. I am not trying to be insensitive to the victim's families. But unless you've been under that kind of control, this may be something you cannot understand. I think he was looking forward to proving to John that he was no longer under his control and could look at him and say, 'You took me into your home and made me a monster,' without backing down or quivering or being afraid."

As the months rolled into years, Malvo arrived at the understanding that no one could inflict as much damage as he could on himself. Many youths who are caught up in the criminal justice system can retrace their problems to when they had been victims of abuse, neglect, abandonment, and a host of other factors that contribute to delinquency. However, Malvo expressed his need to relinquish victimhood, so that he could take charge of his own life. He wrote:

I walked like a victim
I talked like a victim

And so I felt like a victim
I even thought like a victim
And I became a victim.
A victim of my own circumstance
Undone by the doings of these two hands

Without making excuses, Malvo now says he recognizes that his perceived victimhood kept him under Muhammad's control. He questions how he came to believe the lies Muhammad taught him. He questions his own intelligence, if he could have been so easily duped. He thinks of the need to move beyond such questions. And the need to move beyond victimhood to what he calls "survivalhood," the ability to retain one's self through crisis.

As he confronts how his own failure of identity has brought crisis to others, Malvo also confronts the need to move beyond the anger, doubt, and self-loathing that have proven destructive. He views remorse as a positive step—an acknowledgment of the victims he had been trained to deny, and of his connection to their lives.

It has been many years since Lee Boyd Malvo, a.k.a. John Lee Muhammad, took the murderous journey with his mentor and master. Since his formal sentencing in March 2004, he has been on a long and lonesome journey toward self-discovery. He writes in part:

> I have had to accept what I've done, what I had become and how my deeds destroyed, and adversely affected that lives of so many. Going beyond the prison of regret, blame, shame and guilt is not easy, but quite necessary. So, in addition to seeing myself as I am, I've also had to learn what love is, I've had to learn forgiveness. I've been the instrument of loss, loss of lives. Losing is something I know well. I've had to let go what I cannot change. There was a time when I wished for death, I was filled with self loathing. But I have come to recognize my responsibility to create a character I can admire, respect and enjoy living with. Why create myself to be someone I hate? There is no way I can live with so great a self-loathing and carry so great a burden of guilt and be truly alive. This is not to say that I will ever stop feeling remorse; it is the case that I have chosen to use my experience advantageously, to inspire me with a new perception. Recognition of error is not enough; the only true repentance is self-reform.
>
> And so I am learning to accept myself. The only way to be free from shame, blame, guilt and regret is to live wholeheartedly and by putting

forth my best effort to live with awareness. This is by no means easy, but necessary. In fact, there is no easy way out. I can no longer live with the pretense and hypocrisy. I cannot lie to myself with impunity, and so I am learning to make peace with my mind.

At this current juncture, I find myself inspired with a new perception—the only freedom and power I possess is to choose how I think. How I choose to think will dictate how I experience life. The challenge is to put into practice and fulfill the promise of this vision, to take this opportunity to allow the best within me to rule the rest.

All that has been said cannot make amends; for with what currency shall I repay such a debt? The story that has been told in the preceding chapters has been told with the hope that an understanding can be arrived at that children need love, guidance and affirmation. Let's not search for those things in the wrong places. The fanatics of the world are only too ready and willing to turn our youths into child soldiers and suicide bombers. The greatest weapon we have is love and in order to embody so subtle an experience, is to be the change we want to see in the world. I seek to find that change in me.

Malvo, who in 2004 admonished me for mentioning God to him, now finds his comfort in knowing that he is a child of God. He follows the Joel Osteen Ministries on TV and has returned to the faith of his childhood. This is his interpretation of the Lord's impact on his life, written on June 12, 2007.

OUR FATHER IN HEAVEN

I am the miracle
The fruits of thy faith
I am the Light to those who hear me
Cease thy inner grumbling and worship me humbly in silence
For I alone can clothe thee in the garments of thine inheritance
I am the light and the day
I am neither old nor young
Finite or infinite
What is—is—and I am that
So let your lips remember My Name
For in My Name all things are revealed.
I am the life of the Living Word

Know that thou art that
The one reality, Truth everlasting.
I am the beginning and the end of thy journey
I am the light of thy salvation
How far have you journeyed in search of me?
My son . . . Know: Past, Present and Future
I am in you and with you always.

4 A Forensic Mental Health Analysis of Lee Boyd Malvo

Jonathan H. Mack, Psy.D.

A s a forensic psychologist/neuropsychologist, I perform forensic neuropsychological and psychological evaluations, frequently for criminal cases in which a person has been charged with or convicted of capital murder. This involves interviewing the accused; reviewing copious case materials and background information; administering, scoring, and interpreting batteries of neuropsychological and psychological tests; writing forensic reports; and testifying, when called upon, about my diagnostic conclusions and opinions. I have evaluated hundreds of murder cases from a neuropsychological or psychological mental health standpoint in the guilt and penalty/punishment phases of the trial and in the postconviction/appeals phases. I have had some cases in common with Ms. Carmeta Albarus. One involved a young man who killed his sister and two of her children in a dissociated state that had some similarities to the case of Lee Boyd Malvo.

I have been in private practice since 1989, with the first several years predominantly focused on part-time hospital practice and neuropsychological and psychological evaluation and treatment. I have always incorporated forensic neuropsychological evaluations in civil cases and the assessment of neuropsychological and psychological damage in children and adults. In the early to mid-1990s I began to get referrals to perform neuropsychological evaluations of defendants facing capital murder charges. I secured additional training through the American Academy of Forensic Psychology and since about 2001 have focused on forensic mental health evaluation, including a large number of criminal cases.

I graduated in 1983 from the Virginia Consortium for Professional Psychology (through the College of William and Mary, Eastern Virginia Medical School, and Old Dominion University in association with Norfolk State University) with an American Psychological Association-approved doctor of psychology degree in clinical psychology with a fourth-year specialization in clinical neuropsychology. I received extensive postdoctoral supervision and training at the Devereux Foundation Center for Head Injuries and other facilities in the early 1990s. I have performed over a thousand forensically oriented neuropsychological and psychological evaluations and have testified approximately two hundred times in criminal, civil, and family court matters at the municipal, state, and federal levels and in depositions.

In preparation for this analysis, I reviewed extensive discovery and expert reports and testimony as well as Ms. Albarus's biography of Mr. Malvo. I also reviewed many of Malvo's drawings, writings, and poems and some of the materials used in the coercive persuasion (otherwise known as brainwashing) by the older John Muhammad, including the movie *The Matrix*; military-type video games like Tom Clancy's Ghost Recon and Ghost Recon Desert Siege; and the book *The Art of War* by Sun Tzu. I did not perform my own research on Malvo's childhood but rather base my opinions on the information supplied to me by Malvo. I did not evaluate Malvo for trial or litigation purposes and did not conduct my own psychological or neuropsychological evaluation of him, although I do these types of evaluations routinely in other homicide cases. I met him one time, at Red Onion State Prison in Virginia in the regular visiting area, behind a glass partition, for about two hours in May 2009. It was established that Malvo understood my role in the book, and he agreed that I would write my analysis as I saw fit and in as objectively as possible, with the understanding that I did not conduct my own independent mental health evaluation of him.

In general, forensic mental health evaluations—in the context of criminal law and in the particular context of helping to determine the mental state of a defendant at the time of a crime—assist the fact finders, i.e., the jury and/or the judge, to understand why the defendant did what he or she did. The key word is "understand." The forensic mental health evaluator determines any and all mental health diagnoses of the defendant, their etiology and approximate time of onset, and explains how these conditions of the mind and/or brain may have interacted with the events of the case/crimes in question.

The mental health expert's role is to provide scientific evidence and to only argue points of view and positions that are supported by the expert's data and background and by the clinical materials on the case. It is presumed that a competent and ethical forensic mental health witness would argue the same opinion whether he or she was retained by the defense or the prosecution. In other words, the duty of the expert is to uncover and explain the truth in order to promote the judge and jury's understanding of a defendant's actions, whereas it is the job of the attorney to advocate for their side (defense or prosecution, in a criminal case). In Malvo's case, a jury weighed the evidence and concluded that he understood the wrongfulness and the nature, purpose, and quality of his acts, and was therefore legally sane and responsible for his actions in the murder of Linda Franklin.

Here I will provide an explanation of forensic mental health evaluations as they relate to Malvo's case and a mental health analysis of Malvo based on a review of numerous documents, test data, and expert reports; and review relevant diagnostic factors that, in my opinion, predisposed him to be vulnerable to the destructive influence of Mr. Muhammad, and thus to his involvement in the sniper killings.

I will review the roles of the different mental health experts in Malvo's case; define the different types of evaluations performed; and review the psychiatric findings and opinions of defense forensic psychiatrist Dr. Neil Blumberg and defense forensic psychologist Dr. Dewey Cornell, the psychological test findings of Dr. Cornell, the court-ordered second opinion sanity evaluation by Dr. Evan S. Nelson, and the neuropsychological test findings of neuropsychologist Dr. David Schretlen, ordered by the defense.

Other factors worth considering in Malvo's case will also be reviewed, including the effects of chronic abuse, neglect, and abandonment; inconsistent/multiple caretakers; his developmental age at the time of the crime; the concept of youth as a mitigator prior to age twenty-three to twenty-five; possible brain damage; Stockholm Syndrome; and relevant cultural issues. The analysis will end with a section on how to help curtail the epidemic of violence in the United States.

The following represents my independent analysis of Malvo and his situation. I acknowledge that others may hold a different view and that an analysis is not definite proof; however, the opinions presented here are based on my years of experience in the field of forensic and clinical psychology and neuropsychology and review of numerous documents regarding Malvo. My analysis is written with the awareness that the jury in the Malvo case involving the murder of Linda Franklin did not find for the insanity defense argued by Dr. Blumberg and convicted Malvo of first-degree murder, but did not sentence him to death, partly due to his chronological age of seventeen at the time of the crimes and to psychological mitigating factors argued by his defense team.

I do weigh the evidence that I have reviewed and come to my own conclusions about what Malvo's mental health diagnoses were at the time of the homicides. I have developed my own view about what mental health defenses were sustainable in his case, based on the information available to me, acknowledging that I did not evaluate Malvo independently and that not all mental health experts would come to the same conclusions. The standard for arguing a forensic mental health finding is by a preponderance of the evidence, i.e., more likely (51 percent or greater) than not, and I am comfortable with the opinions I have reached within that framework. When a jury convicts of first-degree/capital murder, they are typically doing so to the standard of beyond a reasonable doubt. However, this is not the standard that forensic experts are held to in proffering their mental health opinions.

Acts of tragic violence are often presaged by tragedy in the childhood of the perpetrator. One of the lessons that we hope will be learned from the multiple tragedies of the D.C. sniper killings—of which Malvo himself is a victim—is that abandonment, instability, abuse, neglect, and extreme inconsistency in childhood can cause more problems and, frequently in the case of males, lead to violent criminal acts. The countervailing lesson is that love, security, and consistency in childhood tend to create secure individuals with strong egos, who are better equipped to become productive and law-abiding members of society. These lessons are often overlooked as explanations of adult behavior, amid the pharmaceutical company cant that mental disorders are necessarily incurable diseases, not environmentally induced developmental reactions. If we understand why violence is committed by adults and adolescents, in general and in this particular case, we are in a much stronger position to control the current epidemic of violence by taking steps to improve early childhood environments.

Another point that we would like to make is that interventions that may lead to prevention of future violence need to address the underlying causes of the bad environment, as opposed to masking symptoms with medication or other strategies. Many youths who commit homicide (and suicide) are discovered to be on various antidepressants, as in the case of one of the Columbine High School shooters (Gibbs and Roche 1999). We believe that if even one person had stood up for Malvo to keep him in a positive foster placement, such as with the Maxwells, free from his mother's constant disruption of the positives in his life, he would not have been susceptible to Muhammad's machinations.

We believe that Malvo's childhood set him up for a variety of psychological disorders including chronic Depression, Post-traumatic Stress Disorder (PTSD), and Dissociative Disorders, all of which will be discussed in the following pages. Our thesis is that broken and impaired attachments and emotional neglect and abuse in childhood tend to increase the likelihood of psychological disorders that may help set the stage for future violence.

THE ROLE OF MENTAL HEALTH EXPERTS IN CRIMINAL CASES

Criminal law specifies that for a defendant to be convicted of first-degree or capital murder, the prosecution must prove that his or her mental state at the time of the crime was consistent with intentional, knowing, and purposeful murder. In response, the defense can argue in the guilt phase of the trial that the defendant was unable to form the "mens rea" or culpable mental state during the crime, or can present in the penalty phase of the trial mitigating factors as reasons to spare the defendant's life. Once an individual is convicted of first-degree murder in a jurisdiction that has the death penalty, there is typically a second trial to determine the sentence, which will be either life in prison without the possibility of parole or the death penalty. The decision is rendered by the fact finder—the judge or the jury—based on consideration of the weight of the aggravating versus mitigating factors. In a case like Malvo's, aggravating factors would include the obviously deliberate, merciless, extensive, and multiplicative nature of the crimes and the seriality and number of the homicides that occurred. Mitigating factors would include Malvo's young age at the time, and the fact that at age seventeen the frontal cortex of his brain was not fully developed. Findings from neuroscience suggest that the human brain does not fully mature until about age twenty-three to twenty-five (Walsh 2004). Other mitigating factors would be his history of abandonment, neglect, and abuse; the rather obvious nature of the coercive persuasion (brainwashing) at the hands of Muhammad; and various mental health diagnoses— Dissociative Disorder NOS, chronic Depression, and Reactive Attachment Disorder of Early Childhood, Diffuse Type.

Dissociative Disorder involves splitting off parts of oneself as a defense mechanism against severe stress. Reactive Attachment Disorder is damage to the development of the basic abilities to attach and relate to others as a consequence of early broken attachments and severe disappointments. Malvo's chronic depression was a result of his broken attachments, the loss of an inattentive mother and attentive father and chronically disrupted foster-type placements—replaced by maternal narcissism and both maternal and paternal abandonment. Well-meaning people did try to help, but as soon as they did, their efforts were thwarted by Malvo's mother.

This section will give a brief overview of Malvo's mental health defenses, with some general discussion of appropriate evaluations and procedures in this type of capital murder case, including the roles of the forensic neuropsychologist/psychologist, forensic social worker, and forensic psychiatrist.

Although the word "forensic" is popularly associated with forensic pathology, involving the medical analysis of a corpse for legal purposes, the term implies the application of any field to legal matters, particularly in criminal, civil, or family court. Thus, the forensic social worker, the forensic psychologist, the forensic neuropsychologist, and the forensic psychiatrist are all mental health experts who apply their varied expertise to legal matters. Forensic mental health experts can work for the defense, for the prosecution, or directly for the court in criminal cases.

Criminal law proceedings involve making determinations about the mental state of the defendant at the time of a crime, because serious crimes often involve intentional, purposeful, and knowing actions that comprise some of the elements of the crime. The high stakes involved in forensic mental health evaluation of defendants charged with a capital crime mandate a detailed and thorough approach. If the work is not done thoroughly in the initial trial, the door may be opened for an immensely expensive and time-consuming appeals process postconviction.

In Malvo's case, the defense and prosecution employed a number of different mental health experts. The defense hired what is known as a mitigation specialist, Carmeta Albarus, LCSW (Licensed Clinical Social Worker). Mitigation specialists are usually master's-level mental health professionals with degrees in social work and are frequently Licensed Social Workers or Licensed Clinical Social Workers. The discipline of social work focuses on elucidating and understanding the social and environmental influences on an individual's development, quite suited to the type of background investigation required in these cases.

Mitigation specialists are charged with performing extremely detailed investigations of a defendant's background, often traveling to the places where the defendant was born and raised; interviewing family members, teachers, and others who knew the defendant and his or her history; obtaining all manner of records on the lives of the defendant and relevant family members; extensively interviewing the defendant; and providing summary reports and testimony on the facts of the defendant's life. In murder cases, the mitigation specialist gathers evidence that may be used in the defense's presentation of mitigating factors, to outweigh the aggravating factors presented by the prosecution in arguing for the death penalty. The forensic social worker/mitigation specialist guides the defense attorney to ensure that the full range of mitigating factors relevant to a particular case is presented at trial.

Because the Constitution requires maximum thoroughness in defending a case where capital punishment may be the sentence, all possible factors that may prove mitigating need to be presented to the jury and weighed against aggravating factors. Thus, the role of the mitigation specialist is, in contrast to the role of the forensic psychologist, neuropsychologist, and psychiatrist, oriented to investigation on the defense side, although the information they unearth is relevant to the prosecution as well because it may flesh out possible mitigation or guilt-phase defenses, such as insanity or diminished capacity.

Frequently, the forensic psychologist and neuropsychologist on a capital homicide case will work hand in hand with the forensic social worker/mitigation specialist, who will provide the most complete background data possible to help the doctor form a comprehensive picture of the defendant's background. In rare instances, it may be necessary for the mitigation specialist to assist in gaining the cooperation of the client in his own defense. This tends to happen in cases of defendants who have some type of Dissociative Disorder, as did Malvo, as diagnosed by his mental health professionals and by me. Dissociation is a psychological defense mechanism of the human mind against overwhelming psychological stress and trauma, usually developing in response, initially, to childhood trauma. In the case of Malvo, an adolescent whom Dr. Blumberg argued was in a dissociated state and completely identified with his victimizer, John Muhammad, it was necessary for Ms. Albarus to venture into some critical incident stress debriefing work to break his identification with Muhammad.

Critical incident stress debriefing is a term used in mental health services to describe the process by which a mental health worker, psychologist, psychiatrist, or licensed clinical social worker intervenes in the acute phase of a reaction to a major psychosocial stressor, e.g., exposure to a shooting or violence, a natural disaster, a severe accident, or war crimes. For example, it is fairly common in police work that following a officer's weapon discharge, the officer will be debriefed by a police psychologist to determine if there is any symptomatic reaction to the stress, to educate the individual about the signs and symptoms of PTSD, and to perform any needed mental health interventions.

Ms. Albarus conducted a series of approximately thirty interviews with Malvo to help extricate him from his psychological bondage to Muhammad, so that he could assist his attorney in his own defense at trial. The goal was to help him reconnect with his disassociated self, who was very different from the child soldier he had become at the hands of Muhammad. The fact that Malvo attached to Ms. Albarus so quickly, shedding his complete identification with Muhammad, indicates that the diffuse nature of his attachments was a consequence of broken attachments in early childhood. Diffuse attachments are part of the criteria for Reactive Attachment Disorder of Infancy or Early Childhood—Inhibited Type, which is marked by "indiscriminate sociability with marked inability to exhibit appropriate selective attachments (e.g., excessive familiarity with relative strangers or lack of selectivity in choice of attachment figures)" (*DSM-IV-TR* Diagnostic Criteria, 2000). Malvo's propensity toward diffuse attachments stemmed, in my opinion, from his history of neglect, abandonment, and abuse, leaving him vulnerable to attach—at the tender age of fifteen—to any father figure who would give him positive attention, and able to switch his attachment to Albarus in the course of about seven weeks, even as an older teenager. The fact that Malvo began calling Ms. Albarus "Mom" at age seventeen or eighteen, after having called Muhammad "Dad," is a clear indication of the diffuse and intense nature of his attachments.

Ms. Albarus was a particularly apt choice as mitigation specialist because she is Jamaican and therefore has a clear sense of the cultural issues involved in Malvo's case. The defense hired four additional mental health experts: Neil Blumberg, M.D., a forensic psychiatrist; Dewey Cornell, Ph.D., a forensic psychologist; David Schretlen, Ph.D., a clinical neuropsychologist; and a specialist in brainwashing/induced dissociative disorders and Stockholm Syndrome.

The forensic psychiatrist is a trained physician who has completed a residency in psychiatry. There is specialty certification for this kind of psychiatry. The forensic psychiatrist typically conducts a clinical interview or interviews of the examinee, in some cases performs collateral interviews with other informants about the examinee's life, performs a mental status examination, and reviews available records. The mental status examination is an extremely cursory screening of mental functions that takes about five minutes. It does not include any way to determine if the examinee is lying about their symptoms or exaggerating deficits. The forensic psychiatrist will at times focus on the effects of substance abuse and dependence, issues of mental competency, mental state at the time of a crime, and other forensic mental health issues. The forensic psychiatrist often answers the same questions as the forensic psychologist, but uses a two-pronged approach of clinical interviewing and review of background materials, as opposed to the three-pronged approach of forensic psychologists and neuropsychologists that includes administering reliable and valid batteries of neuropsychological and psychological tests. All these specialists make clear to the examinee the forensic nature of the evaluations, including the particular limits to confidentiality and the fact that there is no treating relationship between the psychiatrist and the examinee.

Dr. Blumberg spent approximately fifty-six hours interviewing Malvo and rendered a number of opinions to the jury involving his mental state at the time of the murder of Linda Franklin. These included the opinion that Malvo was insane at the time: that he did not know and understand the wrongfulness of his actions, having been overwhelmed due to coercive persuasion by Muhammad. Dr. Blumberg argued that Malvo's dissociative state was in reaction to dissociative and depressive tendencies developed in response to childhood trauma.

The structure of criminal forensic mental health evaluation as practiced by forensic psychologists and neuropsychologists in general can be described as a three-legged stool, defined as follows.

One leg is the review of all possible background materials on the defendant, including but not limited to birth records, records and history of family members, school records, vocational records, medical records, psychiatric records, military service records, records related to substance abuse, criminal records, etc. Included in this are interviews of collateral sources, such as parents, siblings, schoolteachers, and so forth. This leg of the stool is frequently supplemented by the mitigation specialist's research in a capital murder defense case.

The second leg is in-depth clinical interviewing of the defendant/examinee. It is explained to the examinee that a forensic mental health evaluation is different than a clinical mental health assessment in that there is very limited confidentiality and that the report, if utilized, will be shared with all the parties involved in the case. The examinee is also informed that there is no treating relationship with the mental health professional, who is responsible not to the examinee but to the authority that has hired the expert—the defense attorney, the prosecutor, or the court. This portion of the evaluation may include screening measures for mood as well as brief structured examinations of mental status such as orientation to person, place, and time, and very cursory measures of short-term memory, attention, word finding, constructional praxis (copying ability), simple reading, and writing. These screening measures do not substitute for detailed psychological and neuropsychological testing.

The third leg of the forensic mental health examination stool is the administration of reliable and valid batteries of psychological and neuropsychological tests. These must include measures to determine symptom validity, in two categories. One category is tests that determine if the examinee is giving good effort, to rule out poor effort or malingering as a cause of poor performance on the neurocognitive tests, such as tests of memory. The other category is tests to determine if the examinee is answering questions about psychiatric symptoms honestly, both in interviews and on psychological self-report inventories. An examinee can give invalid responses (show response bias) in one of two directions: symptom exaggeration or feigning and symptom minimization, defensiveness or deliberately saying that a symptom is not present when it is. Symptom validity testing is mandatory in the context of a forensic mental health assessment, because the individual would benefit from a certain outcome to the evaluation. In a criminal mental health examination where the individual may receive a lesser sentence if they are judged insane or incompetent, there is a temptation to exaggerate symptoms of mental illness or signs of brain damage. In other contexts, such as in an evaluation for fitness to be a parent or fitness to carry a weapon in a law enforcement officer, the tendency is to minimize symptoms so as to not have a child removed or lose a job.

The Test of Memory Malingering (Tombaugh 1996) is an example of a well-validated and reliable test to determine if an individual is exerting full effort on a neurocognitive, in this case memory, task. The Minnesota Multiphasic Personality Inventory-2 (MMPI-2) (Butcher, Dahlstrom, Graham, Tellegen, and Kaemmer 2001) and the Personality Assessment Inventory (PAI) (Morey 1991) are examples of personality tests that have built-in validity scales to help reliably determine whether or not an individual is tending toward "faking good" or "faking bad" in answering the questions.

These tests are self-report inventories performed under the supervision of the psychologist. The validity scales also assess whether the examinee's responses were random or consistent. The Structured Interview of Reported Symptoms-2 (SIRS-2) (Rogers, Bagby, and Dickens 1992) is an example of a measure for assessing symptom malingering in forensic cases, especially the faking of psychotic symptoms.

The point of psychological and neuropsychological testing is that an individual's mind and brain are far too complicated to assess through only a clinical interview, mental status examination, and record review. It is necessary to have test results that are scientifically and actuarially accurate in order to fully assess an individual's personality, the accuracy of the clinical impression, and an individual's neurocognitive function and/or the presence of brain damage (Faust and Ziskin, 1988). This psychologist ensures that the neuropsychological test battery in homicide cases evaluates all major functions of the brain. In *Higher Cortical Functions in Man* (Luria 1966), Dr. Luria defines a useful model for evaluating brain functions. He begins with the fact that the brain has four lobes (frontal, temporal, parietal, and occipital), two hemispheres (right and left), a mesencephalon, and a brain stem. Each lobe handles a specific modality, and each lobe/modality has a primary, secondary, and tertiary cortex. This is a useful model for structuring thorough batteries of neuropsychological tests in forensic cases in particular. This evaluation will cover such areas as:

- intellectual functions;
- attention and concentration;
- memory functions;
- language and academic functions;
- motor and perceptual-motor functions;
- sensory-perceptual functions;
- executive-frontal functions;
- measures of mental effort and response bias;
- summary scores of brain dysfunction (when available), e.g., summary scores from the Halstead Reitan Neuropsychological Battery;
- the assessment of emotional state and personality.

The forensic neuropsychologist and/or forensic psychologist will also frequently administer detailed, objective measures of personality functioning and sometimes tests to answer specific forensic questions, such as the prediction of future violence/violence recidivism, the presence of predatory sexual or pedophilic tendencies, competency to stand trial, or the presence of antisocial tendencies.

CULTURAL SENSITIVITY

It is of critical importance that the forensic mental health evaluator be sensitive to cultural factors and influences that may affect the presentation of a particular client (American Psychological Association 2002). For example, an individual may have been raised in a country different from where the test was normed; this may create error variance in the data interpretation. When English is a second language for a defendant, additional error variance must also be considered, such as a spurious relative weakness in verbal abilities.

In the case of the young Malvo, an issue that came into his trial was the fact that he was reported to have thrown stones at cats in Jamaica as a child. This gained the attention of the mental health experts because cruelty to animals is a symptom of Childhood or Adolescent onset Conduct Disorder, according to the *DSM-IV-TR* (2000). Onset prior to the age of fifteen is a requirement for the diagnosis of Antisocial Personality Disorder (APD). APD is a mental health diagnosis that is not helpful to mitigation and is a formal way of saying that in essence, the individual is a bad person and considered incurable. However, in Jamaica, cats are viewed with suspicion, and it is customary and socially acceptable there to throw stones at them. Therefore, in the case of Malvo, it would be useful to determine if his destructive behavior toward cats was socially appropriate, as opposed to a manifestation of antisocial acting out and/or Conduct Disorder.

MENTAL HEALTH DEFENSES AND
MENTAL HEALTH EVALUATIONS

It is the role of the forensic psychologist and forensic psychiatrist to evaluate certain legal mental health questions pertaining to a defendant's mental state at the time of a crime; the defendant's competency to stand trial at a particular time; the defendant's capacity to have waived a particular right, such as the right to silence in a police investigation, at a particular time; and to determine potentially mitigating mental health diagnoses. The forensic psychologist and psychiatrist present their opinions to the court and the fact finder, which is either the judge or the jury, within a reasonable degree of psychological, neuropsychological, or medical scientific certainty (i.e., by a preponderance of the evidence/more likely than not). Then the fact finder makes the final determination as to whether or not a defendant meets a certain legal standard, such as competency to stand trial or not guilty by reason of insanity or inability to formulate the specific intent to kill at the time of the crime, based on the weight of the evidence presented and on the credibility of the expert(s). In this case, Dr. Blumberg argued that Malvo was technically insane, but the jury did not agree and found him to be sane.

The Ability to Waive Rights

The ability to waive rights refers to whether or not an individual is able to knowingly, intelligently, and voluntarily give up certain legal rights. This issue arises frequently in situations in which an individual might have been, for example, intoxicated or intimidated at the time of waiving his or her Miranda right to silence, thereby giving a confession to the police that may not have been rendered in a fully knowing, intelligent, and voluntary manner, which is the legal standard for a valid confession or statement. The role of the forensic psychologist or forensic psychiatrist is to determine the state of mind of the defendant at the time the relevant rights were waived, and if the waiver was done in an intelligent, knowing, and voluntary manner. Frequently, it is necessary to understand the underlying psychopathology or neuropsychopathology of the defendant in order to do this. For example, it is relevant whether or not an individual has mental retardation; is impaired in spoken language/auditory comprehension; is impaired in the understanding of written language; was in a state of delirium or had dementia; or was schizophrenic and/or in a psychotic state at the time the rights were waived. All such diagnoses would mean the defendant might potentially be unable to give a fully knowing, intelligent, and voluntary waiver of his or her rights.

It is incumbent upon the mental health expert to understand not only the diagnoses of the individual but also the specific facts of the case at the time of the confession. Thus, the mental health expert will frequently review the waiver form used by the police, as well as the actual audio or video recordings of any statements. Forensic psychological and neuropsychological tests may be useful in specifically determining a defendant's comprehension and other issues pertaining to his or her capacity to waive rights.

Dr. Cornell raised the point in his supplementary report (*Supplementary Report* 2003) that Malvo's initial statement to the police that he was the shooter in every one of the homicides was patently false and a direct outgrowth of his state of mind pursuant to coercive persuasion by Muhammad. Dr. Cornell argued that Malvo was so overidentified with and pathologically attached that he confessed to all the shootings as a way of protecting his "father" at all costs. Other experts would agree that Malvo's overidentification with the aggressor "raises serious doubts about the credibility of his confession to law enforcement officers and other statements he made concerning his degree of involvement in a series of criminal acts of violence" (49). These confessions were made in statements that I have reviewed, and I agree with Dr. Cornell's report.

Competency to Stand Trial

The forensic mental health expert is often asked to determine whether an individual is competent to stand trial. This typically involves the defendant having an understanding of the different actors in the legal system, such as the defense lawyer, the prosecutor, the judge, and the jury, and of the significance of different legal scenarios, such as the full consequences of entering into a negotiated plea agreement with the prosecutor, which involves waiving any right to a future trial because there is a plea of guilty. The model for competency to stand trial stems from the case of Dusky v. United States (1960). There are several standardized and reasonably well-validated forensic psychological instruments for evaluating a defendant's current competency, including the Competency Assessment Tool—Mental Retardation, the MacArthur Competence Assessment Tool—Criminal Adjudication, and the Evaluation of Competency to Stand Trial—Revised. However, the forensic mental health examiner must determine the defendant's mental state at the time of trial according to the relevant statutes of the jurisdiction.

In Malvo's case, it appeared to be the opinion of his defense team that he so overidentified with his perceived father figure, Muhammad, that he was initially unable to assist his attorneys in his own defense. For example, he wanted to take all the blame, to be executed and to spare the life of his "father." The fact that Malvo went from accepting all the blame to being a primary witness against Muhammad appears to be a result of the debriefing from his mental health team, especially Ms. Carmeta Albarus. This was further facilitated by interviews Malvo had with significant others from his past, including his teacher, Winsome Maxwell, and hearing the voice of his father, Leslie Malvo. These experiences seem to have helped him get in touch with the old, buried Lee Boyd Malvo, as opposed to the new, coerced John Lee Muhammad identity.

Some experts would agree that Malvo appeared to have Reactive Attachment Disorder of Infancy or Early Childhood, Disinhibited Type (*DSM-IV-TR* 2000). This disorder describes the mental states of infants and young children who have severely broken and disrupted attachments. The effects can be extremely persistent throughout the individual's life. The *DSM-IV-TR* describes two types, the Inhibited Type and the Disinhibited Type. In the Inhibited Type, the child develops an extremely watchful, hypervigilant, and socially withdrawn response set (128). In the Disinhibited Type, the child's attachments are diffuse and the child "exhibits indiscriminate sociability or a lack of selectivity in the choice of attachment figures" (128). This condition is associated with "grossly pathological care that may take the form of persistent disregard of the child's basic emotional needs for comfort, stimulation, and affection; persistent disregard of the child's basic physical needs; or repeated changes of primary caregiver that prevent formation of stable attachments (e.g., frequent changes in foster care)" (128).

Some experts may agree that Malvo's inconsistent attention from his father in early childhood culminating in abandonment at age five, the neglect and abuse from his mother, and the fact that his mother sabotaged every one of his positive placements laid the foundation for an extreme attachment void, leading to diffuse attachments, in which Malvo was extremely vulnerable to the overidentified attachment to Muhammed. This appeared to make it easy for Malvo to quickly attachm to Muhammad as his "father" and also to fairly rapidly switch his attachment to Carmeta Albarus over the course of about thirty visits with her. The fact that Malvo quickly began calling her "Mom" and continued to do so for the next two years (starting at the age of eighteen) is poignantly indicative of both his emotional immaturity and his disinhibited, rapid, and extremely intense attachments. The fact that Malvo was so quick to attach to Muhammad as "Dad" and then to Ms. Albarus as "Mom" in mid to late adolescence is, in my professional opinion, indicative of a diagnosis of Reactive Attachment Disorder, Disinhibited Type.

Diminished Capacity

The forensic psychologist or psychiatrist may be asked to comment on a defendant's ability to formulate the intent to carry out the crime with which he or she is charged, if there were underlying diseases of the mind or brain. This deals with one aspect of the formulation of the "mens rea," or culpable state of mind: intentionality, and the individual's capacity to act in a purposeful, knowing, and intelligent manner (Wulach 1998). If the defendant lacked this ability at the time of the crime, a successful diminished-capacity defense will not eliminate guilt, but may lead to conviction of a lesser crime, such as simple assault instead of aggravated assault, or second- or third-degree murder instead of first-degree or, in some states, capital murder.

Malvo's defense psychiatrist and psychologist argued that he was unable to formulate the specific intent to kill Linda Franklin as a consequence of his underlying psychiatric diagnoses. This involved the Dissociative Disorder Not Otherwise Specified (NOS) diagnosis by Dr. Blumberg, based on the opinion that Malvo developed dissociative tendencies as a child as a defense mechanism against broken attachments, heartbreak, abuse, and neglect. This led to a tendency to dissociate that left him supremely vulnerable to being brainwashed by Muhammad. The argument was in essence that Malvo was so in the grip of his coerced identification and overattachment to Muhammad that he was not in his right mind and was therefore not acting in a manner consistent with his true self. It is my opinion that Malvo's desperate desire to attach to a father figure, combined with his chronological age and his juvenile brain, allowed his former sense of who he was to be completely subverted, and that his crimes were therefore not intentional in the full sense of the word.

Dr. Nelson, who took the opposing view, argued that although Malvo "was highly influenced by John Muhammad [and] Mr. Malvo's background of neglect and immaturity relative to Mr. Muhammad made him more susceptible to this influence," nonetheless Malvo was capable of formulating the specific intent to kill Linda Franklin (2003:25). Specifically, Dr. Nelson opined that Malvo's dissociation, if it did exist, did not "destroy his ability to control his impulses at the moment he shot or aided Mr. Muhammad in shooting Linda Franklin." Dr. Nelson instead argued that Malvo became "desensitized to the experience of killing a person." This is a very fine distinction, and misses the key point that Malvo's ego was subverted by his Dissociative Disorder and by the coercive persuasion perpetrated against him by Muhammad. Dr. Nelson, in my opinion, portrays Malvo as more culpable for his actions than he was.

Some experts would agree that the extremity of Malvo's experience of abuse and neglect as a child and his consequent depressive and dissociative tendencies, in combination with the extreme coercive techniques used by Muhammad, led to a loss of himself that severely diminished his capacity to make independent judgments. In addition, Malvo's ego structure was extremely weak because he was still a juvenile and unprotected by those around him. All this made him particularly vulnerable to Muhammad—the proverbial wolf in sheep's clothing.

Not Guilty by Reason of Insanity

The not guilty by reason of insanity defense stems from the M'Naghten Case (1843). An individual is judged to have been in such an impaired mental state at the time of the commission of a crime that he or she was either unable to appreciate the wrongfulness of his or her conduct or unable to appreciate the nature, purpose, or quality of his or her actions at the time of the offense. The M'Naghten defense is derived from English Common Law recognizing that conviction of a crime requires that the defendant have a culpable or guilty state of mind. Thus, if an individual is adjudicated to have been legally insane at the time of a crime, he or she cannot be held legally responsible and is therefore not guilty. Juries are very reluctant to find a defendant not guilty by reason of insanity for a violent crime, partly because such a person is typically committed to a forensic mental health institution and may eventually be released if found by designated mental health professionals to no longer be a danger to self or others.

Dr. Blumberg specifically opined that Malvo was not able to appreciate the wrongfulness of his actions in the homicide of Linda Franklin due to the influence on and overbearing of his mind and will by Muhammad, and argued that he was therefore technically insane at the time due to Dissociative Disorder NOS, including the effects of coercive persuasion (*Commonwealth v. Lee Boyd Malvo* 2003). Dr. Blumberg also argued that Malvo was unable to formulate the intent to kill, which is the third criterion (after not understanding the nature, character, and consequences of the act and being unable to distinguish right from wrong) of the Virginia statute that defines when a defendant may be considered insane at the time of the crime. Forensic psychologist Dr. Cornell agreed with Dr. Blumberg. The opposing expert, Dr. Nelson, disagreed.

Some experts would agree that Malvo was in a highly dissociated state at the time of the homicide due to his psychological vulnerabilities and the extremity of the coercive tactics used on him by Muhammad, and that this tended to diminish his capacity to appreciate the wrongfulness of his criminal acts. It could be argued that Malvo's will was so overborne by Muhammad's schemes that he believed Muhammad's rants about his ends justifying his means.

Mitigating Factors

Mitigating factors are facts and circumstances used to argue for lessening a sentence or penalty after a person is convicted of a crime. These can include watered-down versions of a diminished-capacity defense, such as inability of a defendant to conform his or her behavior to the requirements of law due to psychiatric, psychological, or neurological damage; extreme mental or emotional disturbance; the chronological age of the defendant and the fact that the prefrontal cortex of the brain does not fully mature until about age twenty-three to twenty-five; or any other factors in the defendant's life that might counterbalance the aggravating factors raised by the prosecution (catchall mitigation).

Dr. Cornell opined that Malvo acted under extreme mental and emotional disturbance at the time of the alleged offense (*Capital Sentencing Mitigation Report* 2003). The disturbance was a consequence of his psychiatric diagnoses, his youth, and his vulnerability to the perceived manipulations and machinations of his "father," John Muhammad. Dr. Cornell also argued that Malvo was unable to appreciate the criminality of his conduct or to conform his behavior to the requirements of law as a consequence of his Dissociative Disorder NOS.

The defense also argued that Malvo's was a juvenile (age seventeen) at the time of the homicide and that therefore he should not receive the death penalty. This was prior to the Supreme Court decision Roper v. Simmons (2005), which made it illegal to execute a defendant who was younger than eighteen at the time of the homicide. The jury accepted that the mitigating factors presented by Dr. Cornell outweighed the aggravating factors and spared Malvo's life.

The neuropsychologist in a capital homicide case should reference the fact that when an individual is at or below the age of about twenty-three to twenty-five, the prefrontal cortex is not fully developed. Specifically, in human beings, the anterior frontal lobes of the brain, which are critical in the ability to inhibit dangerous or socially inappropriate impulses, are not fully mature until about age twenty-four (Beckman 2004; Bower 2004). This relates to the decision of Roper v. Simmons. An additional point to be made in Malvo's case was that he was only fifteen years of age when first exposed to Muhammad. Thus, his twisted attachment to Muhammad began not when he was seventeen, but rather when he was a younger teenager.

Catchall mitigation is the use of anything in the defendant's history that might potentially weigh against aggravating factors. In Malvo's case, many experts would agree that his childhood history of abandonment, constantly changing caretakers, emotional and physical abuse, and his consequent mental health diagnoses constituted catchall mitigators.

PSYCHIATRIC EVALUATION OF LEE BOYD MALVO

Malvo was evaluated by a forensic psychiatrist, Dr. Blumberg. In his guilt phase testimony, the transcript of which I reviewed, Dr. Blumberg stated that Malvo had a Dissociative Disorder Not Otherwise Specified (NOS) as a consequence of his preexisting vulnerability to and the brainwashing and indoctrination by Muhammad. Dr. Blumberg also diagnosed Malvo with Depressive Disorder NOS and Conduct Disorder, Childhood-Onset Type.

Dissociative Disorder involves defenses that enable an individual's mind to cut off aspects of memory and the self that are overly threatening and terrifying. When a person is dissociated, they are in an altered state of consciousness involving feelings of unreality, psychogenic amnesia, depersonalization (feeling like an automaton), and emotional numbness. If a person has the need for this type of defense mechanism, it is a sign that environmental stressors are very severe and toxic, and frequently of early onset.

Depression is, in a sense, the psychological consequence of failed or inadequate defenses, in which the individual feels overwhelmed by their circumstances. Depression can lead in some cases to wanting to die or to suicide attempts. It should be kept in mind that suicide and homicide are both about rage and desperation, either turned inward or turned outward. The outward expression of rage often involves a breakdown of executive-frontal controls that normally regulate behavior, which is one reason neuropsychological assessment can be critical in homicide cases.

Dr. Blumberg conducted twenty interviews with the defendant for a total of about fifty hours. He observed frequent inappropriate laughter. In his testimony on December 23, 2003, Dr.Blumberg observed that

> his presentation though was really very odd. The most notable thing is
> that there was frequent inappropriate laughter. He was almost at times

elated and [had] what I would call a somewhat manic quality to his answers. He was greatly grandiose in the things that he talked about . . . he
seemed to at times . . . [to] go off on a tangent, and I had a hard time
understanding, well, how we got from Point A to Point B. That presentation raised questions what—raised questions in my mind about what
was going on with him at this point, whether we were dealing with somebody who had a bipolar disorder or somebody who might be having an
underlying psychotic process, because it was a very strange and peculiar
presentation at first. (*Commonwealth v. Lee Boyd Malvo* 2003:9–10)

Dr. Blumberg noted that during the second interview on December 19,
2002, Malvo presented with the "same quality of his responses and also
preoccupation with providing kind of a canted summary of political, so-
ciological jargon . . . almost sounding like he was programmed and regur-
gitating this information" (10).

Dr. Blumberg noted that in his first few visits with Malvo, "he related
pretty clearly . . . that he wanted to die, and you know, he really was not
interested in helping himself, and he made comments such as that" (11).
Dr. Blumberg indicated that by the eighth interview, on May 30, he had
come to an awareness that Malvo had been taken advantage of by Muhammad. Dr. Blumberg stated in his direct examination that Malvo perceived
Muhammad as the perfect father who could do no wrong.

Dr. Blumberg discussed how Malvo's mother had left him at the age
of nine, and described Malvo's fascination with and intense attraction to
Muhammad and how Muhammad took care of and doted upon his three
children. Dr. Blumberg described how Malvo was "totally amazed at the interaction that [Muhammad] had with his kids . . . this was something that
was amazing to him as well as something that was, you know, tremendously
missing from his life prior to that. Much of his earlier existence [he'd] been
absent an adequate parent" (13). As Dr. Blumberg explained, due to his
prior experiences of abandonment, abuse, and neglect, Malvo was essentially a proverbial sitting duck to Muhammad's fox. Dr. Blumberg further
opined that Malvo "is a kid, who for a very extended period of time, missed
a parent and was, I think, clinically depressed for much of his childhood
especially after the age of nine when his mom started leaving" (14).

Dr. Blumberg stated that when Malvo began living with Muhammad, he
began following all of his teachings about Islam, the rhetoric of Louis Farrakhan, and "the history of slavery, getting an indoctrination as to what it

might have been to be a very oppressed black person in America. He lost his accent. He [originally] had a really prominent Jamaican accent. He became basically a sponge for all of the rhetoric that Muhammad was willing to give. They exercised. They trained. They ran. He learned aspects of the illegal business that Muhammad was in, and they had contingency plans for what would happen if Muhammad had a problem that he would take over" (17). The vegetarian and Spartan lifestyle, the changing of Malvo's religion and his accent were "the beginning phases of what I had diagnosed as a dissociative disorder, and what it involves is really the beginning deterioration in his own identity and really melding himself with Muhammad, losing his own sense of self, and becoming one with the person that he viewed as his father" (17). Dr. Blumberg further described this process as an indoctrination period. "Indoctrination can cause coercive persuasion, the feeding of information, the controlling all aspects of the individual's behavior, thinking, all of these [factors] can begin to influence their own sense of identity, and again, as part of this process of indoctrination . . . lead[ing] to the loss of identity which is a feature of Dissociative Disorder" (17–18).

Dr. Blumberg described the period when Malvo and Muhammad lived in Bellingham, Washington, as the start of "a whole process of what later became apparent was a clear-cut indoctrination in terms of training, physical exercise, and the use [of] and the training in weapons, all of that became part of the program that he was subjected to" (24). As noted earlier in this book, Malvo registered in school in Bellingham as "John Lee Muhammad." Dr. Blumberg opined that this was not only a name change but also "a literal adopting of the personality, but the more important aspect was not just the name. There were plenty of people who assume aliases. He was psychologically the son of John Muhammad" (24).

Importantly, Dr. Blumberg described that "as a youngster [Malvo] was zoning out, putting his mind elsewhere . . . a dissociative symptom to hide from your feelings, from your thoughts, but when he got to Bellingham, the process was he was becoming one with Muhammad . . . and becoming part of him" (25). Malvo had learned instinctively to use the psychological defense mechanism of dissociation as a way to cope with the abandonment, stress, and neglect he experienced in early childhood, years before he met Muhammad. The fact that Malvo already knew how to dissociate predisposed him, in my opinion, to be especially vulnerable to the coercive persuasion by Muhammad.

Dr. Blumberg also discussed the desensitization to violence that Malvo underwent with Muhammad:

He's being shown various movies of battle movies, sniper movies, video games of a violent content. Training, again, the weapons, the whole process of what I would call a desensitization to various violent aspects. These kinds of things are presented to him as if "we're not really going to necessarily use them, but in order for me to get my kids back." . . . [Malvo] described not only reading and discussing books, history, Farrakhan speeches, Malcolm X speeches with Muhammad, because they made tapes of these where he would go to sleep with these recordings at night. So as if this would be a subliminal message that would be sinking in when he's not consciously aware of it. (26)

Dr. Blumberg continued,

He's taught during this time period to continue to zone out even further the things that, perhaps, made him uncomfortable or anxious. He's learned to control that, to utilize muscle relaxation, deep breaths, all sorts of techniques to reduce anxiety. He's exposed to a variety of criminal types of enterprises, learning to steal things, how to do so with ease. Learning tactics that Muhammad apparently is quite adept at, studying police procedures, studying all sorts of behaviors by authorities, and this ends up being very much of his education outside of that limited schooling. (26–27)

He's developing an increasing intensity of dissociative symptoms, losing his sense of identity, becoming very much desensitized to things of a violent nature, becoming quite detached emotionally from his thinking. Things that would make us all feel squeamish or upset might be bothersome to him, but he's learned to tolerate these things, to not be bothered by them. He's beginning to adopt the beliefs that the government of the United States is evil and oppressive. They've done nothing but oppress the black man. He identifies with being an African American as opposed to having any recognition that he is a young kid from Jamaica, and the thing that although at this point he is fifteen going on sixteen, as this process is—I think he's still fifteen at this point, but this is not the dynamic of an adolescent. (27)

Dr. Blumberg stated that instead of being a typical rebellious adolescent, Malvo was in the psychological state of a child "demanding to be attached to a parenting figure and really can't psychologically tolerate being apart from that parent, and that very much is a childhood dynamic as opposed to what one would expect to see in a typical adolescent" (28). At that point, Dr. Blumberg said, Malvo was "the son of John Muhammad. He no longer has a mother, and Muhammad is really the only parent, the only sustaining figure in his life" (30).

Dr. Blumberg discussed Malvo's killing of Kenya Cooke, who was shot in the face, required the "whole process of desensitization to the violence, the video games, the movies, the practice sessions, teaming that with systematic hypnotic techniques, the zoning out, developing these strategies to control the anxiety and encouragement from Muhammad that that is the right thing to do. There is not right and wrong, what this is [is] sort of the morally justified thing, and, again, it's a command that Lee can't resist" (35). Dr. Blumberg stated that there was a transient period of anxiety after that first killing, but

> that ends up going away very quickly. It's dulled by all of the techniques that Muhammad uses to help relieve the anxiety, the encouragement, the zoning out, the focusing on all of this other, again, political religious rhetoric, the disorder remains the same, and it's a rather intense form in terms of the loss of identity and the prominent use of dissociation of emotions from thinking thoughts and feelings [that] are not there. He's capable of basically being psychologically numb to many of these horrific events that he engaged in." (35)

Dr. Blumberg emphasized the fact that Malvo appeared to be obedient and subservient, and that

> reality . . . [was] what Muhammad says it is, and he's bought hook, line, and sinker the idea that he is on a mission, that the mission ultimately is to destroy the Government, and in the process start a new family, a new society, and any means by which you do that is morally justified. It's the right thing to do even though it may be a crime" (36).

Malvo put himself into a dissociative trance state as a way of handling the violent acts in which he was participating as the spotter until the Montgomery County incident, in which he was the shooter. Dr. Blumberg stated, "He zoned out. He put himself into a trance. This is sort of, again, the disconnect between emotion and thought which is a hallmark of Dissociative Disorder" (43), a psychological numbness. In my view, as I understand the facts of this case, Malvo's going into a trance was not voluntary, but rather a consequence of coercive persuasion by Muhammad.

Dr. Blumberg defined Dissociative Disorder by quoting from the *DSM-IV-TR* (2000:532), as involving "a disruption in the usually integrated functions of consciousness, memory, identity, or perception of the environment." He described Malvo as fitting the third paragraph of the Dissociative Disorder NOS description: "States of dissociation that occur in individuals who have been subjected to periods of prolonged and intense coercive persuasion (e.g., brainwashing, thought reform, or indoctrination while captive)" (532). Dr. Blumberg accurately described, in my opinion, the psychological numbing that took place as a "type of depersonalization where emotion is disconnected from the thoughts, from the actions, from what he actually sees, and so these are really the hallmarks of the . . . Dissociative Disorder, that falls into the Not Otherwise Specified category. It's a combination of identity disturbance and the perceptual disturbance caused by the intense coercive persuasion" (*Commonwealth v. Lee Boyd Malvo* 2003:44). Dr. Blumberg emphasized the "strict and total control over the environment [of Malvo maintained by Muhammad that] may involve rigorous physical training, repeated exposure and desensitization to violent activities, and control over diet, sleep. All of these things can lead to the loss of a sense of identity and again the numbing, the psychic numbing that would make someone very vulnerable to be[ing] manipulated by another individual" (45).

Dr. Blumberg described how Malvo developed the dissociative symptom of psychological numbness as a child to somewhat better cope with the fear, anxiety, and depression caused by the serial abandonment and emotional and physical abuse by his mother, the abandonment by his father, and the multiple and routinely disrupted placements with relatives or friends of his mother.

Dr. Blumberg described his reasons for diagnosing dissociation as a consequence of depression in Malvo. "We're talking about something that begins to affect the biology of the individual, the brain chemistry also, and the history was quite clear that Lee beginning during his childhood years as a result of the abuse and neglect and abandonment experienced a lot of periods of significant depression. Ultimately, you learn to cope with that and try and lessen the depression by dissociating. It's not something that he taught himself or can voluntarily do. It's something that kicks in automatically. It's an unconscious defense mechanism" (47). He continued, "Depression is a very uncomfortable experience and what kicked in with

Lee is his zoning out. When his mother would punish him, he would put himself in another place. We see this in kids that have been subjected to trauma sometimes. When it gets severe enough, you can see them develop split-off personalities" (47).

I would add that in the course of developing Dissociative Disorder, Malvo essentially lost the early foundation of his nascent adult identity. The task of identity formation occurs in mid-adolescence. This key process never occurred in a normal way in Malvo, due to the subversion of his identity by Muhammad. This lack of a clear-cut identity, not knowing who he is, continues to this day, as can be seen in the stilted quality of his writings, as elaborated below.

In my view, Dr. Blumberg aptly described Malvo's dissociative symptoms as being a direct outgrowth of the depression that resulted from his childhood history of abandonment and abuse. He further aptly described that this depression, in combination with the resultant dissociative symptoms, caused Malvo to be (in my words) exquisitely vulnerable to psychologically adhering to Muhammad's racist rhetoric and dictates, and to completely lose his own sense of identity and self in the process.

Dr. Blumberg opined that Malvo first developed marked depression as a result of the loss, abandonment, and abuse he sustained in childhood, and then developed dissociative psychological numbness as a defense mechanism against the depression. Dr. Blumberg said that at times Malvo's dissociative defense mechanisms would become overwhelmed by the events and pressures in his life, and he would then act out. Dr. Blumberg stated, "When those dissociative defenses don't work enough, the anger, the resentment of being abused and rejected gets acted out by a child, and in Lee's child[hood], it took the form of acting out in some theft activities when he was a youngster" (48).

Dr. Blumberg stated that at the time of the commission of the serial homicides, Malvo's

primary illness was the Dissociative Disorder. He was on a mission. He was identified totally with Muhammad. He was one with him. He was going to do whatever Muhammad dictated. He was numb to the effects of violence. He became absolutely convinced that what he was doing was for a righteous cause, which ultimately was to reunite with a family with Muhammad, with Muhammad's family, and in the process punish all of the people who had harmed him, that is, the government, basically, who had, he believed, harmed him during the course of all this. (49)

Dr. Blumberg's ultimate forensic opinionwas, "to a reasonable degree of medical certainty, that as result of these disorders and particularly as a result of the Dissociative Disorder Not Otherwise Specified, Lee was unable to distinguish between right and wrong, and he was unable to resist the impulse to commit the offense" (49). Dr. Blumberg thus opined that Malvo met the first criterion of the M'Naghten defense of not guilty by reason of insanity, due to his inability to know or appreciate the wrongfulness of his conduct at the time. James Wulach, J.D., Ph.D., notes that "The test (for insanity) is essentially one of cognitive impairment, in which the purpose is to determine whether the defendant had sufficient mental capacity to understand what he or she was doing when the crime was committed" (1998:369). The M'Naghten defense has a second criterion: that the defendant was unable to appreciate the nature, purpose, or quality of his acts at the time of the offense. A defendant need meet only one or the other criterion to qualify for a verdict of not guilty by reason of insanity. Dr. Blumberg did not state that Malvo met the second criterion; nor do I.

If the jury had accepted Dr. Blumberg's opinion that Malvo was unable to appreciate the wrongfulness of his actions at the time of the homicide, Malvo would have been found not guilty by reason of insanity and confined to a locked forensic mental institution, and later eligible for release if mental health professionals deemed him no longer a danger to himself or others. However, the jury found him guilty of first-degree murder.

Under Virginia case law, according to Dr. Cornell's *Supplementary Report* (November 2003),

> the defendant may be considered insane at the time of an offense, if as a result of mental disease or defect, the defendant
> —Did not understand the nature, character, and consequences of his or her act; or
> —Was unable to distinguish right from wrong, or
> —Was unable to resist the impulse to commit the act.

Thus, when Dr. Blumberg simultaneously opined that Malvo was "unable to resist the impulse to commit the offense" (*Commonwealth v. Lee Boyd Malvo* 2003:49), he was also stating that Malvo met the third criterion of the Virginia Code of Law specifying insanity.

Wulach writes that "in practice, evidence of mental disease or defect is typically used to disprove that a defendant acted 'purposely' or 'knowingly' in committing an otherwise criminal act. . . . There must be a cognitive impairment that prevents knowing or purposeful behavior, rather than a mere emotional reaction such as rage or impassioned impulse" (1998:366). In essence, then, Dr. Blumberg was stating that Malvo was unable to formulate the intent to kill and unable to understand the wrongfulness of his actions as a consequence of mental illness. Neuropsychological testing may be helpful in elucidating the basis of the cognitive impairment and deficits present in a defendant at the time of the commission of a crime.

FORENSIC PSYCHOLOGICAL AND NEUROPSYCHOLOGICAL EVALUATION

Dr. Cornell conducted a forensic psychological evaluation of Malvo and produced a supplemental report based on review of extensive records/discovery; collateral interviews; numerous videotaped interviews conducted by Ms. Albarus in the Caribbean and by investigator Bob Lesseum in Washington State; and a battery of psychological tests administered by himself, including the Wechsler Adult Intelligence Scale-III, the Rorschach Inkblot Test, the Millon Adolescent Clinical Interview, and the Gudjonsson Compliance Scale. In addition, he reviewed a battery of neuropsychological tests conducted by Dr. Schretlen, including:

- The Wide Range Achievement Test-3 (WRAT-3) (now in its fourth edition), which involves the assessment of academic skills implicating intermodal processing of a variety of brain regions including spelling, arithmetic, and reading. Arithmetic involves spatial/parietal processing. Written spelling involves frontal, parietal, and temporal occipital inputs.
- The Grooved Pegboard Test, a measure of motor sequencing, secondary motor association cortex of the hemisphere opposite to the hand doing the task. This is a task involving posterior frontal cortical functioning.
- Trail Making Test A and B. Trail A measures simple sequencing. Trail B involves assessment of complex sequencing and is at least in part a measure of executive functioning.
- The Brief Test of Attention, which measures attentional abilities that involve subcortical pathways and other areas of the brain.
- The Wisconsin Card Sorting Test, which also assesses executive-frontal functioning involving response inhibition, ability to benefit from environmental feedback, and mental flexibility.

- The Controlled Oral Word Association Test, a measure of verbal fluency involving the recitation of spoken words beginning with certain letters as rapidly as possible for sixty seconds. This involves the processing of the frontal cortex of the left hemisphere.
- The Halstead Category Test, an assessment of concept formation and the ability to learn from environmental feedback, involving frontal-executive and generalized brain functions. Dr. Schretlen administered the portable version, the Booklet Category Test.
- The Boston Naming Test, which implicates left hemisphere functioning and the naming of visually presented objects involving tertiary processing.
- The Rey-Osterrieth Complex Figure Test, which measures the ability to copy a complex figure and involves parietal, occipital, and frontal processing loading relatively on the right hemisphere compared to the left (visual-spatial processing).
- The California Verbal Learning Test, 2nd edition, which assesses verbal learning and tends to implicate medial left-temporal functioning. It is usually best supplemented with other memory tests, such as the Weschsler Memory Scale-IV, which assesses both visual and auditory-verbal memory.
- The Wechsler Adult Intelligence Scale-III, an assessment of skills implicated in overall intelligence. (The standard now is the Wechsler Adult Intelligence Scale-IV.) This tests assesses aspects of verbal/left hemisphere processing (verbal comprehension), visual-spatial processing (perceptual organization), working memory (mental manipulation, an aspect of attention), and processing speed.
- The Brief Visuospatial Memory Test—Revised
- The Conner's Adult ADHD Rating Scale—Self Report, Screening Version, which was administered to measure behavioral correlates of inattention and ADHD.
- Personality Assessment Inventory, a broad measure of different aspects of personality
- NEO Five-Factor Inventory. (*Supplementary Report* 2003:7)

Dr. Schretlen's test battery focused on executive-frontal functioning, which was appropriate given that an issue in the case was Malvo's self-control and judgment. The battery is partly consistent with the model of neuropsychological and psychological assessment that mandates a comprehensive approach to the analysis of brain functioning. Dr. Cornell also consulted with

Dr. Blumberg; Diane Schetky, M.D., a child psychiatrist who examined the defendant; Peter Martin, Ph.D., a psychologist; and Steven Eichel, Ph.D., a psychologist who examined the defendant.

Personality tests administered, include the Millon Adolescent Clinical Interview (MACI) and the Personality Assessment Inventory. These measures are constructed on an actuarial basis, but the MACI does not have any forensic norms and is normed on psychiatric populations, and Malvo was not part of the clinical norm group for that test. The Rorschach Test was also administered. I no longer use this (or any) projective measure because, as some experts agree, these measures are not statistically strong enough for forensic use.

Dr. Cornell indicated that his purpose was to evaluate the defendant's mental condition relative to capital sentencing. According to the Code of Virginia, Section 19.2–264.3:1(C),

> The expert appointed to subsection A shall submit to the attorney for the defendant a report concerning the history and character of the defendant and the defendant's medical condition at the time of the offense. The report shall include the expert opinion as to (i) whether the defendant acted under extreme mental or emotional disturbance at the time of the offense, (ii) whether the capacity of the defendant to appreciate the criminality of his conduct or conform his behavior to the requirements of the law was substantially impaired, and (iii) whether there are any other factors in mitigation relating to the history or character of the defendant or the defendant's mental condition at the time of the offense.

As is typical in such evaluations, Dr. Cornell obtained informed consent before starting. He provided a capital sentencing mitigation report on September 15, 2003, with a more detailed supplementary report on November 3, 2003, which is relied upon herein. In essence, Dr. Cornell was assessing the mitigating factors of whether or not Malvo was in a state of extreme mental and emotional disturbance at the time of the homicide, whether or not he was able to conform his conduct to the requirements of the law at the time of the homicide, and whether or not there were any other mitigating factors to present to counter the aggravating factors (catchall mitigation).

Dr. Cornell described in his supplemental report how strict Una James (Malvo's mother) was, and the heavy degree of corporal punishment she used against him. Dr. Cornell discussed the distress Malvo felt at being abandoned to different caretakers, which, in my opinion, contributed to the development of his diffuse, disinhibited attachments. His mother's disruption of his placements with his aunt Marie Lawrence, his cousin Semone Powell, and the Maxwells markedly aggravated Malvo's development of impaired and diffuse attachments, chronic depression and anxiety, and the development of dissociative defenses as a last-ditch coping mechanism. Thus, some experts might agree, Malvo's history in the first fourteen years of his life led directly to his vulnerability to the brainwashing and coercive persuasion by Muhammad. This was further exacerbated by the horrendous living conditions Malvo endured when his mother left him yet again, forcing him to live in the shack in Antigua with no electricity or plumbing. In essence, then, Malvo was an abandoned child who was set up by his circumstances and consequent psychological disorders to become prey to Muhammad.

Dr. Cornell reviewed the early influence of Muhammad on Malvo. Dr. Cornell noted that when Malvo spent the summer in Florida with his mother, she found that he was an entirely different person who prayed to Allah and ate vegetarian food, and exercised daily in a "ritualistic" manner (17). Dr. Cornell wrote that Ms. James described her son as "emotionally and mentally not there" (17). This is, as other experts may agree, an indication that Malvo was further dissociating, becoming increasingly emotionally numb and detached from his core self.

In the preceding text it is documented how Malvo was instructed to watch the movie *The Matrix* over and over again. In this film, mass slaughter is justified by the need to free the oppressed. As is the case in military training, the types of movies and video games to which Malvo was repeatedly exposed by Muhammad had the effect of desensitizing him to violence, without the natural emotions of guilt, remorse, and horror that typically accompany these actions. Thus, in my view, Malvo began the process of becoming a "child soldier" at the hands of Muhammad.

Dr. Cornell indicated that Muhammad taught Malvo that the concepts of "'right' and 'wrong' were artificial" and relative (37). Muhammad taught Malvo that the government defined in what situations killing was acceptable, such as in war or capital punishment, and unacceptable, and what the government considered to be murder. Muhammad argued that the goverenment's definitions were wrong and that his race war was entirely justified. Dr. Cornell indicated that Muhammad taught Malvo statements like "the truth is what I perceive to be the truth" and "right and wrong do not exist" (37), that "what is bad for you is not bad for me" and "therefore not to think about the effects of his actions on others."

In my opinion, with which some experts will agree, all of the above-cited efforts by Muhammad support the view that Malvo was exposed to extreme coercive persuasion by him. This became part of the foundation for the diagnosis of Ddissociative Ddisorder NOS, discussed below.

Dr. Cornell's diagnoses of Malvo were consistent with those of Dr. Blumberg: Chronic Depression, Dissociative Disorder Not Otherwise Specified, and Conduct Disorder. I would add a diagnosis of Reactive Attachment Disorder of Early Childhood, Disinhibited Type and delete the diagnosis of Conduct Disorder prior to the age of fifteen, and cite Malvo's stoning cats as introducing a measure of cultural bias into the diagnosis that was ultimately, in my opinion, not fully correct.

I agree with Dr. Cornell's assessment that Malvo's "childhood history of repeated parental separations, numerous changes in residence and school, and the accompanying emotional stress and trauma he experienced, had a substantial effect on his personality development and impaired his ability to resist the influence of John Muhammad. Furthermore, his relationship with Mr. Muhammad interfered with his psychological development and prevented him from developing adult maturity and judgment" (49), as well as stunting and damaging Malvo's juvenile, yet developing sense of self and, ultimately, of his adult identity.

It is my opinion that Malvo's ego and sense of self are still damaged. This causes an extremely stilted and unnatural quality in his writings, likely a semiconscious or unconscious defense to put forth a more acceptable image or front to the world than who he feels he truly is deep down, likely exacerbated by his not accepting his actions in the D.C. sniper shootings as part of his true self.

NEUROPSYCHOLOGICAL AND PSYCHOLOGICAL TEST RESULTS

On May 5, 2003, Dr. Cornell administered to Malvo the Wechsler Adult Intelligence Scale-III (WAIS-III). This is considered the gold standard instrument for the assessment of intellectual functioning in adults, now in its fourth edition (WAIS-IV). Malvo's full scale intellectual functioning was in the average range (Full Scale IQ of 98) at the 45th percentile rank. Verbal intellectual functioning was a relative strength at the 61st percentile rank, compared to nonverbal intellectual functioning at the lower end of the average range, the 25th percentile rank. The working memory index was at the 66th percentile rank. Processing speed was a relative weakness in the low average range, at the 18th percentile rank.

Dr. Schretlen did neuropsychological testing on August 2, 2003. He administered portions of the Wechsler Memory Scale-III. Malvo was alert and oriented but was one day off as to the date, somewhat off as to the time of day without looking at a watch, and in the average range (63rd percentile rank) for immediate recall of two short verbally presented paragraphs. On the Brief Test of Attention, Malvo's score was impaired at less than the 2nd percentile rank. The California Verbal Learning Test-II revealed a total score in the average range. On the Brief Visuospatial Memory Test—Revised, Malvo had impairment of total/immediate recall of this information at the 5th percentile rank, delayed recall at the 2nd percentile rank, and intact recognition recall. A Verbal Fluency Test using phonemic (letter) categories was administered and was reportedly a strength at the 91st percentile rank. Two semantic categories yielded a lower score of 39 at the 29th percentile rank, average range. A measure of manual dexterity, the Grooved Pegboard, was administered to the right side-dominant Malvo. Right-hand performance was in the impaired range at the 5th percentile rank. His average score for the two trials with the left hand also placed him in the impaired range, at the 4th percentile rank. On the Rey Complex Figure Test, Malvo's copy score was in the impaired range at less than the 16th percentile rank. Immediate and delayed recall of this information was intact. A measure of simple sequencing, Trail Making Test A, was in the impaired range at the 8th percentile rank with two errors. A measure of complex sequencing, Trail Making Test B, was impaired with a time of 110 seconds, with 3 errors. Measures of concept formation (The Booklet Category Test) and mental flexibility (The Wisconsin Card Sorting Test) were intact. To my knowledge, no tests of mental effort or symptom validity were administered.

It is my opinion that the neuropsychological and IQ score test data raise some significant red flags for neurocognitive/brain dysfunction in Malvo, involving difficulties with subcortical functions including memory, attention, and processing speed. The right hemisphere, visual-spatial processing, and visual memory appeared to be more affected than those subserved by the left hemisphere, including verbal processing and semantic memory. These findings were not brought up in Malvo's trial, although they could have contributed to the overall picture of a damaged youth whose capacity to make independent judgments and decisions, separate from Muhammad, was impaired by a number of factors, psychological and neuropsychological. It is my impression that the neurocognitive deficits displayed in Malvo had to do with exposure to chronic, severe stress, prior to, at the time of, and after the homicides, consistent with the types of brain dysfunction present in cases of chronic PTSD.

It seems likely to me that at a minimum, the severe and chronic stress that Malvo was under starting at younger than age five, culminating in participation in the killings that were against his own suppressed and dissociated moral standards, led to some neurocognitive impairment. This may have improved significantly in prison over time, with the debriefings from my coauthor, positive connections with some key people from his past, and Malvo's own healing process. However, what is relevant here is whether or not Malvo had any neurocognitive dysfunction at the time of the homicides. The evidence suggests that he did.

The Millon Adolescent Clinical Inventory (MACI) administered by Dr. Cornell yielded evidence of introversive, inhibited, and doleful (sad) personality patterns as well as significant identity diffusion and depressive affect. Malvo was somewhat elevated on the Self-Devaluation Scale, consistent with low self-esteem. These scores are consistent with a young man with a weak ego structure who tended to be inhibited, self-effacing, and depressed and was exquisitely vulnerable to coercive persuasion and unhealthy attachments, partly due to his diffuse identity. Furthermore, Malvo's elevated score on the Identity Diffusion Scale supports the idea that he had a poorly formed identity, which made him particularly susceptible to the effects of coercive persuasion/"brainwashing."

The Millon Clinical Multiaxial Inventory-III (adult version) yielded significant scores on the Schizoid, Avoidant, Depressive, Antisocial, Masochistic, and Borderline Personality Disorder Clinical Personality Scales, as well as a marked elevation on the Anxiety Disorder Clinical Syndrome Scale. This test ultimately suggested some core instability in an individual inclined to be socially isolated, in his "own head," depressed, anxious, self-effacing, and self-destructive.

It is my opinion that if more comprehensive neuropsychological testing had been administered to Malvo in 2003, it might have added additional support to a diagnosis of a Cognitive Disorder NOS due to underlying brain dysfunction secondary to a variant of PTSD. This in turn might have lent additional weight to a mental state at the time of the crime defense.

PROSECUTION SANITY EVALUATION

Evan S. Nelson, Ph.D., ABPP, performed a court-ordered second-opinion sanity evaluation of Malvo for the prosecutor. Dr. Nelson reviewed background information and interviewed Malvo. He requested to interview John Muhammad, but this was denied. Dr. Nelson did not do his own psychological and neuropsychological testing of Malvo. His examination was therefore not comprehensive, as it left out the third leg of forensic mental health evaluation. Dr. Nelson formed the opinion that although Malvo was "highly influenced by John Muhammad" and Malvo's "background of neglect and immaturity relative to Mr. Muhammad made him more susceptible to this influence," he was not "brainwashed" or in a dissociative state at the time of the homicide of Linda Franklin (2003:25).

Dr. Nelson also opined that "even if Malvo were 'brainwashed' his capacity to know the nature, character, consequences and legal wrongfulness of his actions was fully intact. His sense of entitlement did not destroy his capacity to know that his actions were legally wrong. In light of Mr. Malvo's most recent letters from the jail in August of 2003, it seems more likely that he agreed then and now with Mr. Muhammad's social philosophy and voluntarily and knowingly cooperated, than it does that he was duped into it. Further, I do not see that there is any basis to conclude that if he was brainwashed then he could not control his impulses because of the power of Mr. Muhammad's influence" (26). Dr. Nelson felt that Malvo was "not experiencing a dissociative episode at the time he shot Linda Franklin" (26). It is my opinion that Dr. Nelson's opinion was contrary to the evidence of the case.

INTERVIEW

I met with Malvo for approximately an hour and a half at Red Onion State Prison in Virginia on May 17, 2009. He was twenty-four. He was behind a glass partition; I was not permitted to conduct a formal mental health examination due to his not having an active legal case at the time of our meeting. My purpose was to gain a preliminary understanding of him, although I would have preferred to be able to conduct my own independent evaluation as a way to come to my own conclusions. I also wanted to get Malvo's permission to work with Ms. Albarus on this book, and to introduce myself and explain my role. I was able to conduct a preliminary interview, but not under normal examination conditions, for which a court order would have been required.

Ms. Carmeta Albarus introduced me to Malvo. He was informed that I was working on the forensic mental health analysis portion of the biographical book written about him, and that there would be no confidentiality about any aspects of his history or his case. He indicated that he understood and that he consented. He seemed fully alert, oriented, and aware. We reviewed the general history of his life in Jamaica, Antigua, and the United States, and his criminal history. Malvo indicated that he had total recall of the homicides in which he participated and of the other crimes committed under the instruction of Muhammad.

The discussion covered some aspects of the training regimen, the maximum four hours of sleep per night/sleep deprivation, the constant listening to tapes of Malcolm X, and endless reviewing of *The Matrix*. Malvo talked about how Muhammad would observe him committing various crimes and would be alert to his displaying any signs of emotion whatsoever, such as anxiety, and would carefully instruct Malvo to void his mind of all emotion. Muhammad taught Malvo that any emotion such as guilt or anxiety was completely counter to the task at hand.

Malvo talked about how Muhammad had three nervous breakdowns. The first one occurred when Muhammad's children were forcibly removed from his custody in approximately August 2001. Malvo said that there were two other nervous breakdowns after that, but did not specify the circumstances. Malvo talked about how Muhammad essentially "lost it," and said that his total commitment to the Nation of Islam and the race war was really cemented after his children were removed.

Malvo talked about the repeated target practice, during which Muhammad would put a picture of Malvo on the target and have him shoot away his old self and replace it with who he was supposed to become: John Lee Muhammad, the son of his true "father."

Malvo talked about how Muhammad was there for him in Antigua in a way that nobody else had ever been. Malvo was somewhat protective of the image of his mother, but nonetheless described her as narcissistic and self-centered. He said she would beat him at times for no apparent reason or for what appeared to be very trivial reasons. He described rampant dislocation, inability to ever be with one family long enough to fully attach, and essentially having no opportunity to put down any roots, with the possible exception of his time at the high school in St. Ann's Parish. Malvo said that his mother beat him for being with people who were taking care of him, such as Semone Powell and the Maxwells.

I also reviewed some of Malvo's drawings and writings. My first thought in seeing them was what a waste of such a bright and talented young man, another of the many D.C. sniper tragedies. In general, these drawings and writings reflect that Malvo was extremely identified with the teachings and directives of Muhammad at the time of the homicides, and that he gradually became remorseful and eventually reidentified with his former self and belief system, following his debriefings by Ms. Albarus. His early writings were relatively disorganized with some mild loosening of association, consistent with his being in a dissociated and disorganized state at the time of the homicides, in my opinion. The sequence of the drawings and writings suggested an improvement in Malvo's neurocognitive functioning over time.

Malvo's writings seem at times to be stilted, overly stylized, and overly mature. I believe that this is because he has not yet formed an adult identity. His identity appears to be stuck in early adolescence as a consequence of severe damage to his self-esteem by the abandonment, abuse, and neglect he experienced in childhood, and by the fact that he has not been able to reconcile his participation in these heinous killings, which went completely against his earlier core identity. Thus, the stilted quality of Malvo's writings seems to reflect his longing to be accepted by others although, fundamentally, he had not, and probably still has not, accepted himself.

STOCKHOLM SYNDROME

Some experts would agree with me that Malvo was a victim of something close to what has been described in the literature as Stockholm Syndrome. Stockholm Syndrome occurs when an individual is under the total control of another, more dominant individual, as in a hostage situation (Namnyak, Tufton, Szekely, Toal, Worboys, and Sampson 2008). This of course was not the exact case for Malvo. However, due to the coercive persuasion by Muhammad of the juvenile Malvo, there is a marked parallel.

Stockholm Syndrome appears to involve the conversion of intense fear and helplessness into a marked, strong, and positive identification with the aggressor or victimizer. This identification, especially in children or adolescents, guards against the formation of intense, overwhelming fear and anxiety that would be engendered by the aggressor's rejection. Malvo's case was complicated by his positive, intense attachment to Muhammad as a father figure, which occurred early in the course of events, prior to the persuasive coercion/brainwashing. This left Malvo extremely vulnerable to the persuasive coercion. There were unfortunately no mitigating, countervailing influences that could have loosened his attachment, because his mother had lost all authority at that point, his father was nowhere to be found, and all of his relationships with his other caretakers had essentially been sabotaged or otherwise disrupted by his mother.

Malvo's intense and coercive indoctrination by Muhammad was extremely severe, all pervasive, and all encompassing. It involved food deprivation, sleep deprivation, indoctrination with radicalized Muslim rhetoric and cant, and anti-Caucasian jargon. Some experts may agree that the regimen of watching *The Matrix*; playing violent video games; reading articles by Malcolm X, Louis Farrakhan, and others; and listening to anti-Caucasian rhetoric even while asleep, over and over again, combined with the sleep deprivation, food deprivation, and rejection when Muhammad's agenda was violated in any way, completely overbore Malvo's nascent, juvenile identity.

Muhammad's teachings and directives were in significant, total opposition to what Malvo had been taught, and represented a complete reversal of his Christian beliefs. The intensity of the indoctrination, combined with the intensity of Malvo's attachment to Muhammad due to his Reactive Attachment Disorder and desperate need for a nurturing parent figure, essentially created, in my opinion, a perfect storm of events that resulted in Malvo's complicity in the serial killings. During the process of the indoctrination and dissociation, Malvo became convinced that the sniper shootings were morally justified as part of a military and religious war and that Muhammad was righteous and in the right.

MENTAL HEALTH ANALYSIS OF LEE BOYD MALVO

The evidence that I have reviewed suggests a number of mental health disorders in Malvo that formed the basis for his susceptibility to the brainwashing and indoctrination by Muhammad.

Malvo had a very unstable caregiving situation throughout his early and later childhood. His father, Leslie Malvo, was there for the first three years of his life, and on an inconsistent basis until he was age five. After that his mother severed the relationship, leaving Malvo paternally abandoned.

According to Malvo's accounts, his mother, Una James's, behavior toward her son was intermittently neglectful, abusive, and extremely inconsistent. Ms. James apparently behaved in a highly narcissistic manner, acting as if her son were merely a tool to better herself or to make herself feel better. In essence, she appeared to consider her son an investment to be used, as opposed to a child to be loved, raised, and nurtured.

In essence, in my view, Malvo's early history and environment set him up to develop symptoms of chronic depression, dissociative tendencies, features of PTSD, and disinhibited attachments. His mild cognitive problems may have been related to chronic stress associated with a variant of PTSD. The instability of the first fourteen years of his life made him susceptible to the three years of manipulation that followed, and extremely vulnerable to the brainwashing machinations of the strong personality of the much older John Muhammad. In essence, Malvo was a victim of circumstances ultimately resulted in his participation in the heinous series of crimes that occurred in 2002.

The poem "In You" by Malvo, exerpted earlier in this manuscript, appears to make clear his broken attachment and sense of loss of his father, which prompted his "search for dad" and the attachment to Muhammad. This poem clearly emphasizes the depth of Malvo'sattachment issues and Reactive Attachment Disorder.

Many individuals who ended up committing violent and criminal acts were subject to environmental conditions that predisposed them to this behavior. Research shows quite clearly that brain damage (Leon-Carrion and Ramos 2003) and unstable, unhappy childhoods (McEvoy and Welker 2000) are both factors that predict future violence, and that when an individual is unfortunate enough to have both, the likelihood of commission of violent crimes in the future is high (Ortiz 2004). This statement is not meant to excuse competent adults from responsibility for their crimes. Yet it is important to understand the causes of violence in order to develop reasonably successful prevention strategies in the future.

I will take each of Malvo's diagnostic conditions in turn.

Depression

The predominant psychological cause of depression in individuals, as some experts may agree, is forms of loss. Malvo was deprived of the consistent love of his father, who ultimately abandoned him. He was deprived of a loving, stable, compassionate mother, and instead was subject to a mother who was what some experts might term a malignant narcissist, as defined by Scott Peck, M.D., in *People of the Lie*. Una was repeatedly verbally and physically abusive on the one hand and neglectful on the other. His mother would abandon him intermittently, and would make matters worse by periodically yanking him out of a relatively stable placement/foster situation and bringing him back into her life, only to abandon him again. This set of circumstances, in my opinion, predisposed Malvo to chronic depression and reactive attachment disorder.

Malvo's will to work through this depression, to go to school and to survive, was strong and remarkable, given the underlying circumstances. If any of the positive placements that his mother had put him in had worked out, he likely would have been better able to overcome the sense of depression and loss through living with stable, loving, and compassionate people. Instead, Malvo became extremely vulnerable to "searching for love in all the wrong places," especially John Muhammad, who appeared to be a loving, compassionate, and present father, the kind of individual that had not been available to Malvo on a consistent basis. When Malvo was sick and alone, Muhammad must have appeared an absolute godsend. His mother's distress about his relationship with Muhammad fell on deaf ears because she had failed to be there for Malvo in the past.

Attachment

I believe that one of the major underpinnings of human psychopathology is insecure attachments in infancy and early childhood. Parents who degrade the child's self-esteem, put the child down, and abuse and/or neglect the child create a situation that may be fundamentally destabilizing. This instability can be so severe that the child will turn against him- or herself in order to produce the illusion that the parent has his or her own best interest at heart. That is, if the child were to see the parent as they truly are, the child would be so terrified that he or she literally could not function. Therein, in my opinion, lies the cause of many self-esteem deficits in individuals as they enter adolescence and adulthood.

Malvo experienced early disruption of his attachment with his father and had a fearful, anxiety-provoking attachment with his mother beginning before age five. It is my opinion that Malvo developed Reactive Attachment Disorder of Early Childhood, Disinhibited Type (*DSM-IV-TR* 2000). This pattern began with Malvo's abandonment by his father between the ages of three and five, and was further facilitated by his mother leaving her son in the care of so many caregivers over time and disrupting each and every placement, often just as Malvo was becoming attached and comfortable. In essence, in my opinion, Malvo was raised in an environment with pathogenic care from an abusive mother and an ultimately abandoning father, along with repeated changes of primary caregivers. The fact that Malvo was able to attach to Muhammad, call him "Dad," then reverse himself and attach to Ms. Albarus and call her "Mom," and become the star witness against Muhammad all support this. In my opinion, Malvo's Reactive Attachment Disorder was a direct outgrowth of the pathogenic, inconsistent, and unstable care to which he was subject as a child. Even in his more recent writings, Malvo's ego still seems weak. His writings suggest that the persona he presents is a false front hiding his lack of identity and broken self-esteem. This would be somewhat predictable, given his traumatic history and the long-term effects of his guilt and punishment.

Dissociative Disorders

I agree with Malvo's forensic mental health examiners that he had Dissociative Disorder NOS (*DSM-IV-TR* 2000). It is my impression that he developed dissociative tendencies from an early age as a way of coping with the extreme stress of the abuse, neglect, abandonment, and "musical" caregivers to which he was subject. His dissociative tendencies appeared to take the form of psychological numbness and ultimately, compartmentalization of his true personality, which became buried beneath the superimposed personality of John Lee Muhammad—the emotionally numb killer created by Muhammad.

When Malvo was forced to leave the Maxwells' after leaving Semone Powell, yet another broken attachment, he subsequently wrote, when he placed his hand on a naked hot light bulb, it seared his flesh but he could not feel the pain. Some experts will agree that this is a clear example of his dissociative defenses prior to his even having met Muhammad.

Dissociation is a defense that typically develops in childhood in response to inescapable and marked stressors. It can take the form of inability to remember important personal information or events that have occurred (Dissociative Amnesia), confusion about personal identity or assumption of a new or partial identity along with sudden, unexpected travel to unfamiliar places with an inability to recall one's past (Dissociative Fugue), the creation of multiple personalities (Dissociative Identity Disorder), persistent or recurrent experiences of feeling detached from one's own mental processes or body with intact reality testing (Depersonalization Disorder), or Dissociative Disorder Not Otherwise Specified (NOS) (*DSM-IV-TR* 2000).

The latter category can include feeling that things are unreal (derealization without depersonalization); states of dissociation that occur in individuals who have been subject to periods of prolonged and intensive coercive persuasion (brainwashing); dissociative trance states, such as acting possessed; and other conditions (*DSM-IV-TR* 2000). In essence, dissociative defenses do not occur unless there is significant trauma in the individual's environment. Thus, some type of dissociation and features of PTSD frequently co-occur.

I agree with Malvo's forensic mental health experts who determined that he developed a dissociative disorder due to the stress of his environment at an early age, and that these dissociative tendencies produced in him a susceptibility to the extreme brainwashing perpetrated by Muhammad. This coercive persuasion, in turn, caused Malvo to become even more dissociated. Although it is feasible that any abandoned fourteen-year-old might have become susceptible to a predator like Muhammad, Malvo's chronic psychiatric symptoms of dissociation, post-traumatic stress, chronic depression, and diffuse/disinhibited attachments made him especially vulnerable. Muhammad did try to ensnare other male youths into his scheme but was foiled by the individuals' caregivers, who showed appropriate concern for their welfare. No such intervention was made soon enough in Malvo's case, and unfortunately, his mother's words, which were too little, too late, had ceased to command any respect due to her history of abandoning, neglecting, and abusing him.

As was well articulated by Dr. Blumberg in his trial testimony, Muhammad did a very thorough and persistent job of indoctrinating Malvo into his semireligious, anti-Caucasian, morality and evil are relative principles view of the world. Malvo's writings state at one point that Muhammad taught him "the mind is your go-between with reality. It is your true eye to the world. Be conscious of your thinking, for what the mind says, the body does. Free your mind." But it was not about freedom, it was about subscribing to Muhammad's twisted and toxic view of the world.

Malvo wrote about the night after his first killing at the direct instruction of Muhammad: "That night Lee Boyd Malvo took his last breath and died," and John Lee Muhammad was born. Lee Boyd Malvo did not completely die, but was in fact dissociated out of his conscious awareness. He was ultimately resurrected by the briefings with Ms. Albarus, after the homicides. Malvo wrote: "I fell into the sea, a sea of bother, vulnerable. I strayed, seeking the comfort of a promise forsaken, forlorn and forgotten. Sunk in an ocean of regret, seeking redemption."

Malvo also wrote how Muhammad made killing seem like a game—hence watching *The Matrix* and playing violent video games again and again contributed to the dissociation of Lee Boyd Malvo and the creation of the juvenile John Lee Muhammad.

The assault upon Malvo's identity was pervasive, sophisticated, and fueled by Malvo's extreme need for attachment to fill the void left by his family. It involved persistent sleep deprivation, total control of his environment, and Malvo's extreme desire to please his "father" Muhammad at all costs. Therefore, some experts will agree that dissociation was a fundamental issue underlying Malvo's criminal actions. Muhammad completely subverted Malvo's superego or conscience. One's sense of right and wrong is learned from family and caregivers, to a large extent. Muhammad subverted not only the young Malvo's ego/identity but also his superego/morality. However, his superego is there now, causing the adult Malvo chronic and severe guilt about the consequences of his actions.

Post-Traumatic Stress

The instability, broken parenting, inconsistent caregivers, and emotional and physical abuse to which Malvo was subject as a child put him under chronic stress. As I did not evaluate him myself, I do not have an opinion as to whether he had PTSD at the time of his arrest. However, it is quite possible, because the crimes in which he participated went totally against his underlying personality and ego structure, causing him, on some level, to be horrified. However, the anxiety symptoms were very likely suppressed, out of awareness and hidden, secondary to his dissociative tendencies and chronic psychological numbness and overidentification with Muhammad.

PTSD, by definition, requires the presence of a stressor that individuals would perceive as life threatening or extremely life disruptive (*DSM-IV-TR* 2000). It also then requires the presence of a number of symptoms, including persistent reexperiencing of the traumatic event or events, persistent avoidance of stimuli associated with the trauma and numbing of general responsiveness, and persistent symptoms of increased arousal. Symptoms can include nightmares and flashbacks, feeling as if the events are reoccurring, intense psychological stress when exposed to internal or external cues that symbolize the event, efforts to avoid symbolic or actual representations of the event, inability to recall important aspects of the trauma, feelings of detachment or estrangement from others, difficulty falling asleep, irritability or outbursts of anger, impaired concentration, hypervigilance, and exaggerated startle (*DSM-IV-TR* 2000).

It is my opinion that the underlying causative factors of PTSD are somewhat different for children than for adults. Because of an infant's or young child's inherent dependence upon his or her immediate external environment, mere neglect or absence of caring or caretaking can be life threatening. If an infant or young child is abandoned, it will die, unable to fend for itself. Therefore, in my opinion, stress, emotional abuse, and abandonment can trigger chronic PTSD in children. The consequences of this disorder on the developing human brain in general have been elucidated by a number of studies (Jackowski, de Araujo, de Lacerda, Mari, and Kaufman 2009). It is clear that chronic stress can cause endocrinological changes, including increased cortisol levels in the bloodstream on a chronic basis, that can negatively affect brain function and behavior, which worsen with the duration of the disorder.

It is my impression that Malvo was exposed to chronic stress during his entire pre-Muhammad life as a consequence of the instability of his environment, negative treatment by his mother, and pathological changes in caregiving. This led to a chronic underlying anxiety, which appears to have contributed to his susceptibility to the predatory advances of Muhammad. The anxiety was often out of Malvo's awareness because of psychological numbing and because of his intense attachment to Muhammad. Malvo became the loyal disciple who could see no evil in his master's behavior.

Malvo did report flashbacks of his mother leaving him and of being molested by a neighbor as a child. He seemed to use dissociation as a defense mechanism to dull his psychological pain. An excerpt of a poem written by Malvo, "The Scent of Death," depicts one of his pre-Muhammad traumatic experiences:

> I was 6 years old
> walking to school.
> what I cannot forget
> are those eyes
> that stared through me,
> burning fear
> into the parchment

of my memory.
The police officer
rounded the corner
immediately.
A shot rang out,
his body sagged
and fell limp

In Malvo's case, the psychological damage he sustained in childhood had a lot to do with the fact that no one was able or available to mitigate the toxicity engendered by his mother—most especially his father, who left the scene and did not come to his rescue at age ten—and the fact that well-meaning individuals such as the Maxwells were ultimately defeated by his mother. Due to this psychological trauma, Malvo was never able to accomplish the developmental tasks of adolescence, most notably creating the foundation for a solid, core adult identity.

Conduct Disorder

Conduct disorder is defined by the *DSM-IV-TR* as "a repetitive and persistent pattern of behavior in which the basic rights of others or major age-appropriate societal norms or rules are violated." This diagnosis was raised by Dr. Cornell and Dr. Blumberg. Malvo did engage in a pattern of illegal behavior and rule violation. Most of this, however, was after his exposure to Muhammad. Also, some of Malvo's pre-Muhammad acting out may have been partly mediated by cultural factors, such as stoning cats. Thus it is my opinion that Malvo's antisocial conduct was predominantly a consequence of the brainwashing by Muhammad, not a core dynamic underlying the criminal acts that he did. It is nonetheless true, however, that when Muhammad undermined Malvo's identity, he also subverted and overran his moral development and conscience.

Cognitive Disorder Not Otherwise Specified

As noted above, the cognitive and neuropsychological test data indicate that Malvo had substantive deficits in processing speed and attention, along with deficits in word retrieval, visual recall, and constructional praxis. Although further testing would have had to be done to maximally solidify this opinion, the available data from the testing by Dr. Cornell and Dr. Schretlen point to the presence of some underlying brain/processing dysfunction in Malvo at the time of the homicides, which likely further increased Malvo's susceptibility to Muhammad. Based on the information available to me, it is my opinion that Malvo likely met the criteria of the *DSM-IV-TR* diagnosis of Cognitive Disorder Not Otherwise Specified. I again note that this condition could eventually improve as he came back to himself and applied himself to studying and learning in a calm and systematic manner. Severe, chronic stress in early childhood is known to negatively affect brain development and may cause or contribute to subtle neurocognitive dysfunction.

The most likely cause of Malvo's neurocognitive dysfunction was the severe chronic stress to which he was exposed in early childhood and adolescence, secondary to the serial abandonment, neglect, and abuse he sustained at the hands of his family—and, catastrophically, at the hands of Muhammad.

Neurological Causes of Violence

Brain damage predisposes individuals, especially males, to committing murder. The neuroimaging research on murderers by Raine, Melo, Bihrle, Stoddard, LaCasse, and Buschsbaum (1998) has demonstrated that many, especially those who committed impulsive killings, had damage to the prefrontal cortex of the brain and to the anterior limbic system. This brain damage appears to predispose individuals to difficulty modulating and controlling inappropriate or antisocial behavior. This is often further aggravated by a tendency to self-medicate to deal with chronic stress, depression, or anxiety with drugs or alcohol, which may have a further disinhibiting effect. Conditions such as ADHD, when properly diagnosed, are known to involve a brain condition with damage to the frontal cortex, especially the right frontal cortex (Boles, Adair, and Jourbert 2009; Miller, S., Miller, C., Bloom, Hynd, and Cragge 2006). ADHD is a predisposing factor to antisocial behavior (Young and Gudjonsson 2006).

Frequently, insecure childhoods are accompanied by events that lead to neurological damage as well. For example, physical abuse of an infant or young child can lead to serial concussions and varying degrees of permanent traumatic brain injury. Living in poverty may place children at risk for exposure to lead paint dust or chips in houses built before 1980 in the United States (McLellan 2002).

PTSD, as noted above, can cause chronic elevations of stress hormones and cortisol levels that can produce permanent, or at least long-lasting, neurocognitive dysfunction over time (McEwen 2003).

When neurocognitive dysfunction is combined with a bad family environment with abuse and neglect in various forms, the probability of future violence in that individual is very high (Raine, Park, Lencz, Bihrle, Lacasse, Widom, Dayey, and Singh 2001).

Mental Health Opinion

The evidence strongly suggests that because of his Dissociative Disorder NOS; his Reactive Attachment Disorder of Early Childhood, Disinhibited Type; his chronic Depression; some underlying features of PTSD and exposure to chronic stress; and Cognitive Disorder NOS that Malvo was unable to appreciate or understand the wrongfulness of his actions at the time of the serial homicides, within a reasonable degree of neuropsychological and psychological scientific certainty, based on the information available to me. Thus, Malvo likely met the criteria for an insanity defense in that he did not know that what he was doing was wrong at the time of the homicide of Linda Frnaklin.

The not guilty by reason of insanity defense was suggested by Dr. Blumberg and argued against by Dr. Nelson. As noted by Dr. Cornell, in Virginia an insanity defense can also rest on the defendant's having been "unable to resist the impulse to commit the act" at the time (*Supplementary Report* 2003:49).

In addition, there was evidence that Malvo was so under the coercive influence of Muhammad that he was unable to formulate the independent intent to kill in the homicides in question. That is, it appears that he again qualified for a diminished capacity defense, in which an element of the offense (intentional, purposeful, and knowing homicide) was negated by diseases of the mind and brain that diminished his ability to formulate the intent to kill. Again, it is my understanding that in Virginia, this would lead to the jury finding a verdict of not guilty by reason of insanity. However, the ultimate decision is made by the jury, not by the mental health experts.

Additionally, Malvo appears to have qualified for a number of mitigating factors that would potentially outweigh the aggravators in the death penalty sentencing phase of his trial, as aptly opined by Dr. Cornell (*Supplementary Report* 2003). These include the facts that:

Malvo acted under extreme mental and emotional disturbance at the time of the homicide of Linda Franklin;

Malvo's emotional and mental conditions impaired his capacity to appreciate the criminality of his conduct and/or to conform his conduct to the requirements of law; and

Malvo had other catchall mitigators, including a childhood replete with abandonment, neglect, and physical abuse.

These forensic opinions would have had to be argued to the jury within a reasonable degree of neuropsychological and psychological scientific certainty, first in the guilt phase and, if convicted of murder, in the penalty phase as mitigating factors.

Mental Health Causes of Violence

Most psychological disorders with non-neurological causes are a consequence of severe stress, especially in early childhood, in my opinion. What children perceive as life threatening may be different from what an adult perceives as life threatening. Due to a child's helplessness and dependence upon caretakers for its very survival, neglect and abuse in and of themselves can be life-threatening. Terror in childhood need not be caused by a gun or a knife. Subtle cues of threatened abandonment, unmet basic needs, and ongoing indications that the child is worthless or that the caregivers would be better off if the child had never been born all can lead to insecurity in a developing mind, surrounded by what is perceived by the child as emotional quicksand. This ongoing stress can also set up a psychological/neurophysiological process that becomes the foundation of later behavioral dyscontrol and antisocial behavior.

Given that positive attachment to a stable caregiver in infancy and early childhood encourages the development of self-confidence, positive self-esteem, and a generally optimistic and forward-looking attitude, what does the opposite produce? The answer is frequently psychological disease in its many forms, including substance abuse, other addictive tendencies, obsessive-compulsive behavior, PTSD, depression, anxiety, dissociative tendencies, and some personality disorders.

It is my opinion that Lee Boyd Malvo was extremely vulnerable to Muhammad due to his psychological problems that were a direct result of the emotional quicksand on which he was raised, and the fact that he had been deserted at the time of Muhammad's advances to him. Malvo had a taste of good parenting from his father, but that ended due to his father's inconsistent presence and abandonment by the age of five, and finalized at age 10 when his father refused to respond to his son's pleas and rescue him from his abandonment. As recounted by Malvo, his mother, Una James, was physically and emotionally abusive, controlling, manipulative, and inconsistently present. Thus, Malvo was a child with no father and an unreliable and toxic mother. This left a huge void, which is why, in my opinion, he was so susceptible to Muhammad.

VIOLENCE PREVENTION

In 1998, the Bureau of Justice Statistics reported that an estimated 283,000 prison and jail inmates suffer from mental health problems. In 2006, that number was judged to be 1.25 million (Human Rights Watch 2006). The rate of reported mental health disorders in state prison populations was five times greater (66.2 percent) than in the general population. Jamie Fellner, the Director of the U.S. Program of Human Rights Watch, stated that prisons were "woefully ill-equipped for their current role as the nation's primary mental health facility" (1). These statistics represent a wake-up call to our nation to recognize and more aggressively treat mental health disorders, and to recognize that mental health treatment is every bit as important as physical/medical treatment in terms of saving lives, especially considering the societal cost of the epidemic of murder.

Childhood-onset psychosocial stressors are critical in the formation of mental illness in general and in causing of violence in particular. If a child has both chronic psychosocial and family problems and neurological illness, the likelihood of their future criminality and violence becomes extremely high. Appropriate parenting, support, and adequate mental health and medical services for children will tend to mitigate against future criminality and violence.

If, prior to the age of fourteen, Malvo had been targeted as emotionally disturbed and needing appropriate psychological treatment and appropriate, consistent caregiving through a foster family, this (although less ideal than living with loving and compassionate parents) might have mitigated against or prevented his susceptibility to participation in the killings in question.

Children require consistent, loving, and stable parenting from both a mother and a father whenever possible. Social programs that encourage paternal involvement and families to stay together, at least when the relationship between the two parents is adequate, should be encouraged. In my opinion, anything that can be done to minimize neurological damage and abusive and neglectful environments will be good for the nation in the long run, by curtailing violence, suicide, and homicide. If a child is shown consistent love, care giving and support, without the presence of abuse, neglect or trauma, criminal behavior is less likely to occur as as that child develops into an adolescent and adult. Individuals who do have some type of neurological damage, whether it be mild to moderate traumatic brain injury, learning disabilities, auditory or nonverbal processing disorders, or ADHD, will do better, and will be much less likely to develop criminal antisocial tendencies, later in life, if given appropriate structure, educational and social services, and parenting.

The availability of appropriate mental health and medical services to children and families is essential in helping to prevent the formation of personality structures that are prone to violence and criminal acts. Genetic tendencies may predispose individuals to certain types of behavior or personality structures; however, the human brain is extremely plastic in its early years, and the ultimate expression of the underlying genotype in an individual human is highly related to the environment in which that child grows up (Grossman, Churchill, McKinney, Kodish, Otte, and Greenough 2003).

Therefore, the development of violent tendencies in individuals can frequently be minimized by early intervention and appropriate parenting. Furthermore, social programs that support, good parenting and good mental and physical health in children should tend to reduce societal costs from violent and criminal acts. Often, once the violent crime has been committed, it is too late. Intervention needs to occur prior to the onset of violent acts.

Finally, the story of Lee Boyd Malvo is one from which we as a nation need to learn, as a testament to the lives of the good people that were lost as a result of this tragedy. Childhood abuse and neglect in its varied forms can have extremely negative effects on the individual and on others who may come into contact with them. I hope that out of the maelstrom of the D.C. sniper killings, people will learn the importance of treating mental health disorders with equal resources and parity to medical disorders, because they are as costly to society in terms of violence and disability as medical illnesses and diseases.

Epilogue

I t has been ten years since the events recounted in the first three chapters of this book. John Muhammad has been executed and Lee Malvo remains incarcerated at Red Onion State Prison, where he has been sentenced to spend the remainder of his life. The extent of the tragedy and trauma cannot be excused or minimized. And yet there are lessons that can still be learned.

In more than two decades of doing this work with a variety of clients, I have been repeatedly confronted with certain themes that were evident in the Malvo story. Issues of neglect, abuse, abandonment, and the missing father prevail. Often the crisis begins with the break in the family unit, with the father either leaving the home or not being in the home. As a result, the mother may be overwhelmed financially and/or emotionally, and the child may become the target of her frustrations. This becomes a developmental burden that often manifests in acting out and learning problems in school, and may contribute to various emotional/behavioral/psychological disorders. This is significant, because it puts the child at greater risk for socially inappropriate behavior, including delinquency, by their teenage years.

For children from poor minority homes, the risk of becoming a statistic in the criminal justice system is greater. According to the Sentencing Project, an advocacy organization based in Washington, D.C., if current trends continue, one of every three black males born today can expect to go to prison. The so-called War on Drugs has contributed significantly to the high numbers of blacks and other ethnic minorities currently in our prisons. More than 60 percent of those incarcerated are racial and ethnic minorities, and three quarters of those in prison for drug offenses are people of color.

For poor urban communities ravaged by broken families and the removal of fathers from the home, this means a greater risk of children seeking attachments and identity affirmation in the wrong places. These might include gangs, drug dealers, and others who fill the void left by the loss of paternal attachments. Certainly this was the case with Malvo, who managed to avoid gangs and the drug culture, yet attached to Muhammad.

Broken homes and single-mother homes are not unique to poor, urban, minority communities—they exist across the socioeconomic spectrum. However, in homes where there is greater opportunity for access to and availability of supportive resources, the child's risk of contact with the criminal justice system is lessened. These resources include but are not limited to:

- stability in residence
- supportive family network
- educational opportunities
- open and safe communication with parents or guardians
- socialization that presents avenues for growth and mobility
- parental involvement in activities
- supervision and guidance
- discipline that is not abusive or detrimental to the physical and emotional well-being of the child
- access to recreational and creative resources

Unfortunately, children from poor inner-city communities often lack the safety nets that could help them avoid a path leading to delinquency or worse. The Lee Boyd Malvo story here has focused on the separation of his parents and his desperate search to find a father, but the horror that took place in 2002 could have been avoided if the authorities had listened to his mother's pleas that her son was in danger. However, her concerns were dismissed, and Muhammad was able to travel throughout the country with this boy because little value was placed on his life. Too often the worth of a child is determined by who the child is—his race, his socioeconomic background, and the community he is from.

Malvo recalls Muhammad impressing upon him that only the United States of America has the resources to make the changes needed to uplift children. In this way, Muhammad demonstrated that resources were allocated discriminatorily so that children like Malvo could not realize their full potential, and therefore Malvo had no choice but to join him. As nefarious as his intent was, Muhammad did not have to go far to show examples of what he was talking about. These disparities unfortunately do exist.

How can we prevent more Lee Malvos? What measures will we as a society employ to avoid horrific days like those in October 2002? The UNICEF Convention on the Rights of the Child, which has been signed but not ratified by the United States, incorporates the full range of human rights for children. The Convention sets out fifty-four articles and two Optional Protocols that spell out the basic rights of children everywhere: the right to survival; to develop to the fullest; to protection from harmful influences, abuse, and exploitation; and to participate fully in family, cultural, and social life. The four core principles are nondiscrimination; devotion to the best interest of the child; the right to life, survival, and development; and respect for the views of the child. The rights spelled out in the Convention are inherent to the human dignity and harmonious development of every child.

> **Part 1: Article 2:** 1. States Parties shall respect and ensure the rights set forth in the present Convention to each child within their jurisdiction without discrimination of any kind, irrespective of the child's or his or her parent's or legal guardian's race, colour, sex, language, religion., political or other opinion, national, ethnic or social origin, property, disability, birth or other status.
>
> **Part 1: Article 2:** 2. States Parties shall take all appropriate measures to ensure that the child is protected against all forms of discrimination or punishment on the basis of the status, activities, expressed opinions, or beliefs of the child's parents, legal guardians, or family members. (www .unicef.org/crc)

The Convention should be ratified, not just symbolically but in substance, by way of policies and resources invested across the board. In so doing we take steps to minimize the risk of creating other pathological relationships wherein our children's future is taken from them.

REFERENCES

American Psychiatric Association. 2000. *Diagnostic and Statistical Manual of Mental Disorders.* 4th ed. Washington, D.C.: American Psychiatric Association.

American Psychological Association. 2002. "Ethical Principles of Psychologists and Code of Conduct." *The American Psychologist* 57 (12): 1060–1073.

Atkins v. Virginia. 536 U.S. 304 (2002).

Beckman, M. 2004. "Crime, Culpability, and the Adolescent Brain." *Science* 305:596–598.

Boles, D. B., L. P. Adair, and A.-M. Joubert. 2009. "A Preliminary Study of Lateralized Processing in Attention-Deficit/Hyperactivity Disorder." *The Journal of General Psychology* 136:243–258.

Bower, B. 2004. "Teen Brains on Trial: The Science of Neural Development Tangles with the Juvenile Death Penalty." *Science News* 165:299–301.

Butcher, J. N., W. G. Dahlstrom, J. R. Graham, A. Tellegen, and B. Kaemmer. 2001.*Minnesota Multiphasic Personality Inventory (MMPI-2): Manual for Administration and Scoring.* Minneapolis: University of Minnesota Press.

Chevannes, B. 2006. *Betwixt and Between: Explorations in an African-American Mindscape.* Kingston, Jamaica: Ian Randle Publishers, 2006.

Clancy, T. 2001. Ghost Recon [video game]. Cary, N.C.: Red Storm Entertainment.

———. 2002. Ghost Recon: Desert Siege [video game]. Cary, N.C.: Red Storm Entertainment.

Code of Virginia, Section 19.2–264.3:1(C) (2009).

Commonwealth of Virginia v. Lee Boyd Malvo, Chesapeake, Virginia. 2003. 03-3089, 03-3090, 03-3091. Transcripts of testimony by: Neil Blumberg, M.D.; Stanton Samenow, Ph.D.; Dewey Cornell, Ph.D.; Mary Marez; Mildred Muhammad; Lindbergh Williams; Euphernia Douglas; Rev. Albert Archer; Peter David; Donald Haaland.

Cornell, D. G. September 2003. *Capital Sentencing Mitigation Report.* Created for Commonwealth of Virginia v. Lee Boyd Malvo.

———. (November 2003). *Supplementary Report.* Created for Commonwealth of Virginia v. Lee Boyd Malvo.

Dusky v. United States. 362 U.S. 402 (1960).

Faust, D. and J. Ziskin. 1988. "The Expert Witness in Psychology and Psychiatry." *Science* 241:31–35.

FBI Report. October 28, 2002. (Items recovered from the dark blue Chevrolet Caprice in which Muhammad and Malvo were arrested.)

FBI Report. July 2, 2003. Forensic Service Division. (Items recovered from crime scenes and the home in Washington where Muhammad and Malvo stayed.)

FBI Report. October 24, 2002. Special Agent J. Jordon and Detective James Drewry, interview with John Allan Muhammad.

Gibbs, Nancy and Timothy Roche. December 20, 1999. "The Columbine Tapes." *TIME.*

Greene, Marcia Slacum. November 8, 2002. "'I'm sure he had me in his scope': Muhammad's Ex-wife Links Killings to Custody Fight." *The Washington Post.*

Grossman, A. W., J. D. Churchill, B. C. McKinney, I. M. Kodish, S. L. Otte, and W. T. Greenough. 2003. "Experience Effects on Brain Development: Possible Contributions to Psychopathology." *Journal of Child Psychology and Psychiatry* 44:33–63.

Heaton, R. K., S. W. Miller, M. J. Taylor, and I. Grant. 2004. *Revised Comprehensive Norms for an Expanded Halstead-Reitan Battery: Demographically Adjusted Neuropsychological Norms for African American and Caucasian Adults.* Lutz, Fla.: Psychological Assessment Resources, Inc.

Horwitz, S. and M. Ruane. 2003. *SNIPER: Inside the Hunt for the Killers Who Terrorized the Nation.* New York: Random House.

Human Rights Watch. September 5, 2006. "US: Number of Mentally Ill in Prisons Quadrupled: Prisons Ill Equipped to Cope." http://www.hrw.org/en/news/2006/09/05/us-number-mentally-ill-prisons-quadrupled (accessed March 11, 2010).

Jackowski, A. P., C. M. De Araujo, A. L. T. de Lacerda, J. d. Mari, and J. Kaufman. 2009. "Neurostructural Imaging Findings in Children with Post-traumatic Stress Disorder: Brief Review." *Psychiatry and Clinical Neurosciences* 63:1–8.

Jarvis, P. E. and J. T. Barth. 1994. *The Halstead-Reitan Neuropsychological Battery: A Guide to Interpretation and Clinical Application.* Lutz, Fla.: Psychological Assessment Resources, Inc.

Knecht, S., B. Drager, M. Deppe, L. Bobe, H. Lohmann, A. Floel, E.-B. Ringelstein, J. Leon-Carrion, and F. J. C. Ramos. 2003. "Handedness and Hemispheric Language Dominance in Healthy Humans." *Brain* 123:2512–2518.

Leon-Carrion, J. and F. J. C. Ramos. 2003. "Blows to the Head During Development Can Predispose to Violent Criminal Behaviour: Rehabilitation of Consequences of Head Injury Is a Measure for Crime Prevention." *Brain Injury* 17:207–216.

Lifton, R. J. 1989. *Thought Reform and the Psychology of Totalism: A Study of Brainwashing in China.* Chapel Hill: University of North Carolina Press.

Luria, A. 1966. *Higher Cortical Functions in Man.* Oxford: Basic Books.

Malvo, Lee Boyd. 2002. Confession, transcript. Montgomery County, Maryland.

Mauer, Marc and Ryan King. "Uneven Justice: State Rates of Incarceration by Race and Ethnicity." The Sentencing Project (Washington, D.C.), July 2007.

McEvoy, A. and R. Welker. 2000. "Antisocial Behavior, Academic Failure, and School Climate: A Critical Review." *Journal of Emotional and Behavioral Disorders* 8 (3): 130. McEwen, B. S. 2003. "Early Life Influences on Life-long Patterns of Behavior and Health." *Mental Retardation and Developmental Disabilities Research Reviews* 9:149–154.

McLellan, F. 2002. "Countering Poverty's Hindrance of Neurodevelopment." *The Lancet* 359:236.

Memorandum, Michael S/ Arif, Esq. to Malvo File re: John Muhammad (John Williams Military Records). July 16, 2003.

Memorandum of Interview conducted with Lee Boyd Malvo by Detective T. Ryan. October 24, 2002. Montgomery County, Maryland.

Miller, S. R., C. J. Miller, J. S. Bloom, G. W. Hynd, and J. G. Craggs. 2006. "Right Hemisphere Brain Morphology, Attention-Deficit/Hyperactivity Disorder (ADHD) Subtype, and Social Comprehension." *Journal of Child Neurology* 21:139–144.

M'Naghten's Case. 1843. House of Lords. Mews' Dig. i. 349; iv. 1112. S.C. 8 Scott N.R. 595; 1 C. and K. 130; 4 St. Tr. N.S. 847. May 26, June 19.

Morey, L. C. 1991. *Personality Assessment Inventory.* Lutz, Fla.: Psychological Assessment Resources, Inc.

Namnyak, M., N. Tufton, R. Szekely, M. Toal, S. Worboys, and E. L. Sampson. 2008. "'Stockholm Syndrome': Psychiatric Diagnosis or Urban Myth?" *Acta Psychiatrica Scandinavica* 117:4–11.

Nelson, E. S. 2003. *Court-Ordered Second Opinion Sanity Evaluation.* Created for Commonwealth of Virginia v. Lee Boyd Malvo.

New Jersey Statutes, N.J.S.A. 2C:4–2 (1990).

Ortiz, A. January 2004. "Adolescence, Brain Development and Legal Culpability." Juvenile Justice Center, American Bar Association (http://www.americanbar.org/groups/child_law/policy/juvenile_justice.html).

Pottinger, A.M. and S. W. Brown. 2006. "Understanding the Impact of Parental Migration on Children: Implications for Counseling Families from the Caribbean." www.counseling outfitters.com/pottinger.htm (accessed July 27, 2010).

Proceedings of the Houston Conference on Specialty Education and Training in Clinical Neuropsychology. 1998. *Archives of Clinical Neuropsychology* 13 (2).

Raine, A., J. R. Melo, S. Bihrle, J. Stoddard, L. LaCasse, and M. S. Buschsbaum. 1998. "Reduced Prefrontal and Increased Subcortical Brain Functioning Assessed Using Positron Emission Tomography in Predatory and Affective Murderers." *Behavioral Sciences and the Law* 16:319–332.

Raine, A., S. Park, T. Lencz, S. Bihrle, L. LaCasse, C. S. Widom, L.-A. Dayeh, and M. Singh. 2001. "Reduced Right Hemisphere Activation in Severely Abused Violent Offenders During a Working Memory Task: An fMRI Study." *Aggressive Behavior* 27:111–129.

Reitan, R. M. and D. Wolfson. 1993. *The Halstead-Reitan Neuropsychological Test Battery: Theory and Clinical Interpretation*. Tucson, Ariz.: Neuropsychology Press.

Rogers, R., R. M. Bagby, and S. E. Dickens. 1992. *Structured Interview of Reported Symptoms*. Lutz, Fla.: Psychological Assessment Resources, Inc.

Roper v. Simmons, 543 U.S. 551 (2005).

Rorschach, H. 1942. *Psychodiagnostics: A Diagnostic Test Based on Perception*. Ed. and trans. Paul Victor Lemkau. New York: Grune and Stratton.

Silver, J., A. Wachowski, and L. Wachowski. 1999. *The Matrix*. Burbank, Calif.: Warner Brothers and South Yarra, Australia: Village Roadshow Pictures.

Singer, M. T. 2003. *Cults in Our Midst: The Continuing Fight Against Their Hidden Menace*. San Francisco: Jossey-Bass.

"Sniper Suspect's Military Records Revealed." October 24, 2002. www.time.com.

Sommers-Flanagan, R. and J. Sommers-Flanagan. 1999. *Clinical Interviewing*. 2nd ed. New York: Wiley.

Stetler, R. 2007. *Mitigation Investigation: A Duty That Demands Expert Help but Can't Be Delegated*. www.nacdl.org (accessed June 30, 2008).

Strauss, E., E. Sherman, and O. Spreen. 2006. *A Compendium of Neuropsychological Tests*. 3rd ed. New York: Oxford University Press, 2006.

Sun Tzu. 1988. The Art of War. Trans. Thomas Cleary. Boston: Shambhala.

Tobias, M. L. and J. Lalich. 1994. *Captive Hearts Captive Minds: Freedom and Recovery from Cults and Abusive Relationships*. Alameda, Calif.: Hunter House.

Tombaugh, T. N. 1996. *Test of Memory of Malingering*. Toronto: Multi-Health Systems, Inc.

Walsh, D. 2004. *Why Do They Act That Way? A Survival Guide to the Adolescent Brain for You and Your Teen*. New York: Free Press.

Wingert, P. May 28, 2006. "'I Thought He Would Kill Me': The DC Sniper's Ex-wife on Life with John Allen Muhammad." *Newsweek*.

Wingert, P. and D. Briscoe. June 5, 2006. "Breaking the Spell: The Young DC Sniper Turns on His Deadly Mentor." *Newsweek*.

Wulach, J. S. 1998. *Law and Mental Health Professionals: New Jersey*. 2nd ed. Washington, D.C.: American Psychological Association.

Young, S. and G. H. Gudjonsson. 2006. "ADHD Symptomatology and Its Relationship with Emotional, Social and Delinquency Problems." *Psychology, Crime and Law* 12:463–471.

INDEX